WINNING
THE
TALENT
WARS

Also by Bruce Tulgan

Managing Generation X

WINNING
THE
TALENT
WARS

Bruce Tulgan

W. W. NORTON & COMPANY
NEW YORK LONDON

This book is dedicated to my wife,
Debby Applegate

For information about permission to reproduce selections from this book, write to Permissions, W. W. Norton & Company, Inc., 500 Fifth Avenue, New York, NY 10110

This book is composed in 9.7/13.8 Versailles Roman with the display set in 29 point Eras Medium. Composition by Susan Carlson. Manufacturing by Maple-Vail Book Manufacturing. Book design by Dana Sloan.

Library of Congress Cataloging-in-Publication Data

Tulgan, Bruce.
    Winning the talent wars / by Bruce Tulgan.
        p. cm.
    Includes bibliographical references and index.
    ISBN 0-393-01958-6
    1. Executives—Recruiting. 2. Organizational effectiveness.
    3. Management. I. Title.

    HF5549.5.R44 T85 2000
    658.4'07111—dc21   00–056857

ISBN 0-393-32300-5 pbk.

W. W. Norton & Company, Inc., 500 Fifth Avenue, New York, N.Y. 10110
www.wwnorton.com

W. W. Norton & Company Ltd., Castle House, 75/76 Wells Street,
London W1T 3QT

1 2 3 4 5 6 7 8 9 0

CONTENTS

FOREWORD TO THE PAPERBACK EDITION   5

PROLOGUE
Welcome to the Talent Wars   9

CHAPTER 1
The New Economy 101   13

CHAPTER 2
Talent Is the Show   31

CHAPTER 3
Staff the Work, Not the Jobs   54

CHAPTER 4
Pay for Performance, and Nothing Else   82

CHAPTER 5
Turn Managers into Coaches   109

CHAPTER 6
Train for the Mission, Not the Long Haul   129

CHAPTER 7
Create as Many Career Paths as You Have People   153

EPILOGUE
**Lifetime Employment Is Dead,
Long Live Lifetime Employment**   175

MEMO TO MANAGERS   178

APPENDIX 1
"Employer of Choice" Life Resources   181

APPENDIX 2
What about Unions?   186

Notes   190

Acknowledgments   208

Index   210

FOREWORD TO THE PAPERBACK EDITION

With all the fluctuations in the economy in this era of uncertainty, one business truth is not going to change: Talent is the number one asset of every organization in every industry. In good times and bad alike, leaders must get more work out of fewer people, and that means the best people are always in great demand. Nearly all projections indicate that, despite ups and downs in the unemployment rate, the supply of skilled talent will be outpaced by demand until at least 2020. That's why the talent wars are not going to end.

Still, a lot has changed since this book was first released. The economy went from boom times to recession. Layoffs reached record highs. And September 11 broke our hearts, made us angry, frightened us, and brought us closer together.

After a year like 2001, many people have wondered aloud whether the much-celebrated "new economy" was nothing but a myth. Indeed, if you thought the new economy was all about dot-coms, magical business models, and never-ending good news, then of course the new economy was a myth. But the real new economy was never truly about such hype.

The real new economy is serious business—driven by the effects of highly interconnected, rapidly changing, fiercely competitive global markets. Business leaders must move resources quickly out of cooling-off market segments . . . and just as quickly move resources into market segments that are heating up. They must make and unmake new business combinations. They must cut waste and increase performance. They must implement new technologies to streamline operations and improve efficiency.

Agility has replaced stability as the key to strategic advantage for organizations of all sizes in just about every industry. Why? Because organizations must be flexible enough to adjust quickly and smoothly to changing circumstances. Sometimes that means hiring like crazy to increase productive capacity. Just as often it means downsizing in droves. In fact, it is rather common for companies to hire substantial numbers of new employees at the same time the firm is downsizing. These changing circumstances have transformed the traditional employer-employee relationship. Long-term employment is increasingly rare, job security is a thing of the past, and employees no longer patiently pay their dues and wait to climb the organizational ladder. That transformation is a fundamental premise of this book.

I've written a lot about the "free agent" mindset that has swept across the workforce—the idea that no matter where you work or what you do, you are ultimately in business for yourself and must vigorously fend for yourself. During the last economic boom, many observers assumed that this mindset was just for disloyal job-hoppers and driven by super-tight labor markets. These observers were convinced that free agency would go away as soon as the next recession came along.

In 2001, when downsizing affected millions of workers and returned to the front pages, many were reminded of the true origin of the free agent mindset: necessity. More and more employees are thinking like free agents because they have no other choice. They cannot rely on their employers to secure their livelihoods. Individuals simply must take responsibility for their own careers.

In boom times, employees have the upper hand in the labor market. When the economy slows, employees lose negotiating power. Why? It's just the logic of the marketplace—supply and demand. This has always been true on a macro level. What is rather astonishing is that, in recent years, market logic has taken over on the micro level as well. Seniority and hierarchy now take a backseat in employment relationships, as the day-to-day details—assignments, schedules, work conditions, rewards—are subject to ongoing negotiations between managers and the employees they supervise.

This puts managers under incredible pressure because they are forced every day to balance the needs of employees with the interests of the organization. Senior executives are breathing down managers' necks pushing for increased productivity and quality. That means managers must get more work and better work out of fewer people. So most employees find themselves hustling double-time nowadays, but they look to managers for guidance, training, motivation, feedback, and rewards.

It is the manager who is on the front lines, who must roll up her sleeves and get into the trenches every day: Keep the talent pipeline full and get the right people in the right places at the right times. Get new people up to speed quickly. Coach, cajole, bargain, inspire, motivate, and reward. Identify and develop the stars and draw them into the organization's core group. Retain the best, and eliminate the worst.

That's why I wrote this book for real managers operating in the real new economy. There is plenty of high-level business strategy throughout the book, but it's the kind of strategy that managers can use—in accord with company policy or in disregard of it.

The philosophy is simple: Forget seniority. Forget hierarchy. Employment relationships are transactional by nature and they are now governed by market logic. So you had better learn to manage people according to market principles. That means every term of employment is on the table all the time. Every employee has a chance to work harder, longer, smarter, faster, and better in exchange for a better deal. But every deal is short-term and every payoff is contingent on concrete deliverables. Flexibility and accountability go hand in hand.

This book is filled with concrete examples of the best practices in staffing, rewards, coaching, training, and retention. There are many stories from the most exuberant days of the economic boom, but those days are not the point of the book. The point is managing people in this new era of uncertainty—when markets are chaotic and resource needs are unpredictable.

In this high-speed, high-tech, knowledge-based, super-fluid economy, what are the best strategies and tactics for getting the best work out of the best people one day at a time? I hope you'll find the answers in this book.

Bruce Tulgan
January 2002

PROLOGUE

WELCOME TO THE TALENT WARS

I was not surprised when Ralph Larsen, CEO of Johnson & Johnson, the $27-billion-a-year health care giant, invited me to his office at the J&J corporate headquarters in New Jersey for a chat. That's what I do. I spend more than one hundred days a year chatting with business leaders and managers about the single greatest challenge they face in the new economy: winning the talent wars.

As I walked into Mr. Larsen's office, three of his senior executives followed me in. They all wore white shirts and dark suits. I was wearing a pair of gray pants, a black sports jacket, a blue shirt, and a red tie. Nobody said a word. We exchanged a few smiles. Then Mr. Larsen appeared in the doorway. He, too, wore a white shirt and a dark blue suit.

As we took up positions on the couches around a glass coffee table, Mr. Larsen looked at me and said, "You know, my first day of work at Johnson & Johnson was a long time ago, but I still remember. I wore a blue shirt, and my manager sent me home to change." "Umm . . ." I asked, "Do you want me to go home and change, sir?" "No, no," he said, "I was just remembering."

Then Mr. Larsen began musing aloud about casual dress. It sounded like the headquarters personnel at J&J wouldn't be dressing down anytime soon, but the dress code was being relaxed in many of the 190 J&J operating companies throughout the world. "People in the operating companies tell me you have to offer casual dress now or nobody wants to work for you," said Mr. Larsen. "I'm not going to stand in the way of that." Soon HQ followed suit, after all.

Mr. Larsen confided that his attitude about casual dress had started to change when he noticed something about one of his own family members. It seems that when he visits at the Larsen home, Mr. Larsen's relative tends to "disappear" for hours at a time. When found, Mr. Larsen explained, he is discovered huddled up with his laptop computer, working. It's not a workday, he's not at work, and he's not dressed for work, but as Mr. Larsen said, "He certainly gets a lot of work done." In that sentiment, Mr. Larsen put his finger on the essence of the solution to the talent wars in the new economy.

For many observers, casual dress is a symbol of these wars. All the media hype would have you believe that the powerhouse companies like Johnson & Johnson are losing all their best talent to the free-wheeling, playhouse corporate cultures of the dot coms. This is the worst nightmare of traditional employers: their key people lured away—Pied Piper style—by a bunch of GenXers sitting around on the floor working on laptops, wearing shorts, t-shirts, and sandals, while their colleagues play Ping-Pong in the "teaming space" near the swimming pool.

How can traditional employers compete with that kind of . . . umm . . . work environment?

Recently I spoke for more than an hour about the staffing crisis to the nearly five hundred managing directors of J.P. Morgan, the $11-billion-a-year financial services company. Although many in the leadership were convinced that they were losing their best talent to dot coms, I insisted, as I do with business leaders every single day, that the talent wars are not just about the dot coms, any more than they are all about Generation X. The talent wars, I explained, are growing out of a fundamental paradigm shift in the employer–employee relationship: from the old slow-moving, rigid, pay-your-dues-and-climb-the-ladder model to the new fast-moving, increasingly efficient free market for talent. Employing people in the free market for talent requires a whole new set of management practices, I urged.

Several weeks later, I was with a handful of senior executives from J.P. Morgan and one of them whispered to me, "I hope you noticed: Just two weeks after you spoke to the managing directors, we went to casual dress." I objected, "But I didn't say a word about casual dress in my presentation." And he replied, "I know, I think that was the only thing we could think of to do."

When the leaders of companies like Johnson & Johnson and J.P. Morgan call on me to help them win the talent wars, I wish I could tell them that all they have to change is the dress code. But we are way beyond that stage.

This is the essence of the talent wars: In the new economy, every term of employment—schedules, location, assignments, coworkers, pay, and more—will be open to negotiation, whether you like it or not. The most valuable talent will have the most negotiating power. Every employment relationship will last exactly as long as the terms are agreeable to all the parties.

Usually, at this point in my discussions with business leaders, most of them are wincing: "How are we going to get all the work done when our managers are spending half their time negotiating and all of our employees are demanding flexible work arrangements?"

This is the dilemma that business leaders are wrestling with every day now.

In fact, Ralph Larsen at Johnson & Johnson and Douglas ("Sandy") Warner, who is chairman of J.P. Morgan, are both visionary business leaders. They are shepherding their companies through the most profound changes in the economy since the Industrial Revolution. Each is seriously tackling the issue of organizational flexibility in what many would think of as stalwart old-economy companies. But as stewards of phenomenally successful enterprises with grand traditions, both Mr. Larsen and Mr. Warner bear a deep responsibility to make great changes with great care.

They, like every leader and manager I know, want new management solutions, but they want new solutions that are already field-tested. It just happens that if you want to move at the speed of the new economy, it is very difficult to identify and implement solutions that have been adequately field-tested and are still cutting edge. That's why they call me.

Since 1993, I have been researching the transition to the new economy from the front lines of the workplace. Back then, my colleagues and I started investigating the work attitudes of the emerging workforce of the time, Generation X. But even as *Managing Generation X* (my first book) was receiving a great deal of attention, I realized that our research was revealing something much more profound than the underpinnings of the new generation gap: the vanguard of free agency.

Through thousands of in-depth workplace interviews, our ongoing research has allowed me to watch the free-agent mind-set sweep across the workforce among people of all ages and create the staffing crisis facing employers today. In hundreds of seminars and problem-solving sessions with tens of thousands of leaders and managers from every industry all over the world, I have searched for solutions to the staffing crisis being field-tested in real time on the front lines of organizations great and small. Some of the most brilliant solutions come from smart managers who simply must get the work done very well and very fast and have no time to mess around. Their ad hoc strategies are often explicitly prohibited by corporate policies. So what? They work.

I don't care where the solutions come from[1] or how subversive they may seem in their corporate settings. I look for strategies that accept the rising tide of free agency, embrace the new free market for talent, and allow organizations to get really good at being fluid. That's what you will find in this book.

From all of our research and our work with leaders and managers, I've been collecting the pieces of a puzzle that begs to be put together—a new set of organizing principles for employing people in the new economy:

> **Talent is the show.**
> **Staff the work, not the jobs.**
> **Pay for performance, and nothing else.**
> **Turn managers into coaches.**
> **Train for the mission, not the long haul.**
> **Create as many career paths as you have people.**

These principles are the foundation of this book. The pages are filled with research and lots of examples of working solutions to the staffing crisis, but I am mindful of something I recently heard from Gary Hamel, who holds chairs at both the Harvard Business School and the London Business School: "You can buy knowledge by the yard today, but insight is still quite rare." If you find that this book contains valuable insight, then I have achieved my goal in writing it.

Chapter 1

THE NEW
ECONOMY 101

Recently I conducted a seminar for leaders of a Silicon Valley–based company with about a thousand employees that makes monitoring devices and is owned by a Fortune 100 company. At the break, a young woman regaled me with this story: The president of the company has been leaning on people intensely to work harder and smarter, use fewer resources, get more done, and so on. Of course, whenever a president starts leaning on his direct reports, the impact cascades throughout the organization. But in this case, the president called a series of meetings because he wanted to deliver the message in person: "Nobody's job here is safe. If you are not producing, you're gone." The young woman continued with her side of the story. She told me, "I was sitting there holding onto both armrests to keep myself from jumping up and saying, 'Ooooh, I'm scared. I may have to go across the street and work for someone else and get a $10,000 signing bonus, and massages at my desk.' What was this guy thinking? What makes him think he has any power over my career?"

Wow. That's all I could think. It's true that I was in the heart of Silicon Valley for this conversation, but still this was a fantastic company owned by one of the longest-standing and most successful mega-companies in the world. Here was no less than the president trying to strike some fear into his workforce. And all he got was silent mockery.

Welcome to the talent wars. Are you a general, a field commander, or a foot soldier?

❏ ❏ ❏

The economy is hot. Productivity is racing forward.[1] Profits are good. The company where you work is more lean and flexible than it used to be. And your job is harder than it's ever been.

You work more hours than you ever have before. You have more authority and greater access to senior management. You get more done than you ever thought possible. You know more every day because you don't have a choice. One thing you know for sure: You (and only you) are responsible for your own career in this new economy, so you'd better not fail. At the least, you'd better keep your options open. Your only source of career security is your own ability to get the job done; to get it done fast; to get it done well; to spot problems that nobody else has noticed (and solve them); to innovate; to motivate, lead, and manage your team of "individual contributors." And you are responsible for a steadily growing number of individual contributors.

You know you are up to the challenge. But you stress about it every day.

"THANKS FOR EVERYTHING, I'M GOING TO BE LEAVING"

Among the worst days are the ones when an individual on your team comes into your office and says, "Thanks for everything. I'm going to be leaving for a new opportunity." Imagine (or remember), this is somebody you really value, somebody you've invested in for weeks or months or years. And that person tells you she's going to be walking out the door with your investment. But: "No hard feelings."

You can't help but have hard feelings. It's debilitating to have an unexpected departure on your team. Everybody has to scramble to fill in the gaps. No matter how much everybody scrambles, details slip through the cracks.

Everybody has to scramble.

You have to get somebody new, fast, and then you're going to have to get that new person up to speed before the rest of the team (and you) can start making up for the time you've lost. More than likely, you'll end up going through a time-consuming (and expensive) hiring process to replace the person you've lost (the more old-fashioned the organization, the more involved the hiring process will be).

The position will have to be "described," posted internally, and placed in advertisements externally. Résumés will have to be reviewed; candidates will have to go through personality tests or some other screening process (some organizations require security clearance, which takes forever); and the candidates who get this far will be interviewed by a battery of managers, including yourself. Each will be assessed in one way or another for whether she is a "good fit." When a candidate is finally chosen, she will be assigned a start date; if she's lucky, there will be some kind of orientation beyond filling out personnel forms. And then, finally, you'll have a chance to get this person up to speed so she can start adding value on your team.

Of course, there is a rationale behind this kind of lengthy and deliberate hiring process: It is designed to choose long-term, pay-your-dues, climb-the-ladder–type employees. It is probably the same process by which you hired that valued team member who just told you she's leaving, "No hard feelings." And the person you hire to replace her isn't very likely to follow the old-fashioned career path either. But that's not your problem right this moment.

YOU NEED SOMEBODY VERY GOOD, RIGHT NOW

Your problem is simple: You need somebody very good, right now to fill the gap on your team. You can look internally for another staff person to fill the role. It's frowned upon to poach talent from other managers in the company, but maybe you can borrow somebody for a while. You probably will, although that person will be stretched thin, as his primary responsibilities are not going to disappear just because you need to borrow him. You could reshuffle the project and outsource some of the work, or you could bring in an independent contractor, a consultant, or a high-level temp. But you may have to go through some red tape (probably the purchasing department or human resources) to make that happen.

The human resources people know your problem very well and want to help. But they are short-staffed too and hamstrung by the same corporate policies holding you back.

Of course, the leaders in your organization, like those in every other company, are focused on the talent wars. And they know that turnover is the crux of the problem. But turnover-reduction programs have been limited in their effectiveness because they are usually focused on two things: (a) creating financial incentives for people to stay, and (b) becoming an "employer of choice," that is, a place where it is such a pleasure to work that nobody would want to leave. The problem is that these kinds of retention strategies thrust employers into bidding wars with other employers. Who can offer more money? Who can offer more perks? And who can offer money and perks in ways that are tied to or encourage (at least some) longevity of employment?

This approach made headlines when many of the big law firms throughout the United States began announcing across-the-board increases in associate pay of as much as 50 percent, intended to stem the tide of young lawyers departing the super–old-fashioned legal career path.[2] Many of the young lawyers I have interviewed recently told me, "I just got a $60,000 raise. Maybe I'll do this for a little while longer now." This reaction is consistent with the findings of research recently reported in the *Harvard Business Review* on the effects of golden handcuffs in the semiconductor industry. The study found that when large financial rewards were distributed, engineers often cashed in their profits and left.[3]

While this desperate financial bidding is most vivid in professional services firms, including a recent increase in salaries for starting MBAs by the leading finance firms, the approach has also been apparent in high-tech recruiting. It has, of late, been creeping into pay schemes from the management level all the way down the line in organizations unwilling to let go of the old-fashioned career path. Of course, the senior executives at these firms are attempting to buy much more than a little more time. They want to keep these young professionals on the old "up or out" path until the senior partners decide whether or not they want each of the associates to stay or go. In pursuing this strategy, however, these firms have (purportedly) locked themselves into very expensive long-term deals that will cause them to (a) pay less to partners, (b) charge more to clients, or (c) require young professionals to work even harder than they already do (difficult to imagine).

Having done this, imagine the feeling of these executives whenever the markets manifest their new, wild gyrations. When the market plummets, they might be thinking, "Oh, no. . . . We've just raised salaries dramatically. Now we are going to be so financially overcommitted we won't know what to do." But of course they are not. Instead they are thinking, "Hmmm. . . . We may have to get rid of a bunch of employees and draw back those pay raises." That's because bidding up pay in the context of long-term employment relationships is at best a pretend game and at worst a foolish business error. Staffing levels and pay must be as flexible as the market is fast.

DON'T GET CAUGHT IN A BIDDING CONTEST

Here's the quandary: The talent wars cannot be won by outbidding other employers. Business leaders who try this strategy will win a few battles, but they are destined to lose the war because their long-term employment model makes them sluggish. Routinely, they will find themselves bloated when they need to be lean and too lean when they need more people. Instead of figuring out how to operate successfully in an increasingly fluid labor market, they are trying to hold back the tide with money.

It's as if these managers are saying to their employees, "If we pay you enough, will you please consider paying your dues and climbing the ladder at least for a little while? . . . Please?" But once the boss is begging and bribing employees to convince them to follow the organization's established career path, you've already lost the spirit of old-fashioned dues paying anyway.

The talent problem facing employers goes way beyond money. Don't get me wrong, money does matter in the war for talent, but employers need only offer enough money to be competitive with others vying for the same talent. By trying to bid against their employees' competing career options, such business leaders are missing the point. The real problem most employers face when it comes to retaining their best talent is that they offer a rigid one-size-fits-all, long-term career path. It is this anachronism that their hot talent is fleeing. Instead of thinking about how they can change their approach to managing their workforce, these employers have decided to pay through the nose so they can keep employing people the same way they always have.

In an environment of constant downsizing, restructuring, and reengineering (every day, newspapers report on the ongoing surgical downsizing in companies in every industry),[4] this old model doesn't work. Employees know better, yet most business leaders and managers are still pretty attached to having the same people they may restructure out of a job tomorrow loyally pay their dues and climb the ladder today. Whole layers on the organization chart may have been removed, but the old structure is still in place.

So employers are paying more and more to get people to play the old game even for a little while. The problem is that with so many employers engaged not just in retention efforts but also in massive recruiting efforts, the retention bidding wars turn into recruiting bidding wars. And it's a vicious cycle, driving up the cost for these organizations of employing the best people, without increasing retention much at all.

The most effective employers in the new economy will avoid old-fashioned wage pressure by employing people in sync with the fluid market. They will employ people only when they are needed and pay them what they are worth on the market one day at a time, rather than trying to make purportedly long-term employment and pay deals that are insulated from market forces.

THE BEST PEOPLE ARE THE MOST LIKELY TO LEAVE . . . BECAUSE THEY CAN

You know turnover numbers are increasing.[5] Guess what? That's only the tip of the iceberg. What should be worrying you much more is that the very nature of turnover is changing.

It used to be that you could pretty well count on the best people you recruited to rise to the top, while the mediocre people would drop off along the way. You didn't expect everybody who came to work for you to achieve a long-term successful career in your organization. Right? There was a challenge hanging out there in front of people when they walked in your door: "Can you make it here?" The best people would rise to that challenge, pay their dues, and climb the ladder, one rung at a time.

In the new economy, the best people are the most likely to leave. Why? Because they can. And they are likely to leave long before they've paid their dues or even paid a return on your recruiting and training investment.

That's what you are dealing with on a regular basis. More and more of your best people are leaving, or talking about it, or thinking about it. You could retain more of them if your hands weren't tied by company policy. You know that a lot of the old rules are obsolete. You want to cut through the red tape, but you have to balance your role as advocate for your team with your other responsibilities. So you do what you can. But as much as you try, some of the changes you know you should make are just "not the way things are done around here." So you keep losing really good people. And you are the one who has to deal with all the problems that causes, but you're not even sure who to be mad at.

> **More and more of your best people are leaving, or talking about it, or thinking about it.**

After all, you have thought about leaving too. Maybe you've fantasized about the dot-com option, or starting your own business. It wouldn't have to be a high-overhead enterprise. You could work out of your living room as a consultant. Or maybe you've started listening just a little when the headhunter calls, just to see what he says. How often does your boss call up and offer that vacation and raise the headhunter has been dangling in front of you? You know you could go work for your former boss or coworker, that supplier you deal with, or any number of your clients and customers. Sometimes it's tempting, especially on the really tough days. It seems like everybody is doing it. If you have to be responsible for your own career, then so be it, you're going to start looking out for your own interests. Who could blame you?

OK. Then what about that valuable individual who leaves your team, walks across the street, and goes to work for the competition, or a former boss, or a supplier, or one of your clients or customers? How can you blame her? But you do. You can't help it. Because she makes your very stressful job much more difficult.

WHERE DID ALL YOUR POWER GO?

Riddle: What's even worse than losing a valuable individual on your team? Answer: When the people remaining on the team begin to realize that it would be easy for them to leave too . . . and they begin to appreciate what that would cost you (and the organization) in time, energy, and money.

Everyone saw how much the last departure hurt, and that makes each person on the team feel more valuable. Suddenly they are aware of how much power they have in the employment relationship. So each person starts pushing for a better "deal" and each person has his own set of demands: This one wants more money. That one wants a different schedule. Another person wants to trade in her responsibilities for a whole new set. This one wants to be included in high-level meetings. That one wants to attend a particular training program. Still another wants to start telecommuting . . . from a thousand miles away.

Soon you find yourself pressed to negotiate about the most basic terms of employment on an ongoing basis with just about every person on your team. Of course, the people you need the most have the most negotiating power (and they know it). Your traditional power as a manager is gone. Never mind recruiting and retaining the best people. How are you supposed to manage the people on your team, drive their performance, and hold them accountable every day when they have so much negotiating power?

After all, you are the boss. Just look at the organization chart. As the manager, you assign the choice projects (and the really horrendous ones). You make the schedule. You decide who is going to work with whom. You may have the power to relocate people from one city to another or even from one country to another. You have a substantial impact on your employees' paychecks and on their prospects for promotion. You do their performance reviews. And you even have some discretionary resources to dole out—office space, training opportunities, exposure to decision makers, time off . . . maybe even cash.

If anything, within the confines of the new "lean and mean" organization, managers now have more control than ever over discretionary resources. You still have all of the authority described above and the corresponding power, probably even more. It's just not very much power, as it turns out.

The power you've lost has a much deeper source, so deep that it is not immediately apparent. In the workplace of the past, managers had power over people precisely to the extent that those people bought into the old-fashioned model of success. According to this model, if you were successful, it was because you had hitched your wagon to the star of an established organization, paid your dues, and climbed the ladder. Not every successful person had worked for the same employer for decades on end, but still, that was the default presumption. That's what success looked like. And that's what most of the best workers aspired to.

Of course, plenty of tangible constraints reinforced this old-fashioned aspiration. Most employee benefits were not as portable as they are today. Job-hopping was generally frowned upon, and a "spotty" résumé could damage your career. When you did change jobs, your new prospective employer would ask quite seriously, "Why did you leave?" Letters of reference from your previous employer could make or break you. And employee poaching was very rare—managers in one company respected (more or less) the sanctity of the employer–employee relationship in another company.

What is more, in the relatively stable environment of the past, company-specific knowledge (the players, practices, and policies) added much more to a person's value. This type of knowledge typically takes a long time to accumulate and, in the past, it didn't become obsolete quickly because organizations were not changing by the minute. Plus the kind of company-specific knowledge most people had did make them very valuable to their long-term employer, but it wasn't transferable: Knowledge specific to one company didn't usually make a person particularly valuable to another company.

As important as these tangible constraints may have been, by far the most powerful aspect of the old-fashioned career aspiration was the aspiration itself, and the social/cultural norms supporting it. Until recently, the dominant norm of success was based on a very small number of long-term employment relationships with established employers. As a result, employers and those entrusted with organizational authority—managers—had a near monopoly on the apparently legitimate success prospects of their employees. Not anymore. And that's how managers lost their traditional power.

THE OLD MODEL OF WORK ISN'T WORKING ANYMORE

Somewhere around the mid-eighties, management experts and business leaders decided the old-fashioned model of work wasn't working very well anymore. And they were right. Technology and globalization and the information tidal wave were (and still are) driving a business environment of increasingly chaotic markets and, thus, unpredictable resource needs. In the new high-speed business world, organizations would have to be able to deploy (and redeploy) resources at a just-in-time pace. Especially human resources. So people would have to adapt from a work environment of relative stability to one of considerable turmoil. The word went out: "Be prepared to do whatever needs to be done whenever it needs to be done, to move from one project to another, from one team to another, to use one skill set today and another skill set tomorrow."

Work would no longer be organized in neat little packages ("job descriptions") that remained relatively constant over time. (This is what Dr. William Bridges, the former literature professor turned business guru, refers to in his many best-selling books as the "dejobbing" of the workplace.)[6] There would still be tons of work to be done. It's just that having individuals go to the same place during the same hours every day and do the same tasks and responsibilities in the same position in the same chain of command was too rigid. That old model and its corresponding bargain of dues paying for job security was constraining organizational agility. Employers decided to loosen up the relationship between employers and employees. So companies downsized, restructured, and reengineered for maximum flexibility.

Remember? The reality of the changing workplace bargain was very scary for a lot of people in the late eighties and early nineties. People were clinging to their jobs like they would to trees in the midst of a hurricane, pleading, "Don't downsize me."[7] What happened? The downsizing hasn't slowed down; it has accelerated. Unemployment is at record lows,[8] but downsizing is at record highs.[9] Why are people no longer afraid? Not because all of a sudden there is job security. That is a great irony. In the midst of the talent wars, there is no job security. People simply got used to all the uncertainty and started taking responsibility for their own success and security.[10]

> **In the midst of the talent wars, there is no job security.**

Most people have found (or are finding) that they can fend for themselves just fine, and a steadily growing number like it much better this way, especially since the changes in the business world are working like a charm on the macrolevel. By loosening up the relationship between employers and employees and thus increasing their agility, companies have been able to drive productivity to previously unheard-of levels—and they're just getting started.

That is the rest of the great irony of the new economy: The surge in prosperity that so many people are enjoying comes directly from the same forces that have demolished job security forever (the same forces that scared the hell out of everybody for about fifteen years). Many have argued that it's technology (not the transformation of the employer–employee relationship) driving the new productivity and profitability.[11] The fact is, without corresponding organizational change, available technologies would be pointless.

Management experts said, "Get rid of the old workplace bargain or your organization will never become agile. Cut people loose to fend for themselves." There have been (and will continue to be) bumps in the road and real human casualties. But overall, let's be honest, it's working: We are in the midst of a transition from a relatively closed (protected), information-starved, slow-moving, and thus, inefficient labor market, to one that is increasingly open (free), information rich, faster moving, and thus, more efficient.

THE FREE-AGENT MIND-SET

Did anybody really think it would be just the people who were downsized who would start thinking like free agents? This is capitalism. If you create a free market for anything, including talent, the people with the most value to sell are going to leverage it for everything it's worth. And that's what's happening. The most valuable people are leveraging their talent in the marketplace for everything it's worth. Success now is defined by the open market, and that means the sky is the limit. No single organizational hierarchy puts a cap on your potential. Go wherever opportunity takes you. That is the essence of the free-agent mind-set.

"You want me to fend for myself?" says the free agent. "Fine. Show me the job you want done and pay me appropriately for doing it, when I do it, with hard, cold cash, not with promises of rewards I may or may not be around to receive down the line. Forget the 'welcome to the family' routine. Pay me now and keep your five-, ten-, and twenty-five-year silver service pins and the retirement gold watch because I don't even know where I will be two years from today, let alone if I will be here working for you."

Work is a day-to-day bargain. (Or maybe it's week-to-week. A senior executive at General Electric once shared with me that Jack Welch, the legendary CEO and prophet of the new economy, liked to tell people, "At the end of the week, we cut your paycheck. You don't owe me anything and I don't owe you anything. We start fresh on Monday.") Success no longer lies in your position on any organization chart, but rather in marketable skills, relationships with decision makers, tangible results bearing your signature (proof of your ability to add value), and opportunities to balance work with the rest of your life. Career security no longer comes from stability and commitments, but rather from options—the more options the better because then you are prepared, at any time, to cash out and renegotiate—or else move on to a new employer.

Of course free agency is still scary to a lot of people. But it's catching on.

The free agent is the hero of the new economy: She is adaptable, technoliterate, innovative, self-reliant, and entrepreneurial. But you know very well, from personal experience, that the free agent is also a pain in the ass to manage. Why? Because he doesn't want to be told what to do, he wants everything his own way, and he's willing to walk away the moment his demands are not met. The more valuable she is, the more negotiating power she has. And she's willing to drive a hard bargain (every day). How do you manage people if you don't have power over them?

"IT'S THE NEW ECONOMY, STUPID!"—THREE PHASES OF TRANSITION

Think of it this way: Phase one of the transition to the new economy was characterized by downsizing, restructuring, and reengineering.[12] That's all very complicated. But the most profound thing that happened in phase one is very simple: Employers disavowed their obligations to employees with respect to job security and sent a loud and clear message that individuals must take personal responsibility for their own careers.

Phase two of the transition is the rising tide of the free-agent mind-set among individuals in direct response to employers' disavowal of job security. Individuals have taken responsibility for their own careers, and now most are looking out for themselves first and foremost in their relationships with employers. Together, phases one and two have set in motion a powerful dynamic between employers (who must remain lean and flexible) and individuals (who must be prepared to fend for themselves).

In phase three, which we are now entering,[13] this powerful dynamic continues to transform the employer–employee relationship from one that was feudal to one that is essentially market driven. Peter Capelli, who heads the Center for Human Resources at the University of Pennsylvania's Wharton School of Business, has been conducting the leading academic research on this transformation. Professor

Capelli finds that companies cannot possibly insulate themselves from today's labor market and that long-term, across-the-board employee loyalty is neither possible nor desirable in a market-driven environment.[14] This means abandoning employment relationships that were relatively fixed, insulated from outside market factors, and governed by each employer's self-contained hierarchy and moving to employment relationships that are constantly renegotiated on the basis of often-volatile market factors both inside and outside the relationship itself.

This shift is already happening, but many employers are digging in their heels and trying to protect their feudal organization charts. They want to stay somewhere between phase one and phase two, and all of their retention and recruiting strategies reflect their deep denial that we are hurtling now to phase three. Employers who make the transition effectively will win battle after battle in the talent wars, at first thwarting, and later slaying, those who do not. In short, phase three is where employers get really good at employing people in a whole new way . . . or else they go out of business.

The really good news is that the simple but gargantuan shift to market-driven employment relationships is great for the economy. Free markets are very efficient (though not without casualties), and efficient systems reproduce effective behavior. Whereas the feudal employment system caused employers to bear much of the risk (and the costs) of fluctuations in the market value of individuals' skills and abilities, the market-driven model diversifies this risk (and the costs) among individuals themselves.

In a market-driven system, the price of an individual's skills and abilities goes up when they are in great demand and goes down when they are not. If the market is efficient, due to constant renegotiation in the face of new information, people are always (or more often than not) being paid what they are worth because the price is elastic. This shift will gradually eliminate the old-fashioned wage-pressure dynamic and, with it, the formerly inevitable long-term macroswings in the economy. In the new economy, the macroswings are likely to be very brief and very fast, reflecting the now critical microswings that will occur in the lives of companies and the careers of individuals. This diversification of exposure to the market puts a lot of pressure on individuals to be really valuable and on companies to be really good purchasers of that labor value . . . and that should be great for the economy as a whole.

GET YOUR POWER BACK

What managers need, if they are going to get their power back—what *you* need if you are going to get your power back—is to move on to phase three of the transition to the new economy. You need a whole new set of flexible management practices designed to embrace free agency and work with it, embrace the fluid workforce and work with it, maximize market-driven employment relationships, and start winning battles in the talent wars. Make the transition to the new economy, with or without your boss, with or without the company where you work. Just make the transition.

Here's the thing: You already know what to do. Right? You know things have to change. You know that work nowadays is a day-to-day (or week-to-week) bargain. You know that you and your colleagues need more flexible staffing options at your disposal. You need to be able to staff up quickly when the right opportunities present themselves, and you need to be able to staff down just as quickly when those opportunities disappear. You know that the best team for one project is not the same as the best team for another: You need to be able to pull the right people together from wherever you can find them, when you need them. You need to be able to get people up to speed quickly so they can start adding value right away, and you'd love people to have access to learning resources on an as-needed basis. You want to pay your best people what they are worth (a lot) when they deliver, especially when they go the extra mile. And there are others you'd like to pay much less and, when they fail to deliver, you'd like to pay them not at all. In many cases, you don't care where people work or when they work, as long as they get the job done very well and ahead of schedule.

Sure, sometimes you mourn the loss of your traditional management power, but for the most part you don't want to manage by fear—you know that you get the best work out of people when you coach them along to success. And you understand that a one-size-fits-all career path doesn't make sense for anyone anymore. You'd like to be able to fast-track some of your telecommuters and slow-track some of the face-timers. You'd rather have someone work part-time or flex-time than lose him altogether. With some employees, you wouldn't even mind sharing them with another employer or letting them leave and come back, as long as they come back.

You are ready to be a flexible manager and negotiate every day to get the best work out of the best people. But there are so many obstacles in your way. Your discretion is limited. You can't just go ahead and change everything about the way the business is run. Many of the things you know you and your colleagues should be doing are against established policies of the company. It takes a lot of planning and careful implementation to change hiring practices, training programs, and compensation systems. Improving the people skills of certain managers would seem to require an act of none other than the Almighty. Plus there are so many intangibles in any organization, you can't just rewrite the corporate culture overnight. There are lots of people (maybe you) who have been in the organization for decades, and they have indeed paid their dues and climbed the ladder. Why would they give up their seniority, authority, and privilege?

You can't just ignore the organization chart. There's a chain of command. In all fairness to your boss and his boss, resources are limited, and they have to be allocated at a higher level before you can start expending them. And you don't have all the relevant information—there must be numerous factors out of your view that you are not taking into account. Having everybody go off in their own direction or do things their own way may sound good, but it's just not practical. It would be an administrative nightmare.

Remove the biggest obstacle of all, the only one that is really holding you back: fear.

There are very real obstacles in your way, and it's very difficult to push past them, no matter how much energy you exert. Let me tell you a basic law of energy flow I learned from a nuclear physicist one time when I was doing a seminar at Sandia, the nuclear weapons research laboratory in Albuquerque, New Mexico: If you exert energy in one direction and an obstacle gets in your way, less energy is required (always) to remove the obstacle than to push past it.

How can you remove all these obstacles in your way? You can't. But you can remove the biggest obstacle of all, the only one that is really holding you back: fear.

You have a lot on the line and you need to be careful about trying to change too much, too fast. You could get yourself fired for doing some of the things you know you should be doing. At the least you could make yourself some serious enemies pretty fast and be ostracized from important power circles. All of a sudden, you could feel like an outsider instead of an insider. You could start getting negative reviews, be passed over for promotions, miss out on some hot projects, lose access to resources, and have your influence diminished to that of a gadfly.

Even if you could get away with bucking the system, becoming a change leader, and managing people differently, it might not work. If you abandon your claim to old-fashioned management power, you may never find a new source of strength. What if it's just a slippery slope? What if you embrace the free-agent mind-set and start negotiating the terms of employment with people on an ongoing basis, and they just demand more? You accept the fluid workforce and try to get good at being fluid and your turnover goes through the roof? All hell could break loose.

That's fear talking. Remove that obstacle and finish your transition to the new economy. History is on your side. The economy is changing right before your eyes. Get there first. No matter where you work, your organization will get there eventually, or else go out of business. Get there first. The free agents are almost there. Get there first.

BE A CHANGE LEADER

You can't change the whole business by yourself.[15] So what? Change the way *you* do business right now. Become the leader who always mobilizes the best team for any project anywhere, anytime—who always gets the job done, gets it done fast, gets it done well, and in the process captures the best innovations of the team. If you become that leader, you will be so valuable on the open market that you'll have absolutely nothing to fear. Sidestep rules if you have to. Don't ask for permission. Make it happen. You will, no doubt, alienate those who are digging in their heels and resisting change. Whatever. They are obsolete. Avoid them.

Ultimately you can't separate your role as free agent from your role as manager. As soon as you are willing to walk away, you have all the power you need to do everything you need to do. Who's going to win the talent wars? I'm going to tell you the ending of the story right here, right now. Talent wins. That's good news because that's you.

❏ ❏ ❏

You are the general, the field commander, and the foot soldier. Welcome to the talent wars.

Chapter 2

TALENT IS
THE SHOW

One question that leaders and managers are still asking is this: "How can we still be known for our people if we can't hire loyal talent anymore?" The question you should be asking is: "How can we maintain access to talent on a long-term basis, so we can still be known for our people?"

One day after a speech I gave in New Orleans, Mr. Chris Welcome came up to me (as people so often do) and said, "I've got to tell you this story." Mr. Welcome is a vice president at Countrywide Home Loans Inc., a Pasadena-based subsidiary of the $2-billion-a-year independent residential mortgage lender Countrywide Credit Industries. He manages a team of six techies focused on the development of artificial intelligence. Here's the story he told me.

For two years, Rita was a "knowledge engineer," responsible for initial problem solving for the branches using the team's automated loan-application-and-approval system. It took the first nine months for a handful of senior people to really get Rita up to speed on the system so she could answer the tough questions when branch-level employees called her at the help desk. It was another twelve months before Rita was a real pro. Then she and her husband decided to move, largely because of a job change for her husband, and she left the company. Soon thereafter, Mr. Welcome lost yet another of his key knowledge engineers.

So he contacted Rita to see if she could fill in. She began working four half-days from home and one day in the office and did so for *almost eight months before she left again . . . this time for her home-land, India. But Mr. Welcome still hasn't given up. He negotiated an arrangement whereby Rita will still handle the help desk, despite the remoteness of her location. She loves the work and needs the job. Mr. Welcome is smart enough to utilize her skills and continue to get a return on his training investment in Rita, while at the same time getting the critical work done that he needs done by the most qualified person. All it takes is a little call-forwarding technology and a lot of vision.*

If an employer has any hope of retaining the best people for the long term in the new economy, this retention will have to happen one person at a time, one day at a time, on the basis of an ongoing negoti-ation.

❑ ❑ ❑

You know very well that a single truly great person on your team is worth two, three, four, or five mediocre ones. The difference in value is hard to quantify, but the truth of the matter is clear: Nobody is more valuable than that person you can rely on without hesitation. That person almost always gets the job done right and ahead of schedule, takes exactly the right amount of initiative without over-stepping, makes the tough judgment calls as well as the easy ones, and makes it all look routine. For me that person is Jeff Coombs. Why can't I have a whole team of "Jeffs"? I've asked myself that question many times, and I'll bet you've asked the same question about the best member of your team.

Access to the best talent has always been critical to the success of any enterprise. That's nothing new. But in the workplace of the past, employers could practically own their most valuable talent, monopo-lizing them through long-term employment relationships. That's no longer possible because employers cannot really offer long-term job security to anybody anymore and because more and more people like Jeff are thinking like free agents.

The irony is that, in the new economy where it is impossible any-more to own the talent you need, access to talent is more important than ever before. Day after day the media reports on the competition for talented workers.[1] Study after study shows that access to the best talent is the number-one challenge facing the business world today.[2]

Why?

Throughout the transition to the new economy, employers have cut staff and invested in new technology, while individuals have assumed the responsibility to "add value" on a daily basis. If lean and flexible organizations are going to succeed, they need to get more and better work out of fewer people. That means those few people have to be very good.

Meanwhile so much work previously done by human beings can be done very well and very fast (twenty-four hours a day, seven days a week, if necessary) by machines. So there is a diminishing amount of low-skill work available for people, while an increasing amount of high-skill work is required.[3] Researchers at Stanford University have been studying the effects of technological advances on skill levels in the workplace. In particular, the work of Professor Roberto Fernandez has quantified substantial increases in skill demand for both high-skilled jobs and what are typically thought of as lower-skilled jobs.[4]

LEARNING NEW TECHNICAL SKILLS IS THE EASY PART

With machines and computers infiltrating almost every aspect of most jobs, everybody has to muster greater technical skill (including human speed and accuracy) to get the work done. And that's just the tip of the iceberg. Even more pressing is the growing need for individuals at all levels to master nontechnical skills such as good judgment and personal responsibility that keep the systems moving when a problem arises (or redirect systems when an opportunity presents itself).

That's why, in the many seminars and problem-solving sessions I lead, I find business leaders and managers in every industry (from J.C. Penney to J.P. Morgan) scrambling to recruit, motivate, and retain the talented people necessary to compete successfully in the new high-tech, high-speed, knowledge-based, superfluid economy. Every day my clients tell me, "We have the right array of services and products, tremendous financial resources, and plenty of marketing savvy to pursue growth. We just don't have enough people with the right skills in place to get all the work done fast enough to seize all the market opportunities." And they are not only talking here about the techies and senior executives of the world, who are the dominant characters in the popular story of the talent wars. In the new economy, the strategic importance of talent goes to every level in every organization in every industry.

Just think, for a moment, of your own experience as a customer, let's say with a bank: You call their "telephone answer center" because you want to transfer funds from one account to another. An automated system answers your call, and you provide the touchtone inputs. You are ready to execute the transaction, but then you realize you have a question. "Is there a minimum balance required in my checking account?" So you bail out of the automated system by pressing "0." When you reach a live customer-service operator, you want to talk with somebody who can answer your question. Of course, once you receive the information you request, another question may come up. "Can I change to an account that doesn't require a minimum balance?" The answer to that question may yield another. "Can I change the account right now, with you, over the phone?" And on and on. Every step of the way, technical skill, good judgment, and effective action is required on the part of the customer-service operator.

You can be sure that automated telephone answer centers put plenty of customer-service operators out of work. Those who remain can do more for you than ever before, assisted by new technology. But they must also learn to operate new software, to navigate new databases, and to respond personally to inputs that the technology does not anticipate. They must think on their feet, exercise judgment, and sometimes improvise to satisfy a customer's needs.

Here's the funny thing: As technology becomes more complex, it also becomes easier to use. The real challenge for human talent is mastering the nontechnical skills necessary to fully maximize the potential of technology. Technology makes instant responsiveness possible, but human beings on the front lines must promptly exercise judgment and take effective action to make it happen.

JUDGMENT IS THE "KILLER APP" OF THE HUMAN BRAIN

The first time I went to Saginaw, Michigan, I spent a full day conducting seminars for all the senior engineers at Delphi Saginaw Steering Systems, the world's largest producer of integral steering and driveline technologies (the machinery that makes the steering wheel work in your car). The steering systems division in Saginaw is part of Delphi Automotive Systems, the great General Motors spin-off success story. In 1999, Delphi became an independent company as part of GM's major shift away from vertical integration. John F. Smith, chairman of GM, says, "The Delphi team has transformed our component operation from a sluggish, internally focused group of in-house suppliers into an integrated and fast-moving team capable of competing head-on with the toughest competitors."

The spin-off means GM has a leaner, faster, more flexible production system that can "anticipate and respond to an ever-changing market and fast-moving competition," according to Mr. Smith. For Delphi, the imperative is to succeed in entrepreneurial terms, now that it has a separate bottom line from GM. This mission promotes innovation.[5]

While I was touring the manufacturing facility, forklifts were zooming around the plant floor, carrying parts to different workstations. I was taken aback when I saw that the forklifts had no drivers. They were not, in fact, forklifts, but robots, taking parts just in time to exactly the right place in perfect sync with the plant's computer-based business-to-business ordering system.

Here's how it works: General Motors orders up, over the Internet, exactly the number and type of steering systems they want shipped . . . in the next ship window (several hours).[6] That's right, it's usually just a matter of hours. Then the process is set in motion: The robots begin transporting the right parts to the right places. The tiny assembly lines and individual workcells do whatever retooling is necessary to adjust to the particular assembly needs of each order. The manufacturing software resets the machinery, and the individual technicians reset themselves. Everything is in place to fulfill the order . . . so it can be shipped exactly when it's needed.

This goes on all day, every day at Delphi and many other reengi-neered manufacturing facilities throughout the world. There's not much need for forklift drivers anymore. The ordering process, inventory management, and order fulfillment are all streamlined, and that streamlined system is fully integrated with the manufacturing process itself through enterprise software. Superlean and highly productive, such a plant can fill the same order much faster and with half the number of people it used to require.

Sure, just-in-time manufacturing is old hat to many in the business world, but think about what this requires of the individual contributors on the front lines of the factory: speed, focus, and adaptability. That's a tall order and a far cry from the image many still have of the UAW card-carrying factory laborer. (By the way, I've included my thoughts about the future of unions in Appendix 2.) No longer does the factory worker do the same thing, day in and day out, a slave to the assembly line. Now she must be prepared to work on one component this morning and another this afternoon. She must keep up with high-speed, high-tech production systems. What is more, with quality controls like Six Sigma[7] in place, there is virtually no room for error. Individuals are expected to achieve an almost machinelike level of accuracy in their work.

Wait: There's more. One of the engineers at Delphi explained to me that the organization is further adjusting its manufacturing operation, to push more of the work away from assembly lines toward small cells of individual workstations. This will give each person on the factory floor even more ownership of the components he is manufacturing and more responsibility for quality. In an assembly line, each individual on the line does one (or one and a quarter) of several steps in taking the component from point A to point B. In the small-cell approach, each individual takes the component from point A to point B himself.

Quality experts believe that, in this setup, individual contributors will be able to identify problems almost immediately, as they are assembling the components. It's not that the workers are expected to exercise creative discretion in the assembly process ("I really like this piece better at two centimeters diameter, instead of three"). To the contrary, exact specifications must be adhered to with great precision. But the workers are being asked to exercise judgment: Do all the parts in the assembly process look right? Are my tools working optimally? Is there a faster or otherwise better way to achieve the result?

To work in the factory of today,[8] it is not enough to know how to operate the machines. Nor is it enough to bring speed, focus, and adaptability to the table. In the new economy, judgment is required of human talent. Judgment is the "killer app" of the human brain, and it is the new standard for human talent in the workplace. Lean and flexible organizations utilizing new technologies can do more work with fewer people, but those people must be high performers. Those who exercise good judgment are worth their weight in gold, because there is no technology other than the human brain that can exercise judgment.

> **There is no technology other than the human brain that can exercise judgment.**

THE WHOLE GAME IS MOVING TO A HIGHER LEVEL

Picture this: You work in the ordering center of a warehouse, receiving orders via phone from field salespeople (who are out calling on customers) and passing those orders to a guy who drives a forklift into the warehouse to collect the merchandise and bring it to a loading area for shipping. If the ordered merchandise is not in inventory, you may call the manufacturing facility to see when new merchandise will be shipped, or you may be able to place a special order. You might even follow up via phone with the field salesperson to let her know the status of the order. Sometimes orders are shipped right away, other times they're delayed. Often it is difficult for the salesperson to let the customer know for sure.

But with Peoplesoft, or one of the other reengineering packages, the salesperson can now check available inventory at an online database herself from the field. She can set the fulfillment process in motion herself online and give the customer an exact timetable for delivery when the customer places the order. If the merchandise is not in inventory, she can check the manufacturing timetable and see what merchandise is coming off the line, what's already spoken for, what's available, and when. The salesperson no longer relies on a game of telephone with the warehouse and the factory. She can exercise her own judgment based on the inventory and manufacturing information available to her online, and she can now let her customer know exactly when the order will be shipped, virtually eliminating unexpected delays in delivery.

So what happens to your job receiving orders via phone in the warehouse? Gone. Downsized. Or, if you are lucky, retrained.

That's where the technical trainers come in and teach people to use the new software package (that does the work formerly done by six people in the warehouse). But the machine does all the easy (for a computer) stuff, like keeping millions of bytes of information organized perfectly and transmitting that information instantly wherever it is needed. The only work left for people at all points in the process is using the software (easy) and knowing what to do with all the information the software generates (not so easy). Now the warehouse manager is a database administrator, and the salesperson must also do the work of an inventory manager.

Because of the tremendous emphasis placed nowadays on technical skills, one could easily forget the growing importance of human judgment in the new workplace. Much of the new learning required of individuals right now is highly technical[9]—people need to learn how to use the new technologies being implemented. When reengineers install SAP or Peoplesoft or some other software package, everybody in the organization experiences a huge change in their day-to-day work. If you survive the inevitable staff reorganization, your new role will likely encompass many of your old responsibilities as well as many additional ones, all of which require knowledge of the new technical system.

It may be hard to appreciate just how traumatic such changes can be unless you have seen people living through them. I was at a management meeting for a company that makes and sells premier exercise equipment, just weeks before their switch to a Peoplesoft-driven sales-order-fulfillment system. One of the big management-consulting firms had implemented it for them, but there was an internal team of techies on the case as well.

When the techies gave their presentation on the imminent switch to the new system, tension filled the room. The groans from the audience were audible. That evening at dinner, I asked one of the most vocal complainers, a sales manager, whether he thought the software might fail. He told me, "I'm not worried about the software. I'm worried about myself and the guys in the field. We were all very experienced at our jobs. Now all of a sudden everybody's job is different." He went on, "Before, if an order went wrong, the salesmen could always blame the warehouse. The warehouse could always blame the factory. And the guys in the factory could say that the salespeople were promising customers too much. Now there is nobody to blame. All the information is there. The whole game is just moving to a higher level."

The whole game *is* moving to a higher level. So there is a growing premium on people, at all ends of the skill spectrum, who can work smarter, faster, and better. You want your people to be innovative (within guidelines), passionate (within reason), and armed with sufficient discretion to make mistakes (as long as they are not too big). Demand for those people is going to outpace supply for the foreseeable future.[10] Technology implementation will continue, organizations will become even leaner, the pace of change faster, competition more intense, businesses more customer focused, expected response times shorter, and productivity expectations will grow.

IN THE NEW ECONOMY, TALENT IS THE SHOW

The market value of results has always been an important equation in business. In the new economy, however, it's the critical equation. And there's going to be a perpetual tug of war between individuals and organizations (between talent and management) over who is going to control and leverage that market value. This reality calls for a more transactional approach to employing people. It's also central to the spiraling fluidity of employment relationships in the new economy.

It's easy to see why talented people are gaining so much power in their relationships with managers and why they are driving such a hard bargain when it comes to the terms of their employment. In lean, restructured companies, people are handling more responsibility, using greater technical skill, and applying more precious human judgment than ever before. Every individual, like every business, has his or her own value proposition to offer employers in the free market for talent, which simply means "Here's what I can do." And that value proposition is strictly business. One really good person is worth a whole pile of mediocre people. Really good people "can do" real things (very well and very fast) that add real value to your bottom line. And they know it. So you'd better learn how to do business with them.

Remember "Jeff"? Jeff is the senior executive talent who turns around a division in eighteen months. Jeff is the programmer who writes two lines of code for every one that an ordinary programmer generates. And Jeff is the call-center operator who dazzles every customer, gathers market research on the front lines, and routinely suggests improvements in the whole system. She's the salesperson in the field who can sell anything to anybody and who also monitors warehouse inventory and the production schedule from her palmtop computer. And the warehouse manager whom everybody knows by name, and who also knows the new database inside and out. Jeff is the factory worker who doubles as a quality-control engineer. He's the nonphysician health professional delivering care previously reserved only for doctors. And she's the soldier operating a laptop computer mounted on a tank in the midst of battle, who turns around as soon as the battle is won and plays the role of peacekeeper.[11]

Every manager wants a whole team of Jeffs. That's why, at every level now, in every industry, talent is the show. And talent drives a hard bargain because they know they add critical value and they want to get paid what they are worth—in both financial and nonfinancial rewards.

Let's take a step back. What can we learn from the first cadres of talented people who realized that they, not their employers, were, in fact, the show? I am talking about professional actors and athletes. They were the first free agents because their market value became transparent more rapidly than the rest of the workforce, due to the oddity of celebrity.[12]

Transparency of value comes from clear, abundant, and available information. Such information may originate from public sources such as the media, from intermediaries such as agents or headhunters, from the personal experience of individuals whose careers expose them to multiple employers, and from a community of peers with relatively fluid careers. These information sources, now turbocharged by the Internet, are rendering the value of talent across the board increasingly transparent. There is great significance to the recent explosion of chat rooms and message boards on the Internet, through which individuals are sharing information about compensation, benefits, and perks, according to the research of Harvard professor Monica C. Higgins. Professor Higgins's important longitudinal study of the career choices and work lives of Harvard MBA students reveals that, especially in times of great change, individuals rely heavily on relevant social comparison with others when making career decisions.[13]

While the real market value of individual celebrities can be measured in terms of ticket price or advertising revenue (the ability to draw viewers), the best way to measure the real market value of other talented people is not always so obvious. For that reason, it will take time for the free market for talent to reach a high level of accuracy and efficiency. But think about this: Celebrities draw viewers because they are known for something. Granted, sometimes that something they are known for is simply being famous. But usually they are known for what they can do—they are known for their talent.

> **Everybody in the new economy is running at least one business, whether they know it or not.**

That's what free agency is really all about. What can you do (very well, very fast)? And how much can you sell it for on the open market?

EMPLOYING PEOPLE IN THE NEW ECONOMY IS A JOINT VENTURE

Everybody in the new economy is running at least one business, whether they know it or not. It's been variously called You & Company; Me, Inc.; Brand You; and so on. That means employing people nowadays is always a business-to-business proposition. It's a joint venture. So all the terms of the deal (what, where, when, how, and how much) are open to negotiation. The venture is only going to last as long as the deal is working for all the parties. This is the fundamental difference between the old-fashioned employment model and the new one.

Let me put this fundamental difference in perspective: Rick is one of the people my company has interviewed as part of our ongoing in-depth interview research. Rick is about forty years old. He has had several jobs, mostly sales related. He's run his own business, a small retail store. Then he went to work as a territory manager for a company called Ecolab, Inc. You may know Ecolab. Based in St. Paul, Minnesota, the $3-billion-a-year company develops and markets sanitation products (ranging from bathroom soap dispensers for the office to restaurant dishwashing systems that can handle thousands of dishes). Ecolab operates in more than 160 countries with 17,800 worldwide employees. To get the job, Rick went through an elaborate selection process that took many weeks. When Ecolab finally hired him, he was psyched and so were they. "Great fit," they both thought.

Rick was given custody of a company van, notebook after notebook of product information, and boxes of product. He was given an existing customer list for his territory and was told that his job was to travel the territory, visiting with customers and increasing sales of the company's products. The best thing about the job, Rick said, was that the more soap products and equipment he was able to sell, the more money he would make. Great deal.

Rick was sent out to a company-run facility for several weeks of training. Most of the training was sales related, with a lot of product information hammered home, but a surprising amount of the training was very technical, having to do with equipment maintenance. When he returned, Rick tagged along with another territory manager for several weeks. Then, Rick's regional manager drove along with him for a few days a month until he got the hang of the job. Ecolab really made an investment in Rick, just as they do with every new territory manager. The company believes, rightly, that it's not enough to bring in the best talent—you've got to train them up to speed and give them the support they need.

Here's the catch: Rick's job wasn't really a sales job at all. Rick carried a beeper. Whenever a customer had a problem with Ecolab equipment, whether it was a soap dispenser or an industrial strength dishwasher, they would beep Rick and he would be expected to come and save the day. But Rick wasn't a skilled mechanic. And you can't learn to be a mechanic in a few weeks of training. Rick was told repeatedly by his regional manager, "Well, it's really something that takes time. You'll get the hang of it." Of course, he did get better at fixing the machines. But Rick still wasn't a mechanic. Plus, all of his incentives were tied to increasing sales, not fixing machines. "That's just part of the job," he was told over and over again.

After a while, the whole thing didn't seem like a very good fit or a very good deal to Rick. Most of his time was consumed with answering equipment-repair calls, so he didn't have time to cultivate sales. His hands were cut up and dirty from all the mechanical work. He was tired of getting called on Saturday evenings to fix the dishwashers at busy restaurants. Rick started to get grumpy. His manager started leaning on him, even telling him that his job was in jeopardy.

Think of the problem from Ecolab's point of view: Shouldn't they have identified Rick's lack of mechanical aptitude (and inclination) during the selection process? Maybe all we have here is a selection problem. But it's probably hard to find people who are skilled at both sales and mechanics. So you have to get a salesperson and teach him mechanics, or get a mechanic and teach him sales. Since the job is largely an equipment-maintenance job, maybe the emphasis should be more on finding someone with mechanical skills. However, it's more difficult to hire a trained mechanic for a job that requires only midlevel mechanical skills than it is to hire a sales type for what is really only a quasi-sales role. At some point, Ecolab decided they were going to squeeze the sales and mechanic roles together, and they must have determined that it would be easier to hire sales types and teach them the mechanical skills. Obviously, this approach has worked fine for a long time because Ecolab is a very successful company.

But in the workplace of the past, Ecolab could expect Rick to stick with the job long enough to get good at the mechanical tasks. So even when he discovered the job wasn't such a great fit, through on-the-job training, he would make it a decent fit over time. Thousands of territory managers have done it. To the extent that a territory manager like Rick felt the job had been oversold to him and that it wasn't such a great deal, he could have been expected to pay his dues through those first rough years of the job anyway. Eventually, it would pay off for him because Ecolab is a strong enough brand that its market share tends to grow even with weak sales efforts in the field. So Rick would benefit from big corporate accounts (like restaurant chains) that have nothing to do with his own sales, but add to the bottom line in his territory (although he also takes a hit when the company loses big corporate accounts). Plus there was always the chance Rick could climb the ladder and become a regional manager. If he just quit his job, in the old economy that would have been a black mark on his résumé.

In the workplace of the past, Ecolab didn't have to be great at employing territory managers. They just squeezed people into their organization chart and made it work. Well, it's not going to work anymore.

Here in the new economy, this is how Rick handled the situation: He sold all of his Ecolab training, his year of experience in the territory, and his relationships with customers to another company. Sofco, Inc., the $200-million-a-year paper goods company owned by the $8 billion giant, U.S. Foods (now owned by the Dutch holding company Ahold), based in Scotia, New York, didn't mind one bit that Rick was job-hopping from Ecolab. In fact, the Sofco manager who interviewed Rick could see right away he was going to get the dividends from Ecolab's considerable investment in Rick and he snapped him up right away. In his new job at Sofco, Rick just sells, which is what he wanted to do from the beginning. His rewards are really and truly tied to his own performance as a salesperson and he is earning good bonuses every quarter. This one is a great fit. And both parties to the negotiation feel they got a great deal.

Rick's territory is just about the same as he had with Ecolab, and he has many of the same customers. And get this: Rick sells, along with paper goods, many of Ecolab's soap products. That's right. Ecolab often uses other companies' salespeople to represent their products, right in the same territories where they have territory managers scrambling to sell and repair, repair and sell. Now Rick's old regional manager from Ecolab calls him on the phone periodically to "touch base" and make sure everything is "cool" between them. Why? Because Rick is a valuable outsourced salesperson, especially now that the regional manager is having a hard time filling Rick's position.

So who wins this battle in the talent wars? Sofco, right? And Rick too. But Ecolab loses big. Why? Because Ecolab's approach to talent is that talent doesn't really matter. What matters is filling the territory manager position. It's as if they decided, "We need a pitcher, but we'll just take a second baseman and turn him into a pitcher . . . and he can cover second base a little bit too. We've got time. We've been doing it this way for years." Good luck.

If I were the regional manager for Ecolab in this situation, here's what I would do: Outsource all of the sales in the territory to Sofco and keep getting a return on the investment Ecolab has already made in Rick. As for the equipment maintenance, one solution would be to hire a mechanic for that job and tie his or her rewards directly to the repair work. Another solution would be to contract with several local mechanics and pay them only for the calls they actually make. A third solution would be to give customers a limited warranty and let them deal with their own maintenance after the warranty expires. One thing I wouldn't do in a million years is let that training investment in Rick walk out the door forever.

You may be thinking, "This is just one case. Why should Ecolab retool their entire territory management system just because of Rick?" Of course, the answer is not a new system, company-wide, that works in the "Rick scenario." What Ecolab needs to do is retool, not its territory management system, but its way of employing people in the field so as to get all the work done very well, very fast in the best possible way. Managers need an approach to employing people that is flexible enough that they can mix and match staffing options to fit the changing situations in which they find themselves. Managers in the field need to be able to make a good fit between their needs, at any given moment, and the best talent available to them, at that same moment.

Should you be changing the work to be done so it fits the talent that is available? Of course not. But when the talent you have doesn't fit the work as it is currently arranged, the best solution is often to unbundle the tasks of current jobs and rearrange the work so it does fit. Michael Dell, the CEO of personal computer giant Dell Computer Corporation, is fond of telling people that business structure should "come last, not first," otherwise an organization is too rigid. Dell proudly reports that at his company, managers regularly separate the tasks that would normally make up one job, dividing responsibilities so they can maximize the best talent available to the company at any given time.

Had Rick's regional manager at Ecolab used that kind of flexible staffing approach, Ecolab would still be maximizing Rick's talent selling Ecolab's products in the territory. Now Softco is Rick's joint-venture partner, and Sofco is leveraging Rick's ability to sell, instead of Ecolab.

FACE THE CHALLENGES HEAD ON: GET REALLY GOOD AT BEING FLUID

It is time to let go of rigid organization structures and long-term employment models. Whatever it takes to get the work done, do it, no matter how much it stretches your current business practices. Explode the organization chart. It's only holding you back. Several leading researchers at the Stanford Business School have confirmed that when companies get locked into a particular way of organizing their workforce, they limit the options of managers trying to respond to shifting demands in the marketplace.[14] Don't limit your options. You need more ways to employ people.

> **Explode the organization chart. It's only holding you back.**

Take a look at the bleeding edge of the new economy: In the fast growing world of e-commerce, talent is so hot, there is simply no other choice but fluid staffing. Andrew is an e-commerce architect with a mortgage finance organization based in Washington, D.C. He tells me, "It is seriously a tough market. . . . The Washington, D.C., area has a significant number of high-growth companies that offer unique opportunities. There's AOL that offers folks the ability to participate in the 'Internet lottery' . . . while still having a measure of security. . . . And there are countless other (mostly small) e-commerce and other high-growth companies that offer the potential for even greater rewards along with the risk that the company may not survive."

How does a traditional finance company compete in an environment like that? "It is a constant struggle. It seems as soon as you've hired folks to fill the slots you need, current folks leave for some of those high-growth opportunities." So then what's the solution? "We use a mix of contractors, employees, part-timers and some-timers (the last two groups by keeping in touch with the really good folks that leave)." How does Andrew pull off that kind of flexible staffing in a company where the leadership prefers the organization chart? Of course, not everybody is going along with the new way. "It is frustrating to me to see significant numbers of management folks that just don't get it. They don't want the 'trouble' of flexible work arrangements. I've heard a number of stories where a really great staff member is leaving and willing to work part-time in a consulting role but the management folks in their group refuse. They usually say that 'it would be bad for morale to let a former employee make more money by contracting back.' They just don't get it. I approach it as a team of technical specialists working together to solve the problem. I take the lead in guiding the group's design solution and help folks get work that meets their goals.

"Part of our 'success' (at least we are close to keeping up with our needs) is that our group's management team is open to flexible staffing arrangements." Andrew reports that not only do these arrangements help his team meet productivity goals, but working with outsiders is also a boon to effective professional learning. He says, "I am actually working with a guy right now (contractor) on an e-commerce project where we essentially take turns coaching each other. He has about five years less experience in development than I do, but he's done a lot more e-commerce work. As a result, I have been able to fill in gaps in his experience in areas like building transaction systems for large companies, and he has, in turn, helped me better understand the emerging e-commerce Internet development space."

Perhaps the retail sector is a less obvious example of successful organizational fluidity. Having been a consultant to more than a dozen different retail organizations, I can tell you that high turnover is an operational norm throughout the industry, and supermarkets have the highest turnover. For that reason, there is much to be learned from the retail sector, especially supermarkets.

One of my clients, Publix Super Markets, a $13-billion-a-year chain that employs over 120,000 people in approximately 600 stores, is the tenth-largest supermarket chain in North America. How is it that Publix can have massive turnover among their store personnel and still be the number-one company in the world in any industry when it comes to customer satisfaction?[15] The answer: They have mastered both a strong core and a robust fluid-talent pool.

Some sixty thousand part-timers flow into Publix Super Markets as employees and then flow out again in any twelve-month period. That's 100 percent turnover. But Publix fills nearly twenty thousand full-time positions every year from the ranks of part-timers. Where do those full-timers come from, if all of the part-timers are leaving? The answer is that the part-timers leave and come back. Those who keep coming back eventually move into full-time positions. Among the sixty thousand or so full-timers at Publix, roughly one-third leave every year. Again, many come back. The best people move into management positions where the company has virtually no turnover. Publix hires absolutely no retail managers from outside the company. None. They select people into their core group exclusively from their fluid-talent pool. Publix maintains a strong and enduring culture because it is driven by people who understand fluidity from firsthand experience. And in seventy-one years of business, they've never lost a corporate officer to another company.

One Publix store manager told me at the company's 1999 annual management meeting, "When good people leave my store, they are always welcome to come back. Everybody who works for me knows that. So even if somebody has one foot out the door, he knows it's in his best interest to do a good job, to stay on good terms. You never know when they'll want to come back or get their brother or sister a job working in the store. I demand a lot, but the more you give me, the more flexible I am going to be."

This attitude is common among people in retail organizations of all sizes. Terri Freiman is director of human resources for West Point Market, a specialty food store with 177 employees in Akron, Ohio, that has been featured in the *Wall Street Journal,* the *New York Times,* and *Bon Appetit* among others. To go along with that cool store, Ms. Freiman has a very cool attitude about the people who work for the store. She asks rhetorically, "Isn't developing relationships what we do all the time?"

Ms. Freiman knows that enduring relationships with good talent can't always be maintained through uninterrupted employment alone. People leave West Point Market and come back again, all the time. The key to making that work is in how you handle people leaving. "In our employee break–room there is a big sign over the bulletin board that says 'Protect Our Good Name.' How can I help protect the company culture, reputation, and name if I have people leaving angry, hurt, and disgruntled?" She explains, "If I can make a call to another retailer and I can recommend a person who is leaving, I'll say, 'This person wants to work for you instead of me, will you talk to him?'" She continues, "How do I win if I am giving my employees away?" Because the relationship is ongoing, "What it does is insure that I haven't closed any doors from my side."

I know that, to those unaccustomed to thinking this way, managing the new superfluid workforce seems daunting. For starters, it sounds like an administrative nightmare. And then come the tough questions: How do you maintain any internal and external continuity? Will anybody work for you long enough to acquire professional depth? At what point will you get a decent return on your training investment? How will you have enough leverage with people to demand very high levels of performance? These concerns are very real. That's why most efforts to deal with the staffing crisis are still focused on holding back the inevitable tide.

But trying to hold back the tide is keeping business leaders from seeing the obvious answer: Jump in and learn how to swim. Your organization is going to get fluid. The free market for talent will take care of that. The challenge is to get really good at being fluid by becoming incredibly flexible. The way to do that is not to scrap long-term employment relationships, but rather to reinvent them.

LONG-TERM EMPLOYMENT REINVENTED AS FLUID AND FLEXIBLE

You can reinvent long-term employment, and thus save it, by having a wide repertoire of ways to employ people. Actually, you'll need an infinite number. And you might as well get started because this outcome is inevitable in a free market for talent. Think about it: In a free market, you get what you can negotiate. That's it. Every negotiation turns out differently depending upon the value proposition at stake, the skill of the people negotiating, and the degree to which each party can compromise. Obviously the deal you will make with a cashier in a grocery store is going to look quite different from the deal you make with the manager, and that deal will look quite different from the deal you make with the software developers on your e-commerce team.

You can reinvent long-term employment.

If every condition of employment—not just pay, but schedule, duration of employment, location, assignments, and so forth—is on the table, your negotiating position as a manager is stronger, not weaker. Instead of negotiating with your hands tied, you can make the best deal that makes sense in every situation. Ultimately, the more terms of employment that are on the table, the more ways you have to employ people, get the work done, and retain your workers.

The flip side is this: In a free-market environment, the best people at every level will be able to negotiate the best deals. That's the way it should be. In fact, the very best people at every level can just about name their own terms, as long as they get all the work done. As long as they get all the work done, why shouldn't they name their terms? That's a pretty good deal for everyone involved.

Just ask Deborah Carter. She's one of those superstars everybody wants to hire. Truly global, Ms. Carter carries dual Canadian and British citizenship and has lived in both of those countries, the United States, and various parts of Africa and Europe. She has bachelor's and master's degrees in journalism and has held several prestigious fellowships. Ms. Carter has worked in print, television, and Internet media for organizations including the Tribune Media Company and the *New York Times*. By the way, she is thirty-one (at this writing).

When she decided to look for a breakout career move, Ms. Carter knew exactly what she wanted: A ground-floor opportunity in business development with a company based in Europe focused on new media convergence (television and the Internet). She told me, "I'd worked for large companies where at times, I felt that I was more or less a cog in the wheel with very little opportunity to exercise my talents and spearhead meaningful projects. I'm tired of the unequal power balance which has given employers far too much control over the direction of my career and lifestyle." In short, Ms. Carter was intent on selling her talents not just to the highest financial bidder, but to the company that would make her a joint-venture partner in her dream job on her own terms.

Good luck, right? What kind of company is going to be able to offer her that?

Actually that would be Van Dusseldorp & Partners, a Dutch startup research and consulting firm focused on technology and the media, founded by Monique Van Dusseldorp, the former director of communications for the European Institute for the Media in Dusseldorf, Germany. Van Dusseldorp & Partners is really good at being fluid.

The majority of the firm's full-time employees are based in the home office in Amsterdam. But this core group works in close collaboration with a fluid-talent pool that includes strategic partnerships with other new media ventures, an advisory council of high-profile executives from companies such as CNN Interactive and BBC Online, and a huge cadre of freelancers who work on a project basis.

At Van Dusseldorp & Partners, there is constant movement of talent. New people join as staff members or associates while others move on. The firm stays in close touch with those who leave, offering them freelance work in their areas of expertise, acquiring valuable business referrals, and periodically extending opportunities to return. Researchers are hired to work on specific projects, usually conducting research commissioned by clients in areas where the researchers have specific expertise. Many are university students who are also completing graduate degrees. Others are professors and directors who work for European research institutes.

"In this company," says Ms. Carter, "I'm getting a return on my involvement with the company immediately and irrevocably—compensation, recognition, contacts, experience and knowledge—and my value is tied to my performance. It's really an amazing way to expand my horizons, increase my marketability, and live and work the way I want to live and work."

What is the best thing about working for Van Dusseldorp & Partners? Ms. Carter will probably be an employee for life, even if she decides to move on tomorrow. Regardless of how long she is part of the firm's core group, Ms. Carter will be talent that Van Dusseldorp can leverage as an asset because they have such a wide repertoire of ways to employ people. Ms. Carter may be a freelancer one year, serve on the advisory council another, and participate in a strategic partnership at some other time. Very likely, she will have other employers throughout the course of her career. But she will always be part of Van Dusseldorp's fluid-talent pool.

That's what long-term employment is going to look like, at its best, in the new economy.

BE A CHANGE LEADER

You can have long-term employment relationships with the very best people, but you'll have to learn to employ people in many, many different ways. Learn to employ people wherever, whenever, and however they are willing and able to add the value you need from them. That means you'll need to regularly assess and reassess the people who work for you today, yesterday, and tomorrow. How transparent is their value to themselves? How transparent is their value to you? You have to know what every person is worth—to you and your organization—if you are going to negotiate effectively.

Don't let a rigid organization structure or the old employment model limit your options when it comes to maximizing available talent. Rearrange the work to fit the people you have today. When there is a change in the work, or in the available talent, rearrange it again. Remember what Michael Dell says: Structure should come last, not first.

In the new economy, just like always, you will be known for your people. But you can't do it the old-fashioned way anymore. In order to have access to the best work of the best people on a consistent basis, you just need to know where to find those people when you need them, and have good enough working relationships that you can bring them in when you need them. And accept that they will work for you only when they are available. As long as you can maintain a deal that makes sense for you and for your best people, the best people will keep serving you well when you need them and when they are available.

Chapter 3

STAFF THE WORK, NOT THE JOBS

One question that leaders and managers are still asking is this: "How am I going to fill all the open positions on my organization chart?" The question you should be asking is: "How am I going to get all this work done?"

Microsoft has developed an ingenious way to get tons of its most important work done by a relative army of more than 125,000 highly skilled techies who don't even work for the company. Not only are these techies not on Microsoft's payroll, but they actually pay Microsoft for the honor of doing the work. Empowered by Microsoft through its system of "Microsoft Certified Solution Providers" (MCSPs), this army is made up of individual experts who work for businesses of all sizes. They help end users make use of Microsoft software. They do work such as designing and developing business applications, installing and managing networks, administering databases, developing Web sites, and so on, all, of course, using Microsoft products. Indeed, many companies using Microsoft systems employ Microsoft Certified Systems Engineers (MCSEs) as full-time technical support. The program is so effective for Microsoft that they have launched efforts to recruit students, senior citizens, and departing military service members into this career path.

To become an MCSE, individuals take one of the many training programs offered for a fee by Microsoft (or an independent training vendor licensed by Microsoft). They must then pass a series of exams.

Once certified, MCSEs must stay current through new exams. MCSPs enter into annual agreements (for a fee) with Microsoft that provide them with support from the mother ship, including early access to new Microsoft products, technical resources, online support, networking with other MCSPs, and licenses for new products to encourage evangelism on behalf of Microsoft products. Microsoft remains in regular communication with this army through newsletters, e-mails, and seminars, and supports the MCSPs with software- and hardware-development kits, sales kits, and marketing kits.

Because all of this support helps MCSPs build their own businesses by selling and supporting Microsoft products, the arrangement is completely win-win. Through the entrepreneurial spirit of MCSPs, supported and guided by Microsoft, absolutely necessary and incredibly valuable work of the Microsoft enterprise is accomplished every day.

❑ ❑ ❑

Why would you ever hire anyone anyway? My guess is you have a bunch of work you need to get done and you were hoping to find some people to help you. That is the essence of every staffing challenge. It always was and it always will be.

Why would you ever hire anyone anyway?

In the workplace of the past, the best way to find help was to look inside the organization and draw from its stable of full-time employees. Or you'd hire someone new into that stable. Most organizations had one main way to employ people: full-time, on-site, uninterrupted, and exclusive. (*Exclusive* means they just work for one employer, nobody else. *Uninterrupted* means they don't leave and come back.) The vast majority of the work was done by a relatively static pool of talent, all of whom were kept on the organization's payroll and at-the-ready for assignments that fell within their particular job descriptions. The main advantage of the old system was reliable access to the talent you needed when you needed it, guaranteed by a large at-the-ready, full-time workforce. But it was too much bloat. Productivity was slow. Profits were low.

Remember?

The reengineering gurus decided to change all of that. Cut the dead wood. Streamline business processes using new technologies. Break up the fiefdoms known as departments. Restructure the new lean staff around the new streamlined work. Get lean. Get nimble. Get fast. Rejoice. The revolution worked like a charm.

But now the staffing crisis has many business leaders pining for their predownsizing workforce with its bloated staff levels and "organization-man"[1] attitudes. After all, if you don't have the right people in the right places when you need them, you can't get the work done fast enough. You start losing out on market opportunities. You start worrying, "Maybe we are too lean for our own good. We are short staffed in a tight labor market. We need a massive recruiting and retention effort." That's the red herring of the talent wars. And it is precisely because employers are still trying to meet their staffing needs with that obsolete approach that most are facing a seemingly intractable staffing crisis.

Just think: What if your massive recruiting and retention effort works? You bid high enough on the open market for talent with whom you successfully fill up positions on the organization chart. You offer golden handcuffs that make it very difficult for them to leave. By investing heavily in the old-fashioned career path, you might convince enough of the right people to return to it, at least for a while. But that wouldn't solve your staffing crisis, rather it would make your organization overcommitted (financially and morally) and unable to respond quickly to shifting market forces. You'll have undone all the good of that painful downsizing, reengineering, and restructuring.

Remember the business need that got this ball rolling in the first place? The new economy requires staffing flexibility: The person you need today and tomorrow is often not the person you needed yesterday. New opportunities will force you to staff up in one skill area very fast. When those opportunities wane, you staff down even faster. How'd you like to have been a Y2K programmer in 1999? What about 2000? See what I mean? This is not rocket science. What do retail stores do with their staffs around Christmas season? What about late January? These are not isolated examples.

STOP PRETENDING THAT STAFFING NEEDS ARE STABLE

One of my clients, a multibillion-dollar-a-year electronics company, has recently pulled out of an entire segment of the electronics business, sold off several units of the company, downsized thousands of people, and refocused all its energies on a particular market—the digital signal processor market. Why? Because the other markets they were in cooled off, while the digital signal processor market is smoking hot (as of 2000). They want to exploit the market opportunity immediately, knowing that in today's environment, what's hot today may not be hot tomorrow.

Now they are frantically trying to hire more than a thousand high-level technicians to work in a high-tech production facility. Still, no matter what they do, they are having a very hard time recruiting enough people. So I asked the group of managers with whom I was problem solving, "Are you trying to sell people on the company's long-term career path? Are you telling them about the company ladder and how, if they sign on and pay their dues, they too can climb the ladder?"

That's exactly what they are doing. Why? Because that's still the only way the organization knows how to approach their staffing needs. They don't want to hire high-level technicians as temps, independent contractors, or interim employees with an uncertain duration of employment because they see these new technicians as being extremely important to the company's success, which they are. So they are busy creating new long-term positions on the organization chart and trying to fill these positions with the new technicians they need (right now).

The painful reality is that they cannot really predict how long these new positions will exist. Certainly they cannot be sure how long more than a thousand high-level technicians will be needed to do wafer fabrication for the digital signal processor market. Maybe the market will heat up even more, and they'll need a thousand more people in this area. But maybe the market will cool off, and they'll need fewer than they thought. There could be a substantial dip in the market, followed by a strong resurgence. Or maybe two years from now they will decide it was all a big mistake and that they should put their resources into a totally different product, requiring people with different talents and training.

Yet they are scrambling to find enough people with the right skills willing to sign on to a long-term career commitment in positions that are full-time, on-site, uninterrupted, and exclusive. The potential recruits know the score. They are being offered a "starting salary" that will escalate as they "climb the ladder," even though everybody knows the real potential for ongoing downsizing and restructuring. Don't forget, because they are still pretending, the company needs to use selection criteria to identify people to whom the company is willing to make a long-term commitment (at least in theory), and that narrows the hiring pool substantially. New hires must be approved as the kind of people the company would like to keep around for decades on end, even though it's all a pretend game.

Any employer determined to limit itself to one cumbersome staffing option will be fighting for crumbs in the new economy. They'll be beaten to the market every time by competitors simply focused on getting all the work done as well as they can and as fast as possible—with full-timers, part-timers, double-timers, flex-timers, telecommuters, former employees, people working three jobs, independent contractors, temps, and whatever else it takes. Wherever, whenever, and however they can get the work done.

> **Any employer determined to limit itself to one cumbersome staffing option will be fighting for crumbs in the new economy.**

In the case of the electronics company in this story, I found, upon further examination, that this was exactly how the managers on the front lines were actually solving their staffing problem, on an ad hoc basis, because they had no choice. The more we talked about it, the more relieved the managers in the room became. "What you are doing is dead-on," I told them. "You just need to stop looking at this as the problem and start seeing it as the solution. And you need better systems to support this approach to staffing."

You see, almost every manager in the real world who is actually meeting his or her staffing needs is doing so with a mix of solutions that run counter to the old-fashioned norms of long-term employment. But often their minds are still trapped in the old paradigm, so they see these square-peg solutions as part of the problem. But square pegs are what you need. Instead of trying to fit the square pegs of a fluid workforce into the round holes on the old-fashioned organization chart, scrap the old-fashioned organization chart. It's obsolete.

OUTSOURCE EVERYTHING YOU POSSIBLY CAN

If you're not great at it, whatever it is, stop doing it, or else outsource it to a vendor that is truly great. The financial reason is diversification of risk and cost. But there is a much more important reason: diversification of excellence.

Be clear about your real sources of market differentiation. That's equally true whether you are making decisions for a multibillion-dollar company or your individual career. What sets you apart in the marketplace? Whatever that is, you can never outsource it to anybody. Why would you? If you are not known for your core competency,[2] you will never be known in the marketplace. But you can only be truly great at just so many things. So you must also become known for integrating the core competencies of other truly great vendors into your day-to-day work process and ultimately into your final products and services.

This is very important: You need to be better at outsourcing than your competition . . . much better.[3]

Maybe you think of outsourcing in terms of relatively short-term or isolated needs: You hire a law firm if you get sued. "Maid-for-a-day" provides you with janitorial services. A security firm guards your building. Car services drive your employees around, airlines fly them, and hotels lodge them. Maybe you use a travel agency for all your travel services. FedEx or UPS does most of your package carrying. You send out for lunch. A small Internet consulting firm designs your Web site. And when there's too much photocopying, someone takes it to Kinko's. These are all sensible ways to use outside vendors, but not strategically significant.

I'm talking about integrating outside vendors, horizontally, into the day-to-day operation of your business. What if Kinko's comes into your office, sets up an in-house photocopy center, and runs it for you? The consulting firm not only designs your Web site, but also provides a Webmaster who updates the site daily and retools it regularly. On the third floor of your building, the caterer opens a restaurant dedicated to your employees. And so on. That's horizontal integration. That's what I'm talking about.

I see examples every day in my work with business leaders, all along the chain of supply, production, distribution, and marketing. The vast majority of goods manufacturers are happy to outsource the whole sales process to wholesalers, or retailers, or direct-mail/catalog outfits, or e-commerce companies. Automobile, airplane, locomotive, and boat manufacturers routinely outsource the assembly of component parts, as do the makers of refrigerators, washing machines, telephones, televisions, and virtually every other household appliance. Millions of backroom white-collar jobs (data entry, writing computer code, and so on) are currently being outsourced by Western companies to an emerging industry in India—the distance doesn't matter one bit.

Why does Barnes & Noble do business with Starbucks? Because they wanted to open coffee shops to make their bookstores destination places and they knew they weren't the best in the business when it came to coffee. Their customers have to be thinking now, "Not only is Barnes & Noble great at selling books, they are also smart enough to recognize the very best in the coffee business and be the ones to deliver that coffee to me in their stores."

Regardless of your size, you can outsource to firms as small as one-person niche operations or as large as IBM or GE. Think strategic alliance.

When Ogilvy & Mather, the international advertising firm that buys more media time every year than any other agency, found that a lot of creative talent (artists, writers, directors) was leaving to start their own small firms, the ad giant simply became the best client to their best former employees. Ogilvy & Mather formed what they call an "outside syndicate" of small firms to which they outsource work on a preferred-customer basis. The same work that was being done internally by employees is now being done externally, and only as needed, on an outsourcing basis.

More and more business leaders take the same idea one giant step further by investing in promising start-ups led by their departing employees. John Chambers, the CEO of Cisco Systems, is well known for this practice. Walker Digital, however, has made an entire business of it. Walker is the business-development company based in Stamford, Connecticut, that is responsible for priceline.com, among many others. They recruit and cultivate high-tech inventors, teach them how to run a business, and help them create breakout companies, owned in part, of course, by Walker.

Meanwhile, in a move that may seem counterintuitive to many, one of the fastest growing businesses at IBM is the company's role as outsource to other businesses—small, medium and large. IBM will host your Web business at one of its massive data centers (so will Intel or Exodus or one of the others). But they go way beyond hosting. IBM's army of 130,000 consultants handles assignments ranging from Internet strategy to Web page design. And IBM's National Testing Center in the Washington, D.C., area will even stress-test your Web system, heaping huge amounts of traffic on your site until it buckles.[4]

And get this: Sun Microsystems Finance (SMF), a division of Sun Microsystems, the $12-billion-a-year Palo Alto–based computer networking company, is an operation with roughly 110 people. But only thirty of them actually work for Sun Microsystems. The rest are on the payroll of GE Capital, the Connecticut-based financial services division of General Electric, although they carry SMF business cards and their e-mail addresses are @sunlease.com. This $1.5 billion computer lease financing operation is almost entirely outsourced.

It works like this: An end user, say an accounting firm, buys eighty Sun Microsystems computers for their local area network. Instead of buying the fast-depreciating equipment outright for, say, $200,000, the accounting firm takes lease financing from SMF, paying off the equipment over time, with interest. The end user will upgrade to new equipment in a couple of years anyway, at which point they renegotiate the lease. Accountants know this is good business for them, because they are able to expense the lease payments (instead of amortizing a capital investment). For Sun, the financing arrangement is a lubricant to help move new machinery into the marketplace at a steady pace.

What's great for Sun is that they can focus on what they do best, which is making computers. Meanwhile, they have the best in the business, GE Capital, handling the lease financing. Of course, as a lease-originations manager who works for GE Capital (sort of) told me, now that Sun is learning the financing business from GE Capital, maybe they'll acquire the division at some point and go into the financing business themselves. I asked this gentleman how he would feel about that. He said, "Whatever."

You might be the only "employee" left in your business.

Whatever you don't outsource, you'd better be great at. If you can't find a vendor who is great at it, then you are going to have to get into the "it" business, whatever it is. Just think of the implications of that business model. Before we're through, you might be the only "employee" left in your business.

YOU ARE ONLY AS GOOD AS YOUR ROLODEX

What if you are the only "employee" left in your business? So what?

I spend a lot of time at big corporate meetings that cater to thousands and thousands of participants. These are monumental events requiring months, sometimes years, of preparation and huge budgets. First a large venue, perhaps a convention center, must be identified and secured for a particular date. Then blocks of rooms at numerous hotels must be reserved for all the attendees. Several days' worth of keynote speeches and classroom seminars must be scheduled, which means that well-known speakers like Colin Powell and Stephen Covey must be chosen, retained, and managed, not to mention dozens of lesser-known seminar leaders. And arrangements must be made for recreational activities ranging from museum visits to bar crawls.

Meanwhile databases of potential attendees must be acquired, informational mailings sent, followed by invitations, registration forms, and one follow-up mailing after another. Of course large meetings include huge trade shows where hundreds of companies display their wares in gigantic exhibition halls. As trade-show exhibitors and meeting attendees sign up, registration lists must be maintained. Head counts must be assessed and reassessed as the event draws near. When the event finally happens, the whole conference must be put together physically: registration booths, the trade-show floor, ballrooms, smaller classrooms, and so on. Audiovisual equipment must be in place for every presentation. Meal after meal is served. Receptions are held. Tote bags, pens, and pads are given away. And on and on and on. Thousands of details must be attended to until the whole event is over, and then the whole shebang must be taken apart.

I tell you all of this because such events are almost always run by production companies, or "show organizers." One time I was talking with a show organizer at one of these monumental corporate meetings. His company put this whole, immense thing together. I asked him, as I tend to do, about his company. "How many people do you have working for you?" I asked. "Oh, it's just me," he said. "Me and my Rolodex. When I get a contract to run an event, I just start lining people up. In this business, you're only as good as your lists. You need to have really good lists of people and vendors and really good working relationships with them. You need to know who can do what for you and whom you can rely on. And they need to know what it's like to work for you."

There you have it. Incidentally, this business structure is known as the "production company" model.

If you are going to build and maximize an incredible pool of talent, you need a system for organizing those resources. You need really good lists. To be that good, a list must contain the following data on each person or vendor in your talent pool: up-to-date contact information, accurate skill profiles, and (this is critical) detailed notes about each person's/vendor's track record of working with your organization as well as others.

You will also need effective methods of communicating with your talent pool so you can quickly assess availability and line up individuals and vendors when you need them. The telephone works pretty well—you run a list of people or vendors who fit your need and start calling through your list until you find enough matches. E-mail works even better.

CREATE A BROAD NETWORK OF TALENT

Your lists and your systems for communicating with people on those lists are what Ray Kotcher calls "the digital glue keeping your talent network working together." Mr. Kotcher is the president of Ketchum, Inc., one of the world's most successful public relations firms with $125 million in annual revenue and more than fifteen hundred professionals in twenty-nine offices around the world. In less than five years, Ketchum has increased its profits more than fivefold. How did they do that?

One of the first things I noticed when I started consulting to Ketchum was that the number of employees technically working for the firm is quite deceptive. In contrast to the production company model, Ketchum seeks to employ just about every talented person in the PR industry. I mean everybody. But not as employees.

"The power of Ketchum is our broad talent network," says Mr. Kotcher, confidently. "We no longer need to own talent to have control over the quality and consistency of the work. We just need to forge relationships, whether it's through using freelancers or alliances and joint ventures with other firms. Overall the goal is to enlarge our network as much as possible so we have access to as wide a range of services as possible. It's just an amazing pool of resources we can deploy to meet the needs of our clients in ways we never would have been able to before."

When a new piece of business comes into the agency, the first step is an assessment of the work to be done. It doesn't matter whether the client is in St. Louis, San Francisco, or Frankfurt, all the resources of the firm's talent network throughout the world can be called upon to staff the project, from any of the firm's six practice areas. Every element of the project is assigned to the very best person for that particular assignment—that is, the person with the most relevant skills and experience who happens to be available.

Let's say a global company in the high-tech sector comes in with a need to communicate its new health care plan to all of its employees. The account executive might pull together a team from the high-tech practice in Silicon Valley, the health care practice in New York, and the corporate communications practice in London. It all depends on the particulars of the project. If the health care plan itself still needs shaping, somebody with deep knowledge of corporate benefits packages might be needed. Or maybe the policy is settled but it needs to be clearly articulated, so the team will need a good technical writer. Or maybe the plan is to be communicated in as many different media as possible, so the team will need experts in audio, video, print, and Web-based communication, and the firm would draw from its resources around the world. Perhaps the policy has already been written up and published, but the client's employees are responding badly. The team will need someone with experience in employee relations. And so on. Whatever roles need to be filled, they will be supplied as necessary with the best person available from anywhere in the firm's talent network, whether those people are traditional employees or not. Ketchum calls this approach their "Best Teams" strategy. What does your best teams strategy look like?

This approach is a clear departure for Ketchum and from the standard operating procedure of most professional services firms. Typically when a client comes to a professional services firm with a piece of business, the particular practice group in the particular office where the client walked in the door would tend to be very proprietary about the project. "That's our client. That's our business." And because rewards were allocated based on office billings, that made a lot of sense in terms of each individual's self-interest.

Not anymore at Ketchum, and more and more other professional services firms are following suit. "The point is to look at the client and the client's needs first and tear down every barrier that would be an impediment to delivering what the client needs. And those barriers can be both geography and specific practices. So companies that were organized only around geography or only along practice sectors would also become isolated. The goal for the client is best served by moving across practice groups and accessing people from throughout the firm," says Lorraine Thelian, senior partner for North America at Ketchum.

Mr. Kotcher says, "We started to look at what our clients were asking for and that was the very best service in real time on a global basis twenty-four hours a day, seven days a week. That was just no longer something you could handle from one geographical location or one knowledge base, no matter how great the knowledge of one office or one practice group may have been. But it was definitely something we could do by drawing on the resources throughout the firm and outside of the firm. We had to teach our account people about all the resources at their disposal throughout the organization and to be facile enough to access and bring those resources to bear on any problem in real time."

The local offices of Ketchum are still the gateways into the firm for clients, but every office is as great as all the resources in the firm's talent network. Says Mr. Kotcher, "When we started removing the boundaries of the office and the practice group, our value proposition became simply our ability to access and deploy talent from any source in the firm and bring it to bear on our client's needs." Now 50 percent of Ketchum's profit is from business shared between offices and practices, a dramatic increase.

Ketchum's new fluid structure is a beautiful illustration of what Michael Tushman and Charles O'Reilly, professors at Harvard and Stanford respectively, have dubbed "ambidextrous organizations." In their research, professors Tushman and O'Reilly have found that companies are much more effective at turning shifting markets into business opportunities if they adopt flexible structures capable of maximizing resources (especially human resources) from anywhere within the organization, and even more important, from without.[5] The promise of the ambidextrous organization has paid huge dividends for Ketchum.

The initial success of the talent network without boundaries led Ketchum to start including nonemployees, quasi employees, and plenty of outside niche firms in its "best teams." Once they did that, the floodgates were open for new kinds of relationships with traditional employees too. Mr. Kotcher says, "This approach gives employees the opportunity to move in and out of the agency (and back in if they want) more freely. They can leave and still be as much a part of Ketchum as they were when they were account supervisors, because they are still part of the talent network as a service provider. We have access to them, but in a different way. We've invested so much in them and they in us, it just makes sense to keep working together."

Ms. Thelian points out that the talent-network/best-teams approach also facilitates the career customization needs of today's ambitious free agents. "We've just moved one of our very senior people in Washington in the health care field to London to run the European health care practice. If we hadn't done that, we might well have lost him. Instead of losing him, we are keeping him and his talent in the agency. Because of the talent-network/best-teams approach, it is pretty easy to move people from one role to another, from one geography to another, from one practice group to another. We can't meet every single need, but it is much easier to do it now."

She continues, "We created this as a way to better service our clients and what we found out is it has been a tremendous asset as far as attracting and retaining the best people as well. It gives people access to continual challenges. We can open a new practice area to them, or a new geography to them. When we recruit, we talk about that a lot. We say, 'We are hiring you into this job but we can move you into other jobs along the way.' Some people want more balance in their work, but others just want more work. It also depends on what their passion is. And whatever it is, we have a multiplicity of opportunity for them."

As a result of the firm's fluid structure, its turnover is consistently 15 percent (or so) less than the industry average, but that figure is deceptive as well because Ketchum is redefining turnover. Even when people leave Ketchum as full-time employees, they often return again, largely because even when they leave, through the talent network, they never stop working for the firm.

BRING IN THE SWAT TEAM

When my team was interviewing professionals in the merchandising organization at Mervyn's, a California-based chain of 268 department stores owned by the $33.7-billion-a-year Target Corporation (formerly Dayton Hudson Corporation), we found that many people were frustrated with the rigid, hierarchical, one-size-fits-all career path. There were nine levels on the buying food chain, and the hierarchy was as strict as any I've ever seen. In one interview after another, individuals spoke fondly of Mervyn's and of their merchandising profession, but it was clear that they hated the "up or out" career path available to them. One person after another—whether a buyer of shoes or sweaters or cosmetics, it didn't seem to matter—told us, "I'd love to keep working here, but I think I'm going to be moving on soon." So our interviewers asked each person, as they do in our ongoing research, "Is there anything that would convince you to stay?" And most said the same thing, "Well, if I could join the SWAT team, I'd probably stay."

> ## "I'd love to keep working here, but I think I'm going to be moving on soon."

"The SWAT team . . . ," our interviewers inquired repeatedly. "What's that?"

It seems that several smart managers had been confronted one at a time with some very talented people who wanted to opt out of the merchandising organization's rigid career path. These talented individuals were not acting in concert in any way. Yet each was prepared to say, "Thanks for everything. . . . I'm going to be leaving." And of course, each of them had different needs and desires, but they were all sick of going to the same place every day during the same hours and doing the same work in the same position in the hierarchy and waiting to move up the ladder. Each person was looking for a greater mix of responsibilities, exposure to different aspects of the business, new learning opportunities, contact with people other than those in their immediate department, and more control over their own schedules. And none of them really cared about moving up the ladder (except for the fact that it seemed to count for so much in the organization). They all were looking simply to grow their careers in their own directions and their own ways.

How did their managers respond? Rather than saying, "That's just not the way we do things around here," they decided not to lose these people altogether. "Maybe we could create a special working relationship that would give you what you need, and meet the organization's needs as well," their managers must have said. And one by one, these special relationships were created. Each person was taken out of the traditional career path, but they remained exclusive employees of Mervyn's. Instead of going to work for other companies to reinvent themselves, they would do it in the merchandising organization on an ongoing basis. They were put on unassigned status and would remain available to fill gaps in the staffs of the nine different divisions (shoes, cosmetics, etc.) internally as those gaps occurred. Those gaps occurred a lot. In many cases because talented people were leaving (and their managers weren't gutsy enough to create special working relationships with them). But mostly because different departments would be very, very busy sometimes and not so busy other times. While some of these fluctuations are easy to predict (toys in December, bathing suits in June), others are not so predictable (Pokemon paraphernalia, Ally McBeal–style short skirts). Of course, the staffing levels of the various divisions, in the traditional model, certainly couldn't take into account sudden unpredictable demand for very specific merchandise. So the divisions were overstaffed plenty of the time, and occasionally they were plunged into a staffing crisis.

As you can imagine, when those staffing gaps did occur, these unassigned individuals were sought after and much appreciated. After all, they already knew what they were doing, for the most part. They might have to get up to speed on Pokemon paraphernalia, but so would the most experienced toy buyer. "We are scrambling to get all this work done," people in the toy department might have said. "Isn't Joe unassigned now? Let's see if Joe is available to help us out." If he were available, of course, Joe would come in—like a police SWAT team—and take the pressure off. That's how the SWAT team got its name. Still, the SWAT team was small. More often than not, Joe wasn't available. He was busy helping the women's clothing team acquire a bunch of Ally McBeal–style short skirts, or filling in somewhere else for somebody who had just quit, or for somebody who was out sick, or whatever.

In no time, those in the SWAT team, that band of roving unassigned talent, became some of the most valuable people in the merchandising organization. When we asked managers if there were one thing they would do to improve their staffing situation, almost every one of them said, "We need more people in the SWAT team."

Eureka!

Now when talented people want to opt out of the traditional career path, Mervyn's has a great career option for them and a great way to retain them. It's working like a charm. What started as an ad hoc solution to retain a handful of talented people grew into a successful method that deals with a whole range of flexible workforce issues. Now the SWAT team is becoming one of the most important staffing strategies in the company. In 1997, the SWAT team had nineteen members; in 1998 the number grew to thirty-four.

In addition to helping Mervyn's manage its unpredictable staffing needs and providing talented people with more flexible work arrangements, the SWAT team promotes knowledge sharing and best-practice migration across divisions because members have such broad exposure throughout the company. This exposure, and a proven ability to adapt quickly and achieve tangible results (required traits on the SWAT team) also puts members high on the list of managers seeking core-groupers for their divisions.

It is now very common for people who have served on the SWAT team to be hired away from the team into high-level positions, often leapfrogging rungs on the traditional career ladder. Now that the most ambitious stars in the company realize they can move back and forth between the SWAT team and the core groups of the various merchandising divisions, the SWAT team (not paying one's dues and climbing the ladder) has become the fast-track career move of choice. Due to managers' recruiting from the SWAT team into their core groups, by mid-2000 the SWAT team was back down to just a dozen members.

The SWAT team is here to stay at Mervyn's, and its value to the organization is precisely that its numbers can rise and fall as necessary. What Mervyn's has successfully created is a high-profile, high-prestige, highly flexible, highly rewarded alternative to the old-fashioned career path. And they've met some of their most pressing staffing needs in the process.

The essence of a SWAT team is that it is made up of unassigned internal talent, people who can be moved around wherever and whenever they are needed, so long as they are available. Formally and informally, there are lots of internal fluid staffing examples that follow this model. It works in organizations that are high tech, low tech, or anywhere in between.

When I first began working with the Sandia National Laboratory, the New Mexico–based national security laboratory responsible for all nonnuclear components for the United States's nuclear weapons arsenal, I discovered that all of their company's more than three thousand nuclear scientists are, in many ways, unassigned. When one scientist gets grant funding for a project, she will start shopping around for the most appropriate talent to make up her team. On the other hand, scientists without grant funding are always selling themselves, their skills and time, to get onto the grant-funded research. At Sandia, this is known as "manager shopping." On an ongoing basis, the more junior scientists negotiate with the more senior scientists to get staffed onto the best projects. The best managers with the most to offer routinely attract the best talent to their projects, while the best people without grant funding are in greatest demand and, therefore, have the greatest choice of assignments. It is an efficient internal marketplace that is, de facto, fluid and leads to optimal matching between available talent and the work that needs to be done. The system promotes the highest levels of excellence in a community made up, literally, of rocket scientists.

At the other end of the skill spectrum, the checkout lanes in the best retail stores provide another example of internal fluid staffing. Market leaders like Target (the parent of Mervyn's) and Home Depot have solved the front-end staffing dilemma (it is always hard to properly staff the checkout lanes; almost always, you have too many people or too few). What the leading retailers have done is cross-train most of the workers in the store. Regardless of one's role, whether a person is a hardware woman at Home Depot or a jewelry man at Target, each employee is also trained to work the cash register. As soon as lines start to form, the announcement comes over the loudspeaker, "Backup cashiers to the front please." People are expected to leave their very important, but less urgent, work—wherever they are, whatever they are doing—and take up a cash register until the lines disappear. That is just-in-time staffing at its best (especially if you are a customer waiting in the checkout line).

It will work differently in every organization, but you can create your own SWAT team and discover the value of having a pool of unassigned workers who are cross-trained and ready to take up work where and when they are most needed.

BUILD YOUR OWN RESERVE ARMY

Your pool of unassigned workers need not even work for you . . . anymore.

My company has had the great honor over the years of working with the United States Army. One time I was at Fort Leavenworth addressing a group of generals about best practices in business. I was telling them how many business leaders are becoming so concerned about turnover and so intent on not losing the training investment they make in their employees, they are going to great lengths to retain people in less than traditional ways. Rather than lose people altogether, some employers are retaining people part-time, flex-time, as telecommuters, and in other nontraditional manners. Many employers are letting their people leave and come back. And in some cases, employers are even saying to people, "Hey, you can go work for our competition. We'll still welcome you back."

I guess I wasn't thinking about my audience. Later, one of the generals said to me, "Son, when our employees go work for the competition, we shoot 'em."

But I learned something that day that was extremely valuable. The generals, I discovered, know very well the value of the training investment they make in their soldiers, just as other employers do. Indeed, the U.S. Army has developed a very effective method of continuing to get a return on that investment long after soldiers finish their periods of service. The army calls this method the "reserves." Indeed, in the U.S. Army itself, the reserves (and the National Guard) actually outnumber the active duty force (564,000 to 479,000, as of the year 2000). While hundreds of thousands of reservists were called up to support the Persian Gulf War, back in 1990–91, the reservists were largely called upon to backfill the stateside roles of those active duty servicepeople who were deployed abroad. Not anymore. Increasingly, reservists are integrated into missions overseas, such as the seven hundred men and women of the 49th Armored Division deployed to Bosnia in February 2000 for a nine-month assignment to take command of the American sector of NATO's operation there.[6]

Why not borrow a staffing strategy for winning the talent wars from one of the greatest fighting forces in the history of the world? Build your own reserve army.

You won't have the force of law to compel your former employees to return to service, but still, you can call upon your former employees (those who have left on good terms, of course) when you need them. If they are available, they might return to help you, even if it's only for one assignment . . . or two or three. Many managers already do this, informally and without good support systems: "Hey, I wonder what John is up to lately? I wonder if he'd be able to help us out with this project. Let's call and see if he's available."

Al Barea has been using a small reserve army for several years at Baptist Healthcare System, a billion-dollar-a-year Kentucky-based company where he is the chief information officer. Mr. Barea says, "I have spent the last three years building my team to help execute what I believe is the vision of information systems in health care for the future." To cope with the staffing challenge, Mr. Barea has borrowed a fluid staffing practice from the nursing field and applied it to his information-technology team.

"In the health care industry many times we keep nursing and other allied health professionals retained on an as-needed basis. These individuals may hold full-time positions at other employers and squeeze us in if they can. I have taken this concept and applied it to IT staffing as a means of desperation more than a well-thought-out strategy. It just happened to benefit our operation very well. If we have an employee who decides to leave us for another local job and we have had a good relationship with that individual, we may ask them to help in a pinch. This allows us to keep them on as needed and pay them for work they may do at night or on weekends. Typically their other employer has no problem. I maintain a good relationship with competitors and would not put these employees in compromising situations. This has worked out well over the last three years with about three or four individuals."

> **Your best former employees can quickly become backbones of your fluid staffing strategy.**

Your best former employees can quickly become backbones of

your fluid staffing strategy. Don't you think so? They already know how to do business in your organization. You've already trained them. They already know you and many of your colleagues, and probably plenty of your vendors and customers. Whose skill and performance abilities do you know better than the people who have already worked for you? When they come back, you'll probably have to fill them in on some new developments, but it's going to be a lot like riding a bike. Once they're back on the bike, working with you will be almost like second nature.

Maybe in the time they've been gone, they'll have discovered that the grass isn't so much greener on the other side. In some cases, before long, they'll be angling to get rehired again as full-timers. If you are smart, you'll let people flow back into your core group as easily as you let them flow out.

TURN YOUR HR DEPARTMENT INTO A STRATEGIC STAFFING WAR ROOM

Your human resources department can no longer be on the sidelines for the talent wars. They must become strategic staffing war rooms, central to the daily scramble. (Especially now that so much of the work traditionally done by HR is being outsourced by most companies.) Having interviewed dozens of HR professionals and conducted seminars for thousands of them, I can tell you that most of them already know this. And they are doing their best every day, but most simply don't yet have the organizational support or the necessary resources to do what must be done. That's why it is so important to retool the role of HR to give them the budget and the technology and the authority they need to be the key strategic partner to managers on the front lines.

Why is the Internet the fastest growing venue for job search by employees and the fastest growing venue for recruiting by employers? Because the process revolves around a proprietary database indexed by the important information necessary to match available talent with available jobs.[7] And why can a good temp[8] agency almost always meet your last-minute, short-term staffing needs? Because it maintains a proprietary database including the names, contact information, and other key data on people who may be (or probably will be) available for short-term assignments.

Why not combine the strengths of the Internet and temporary staffing and bring the whole process in-house, run by your own HR professionals? Develop your own proprietary talent database, instead of sharing one with every other employer in your vicinity (temp firms) or every other employer in the world (the Internet). Create an HR team dedicated to helping managers draw staff just in time from your own killer talent pool. Build your database around your organization's particular staffing needs. Does it look like Ogilvy & Mather's outside syndicate of niche firms? Ketchum's talent network? The "production company" Rolodex? The SWAT team? The reserve army? It should be whatever combination fits your business needs. In order to select individuals and companies from as many sources as possible, you'll have to be recruiting into the database all the time, not just when you have open positions.

One manager, who works in computer information systems at Fannie Mae, the $35.5-billion-a-year mortgage finance company, told me during one of my seminars that he constantly recruits candidates into his own proprietary talent database, even when there is no "open position" on the org chart to fill. At Fannie Mae, this is a violation of procedure. So what? He said, "By the time you hire somebody 'by the book' it's too late. So I always keep a steady stream of people in the pipeline. I advertise vacancies on my staff all the time, whether there are open positions or not. That way, I am always interviewing people, putting them through the screening process, and I always have a ready list of 'finalists.'" That's the idea. You need a database that is a ready list of finalists in the pipeline all the time. But your managers on the front lines shouldn't be managing the process; HR should be.

The most important things to remember: Index your talent database by skill profile and performance track record. And include good current contact information. Remember Ray Kotcher's "digital glue."

Staffing is destined to be a perpetual challenge in the new economy. You need to have dedicated professionals helping managers get the right people in the right place at the right time to get the work done very well and very fast, whatever the work may be on any given day. And that—whatever the work may be on any given day—is going to be a moving target.

That's why every staffing need—every day, every week, every project—must begin with a clear assessment of the work: Exactly which tasks, responsibilities, and projects need to be done? Once you have a clear picture of the work itself, the remaining questions are obvious: Who is the best person (or who are the best people, what is the best team) to do this work? Where will you find the people you need? And are they available when you need them? What is the best mix of people you can pull together on an ad hoc team[9] to get the work done very well and very fast? That mix might include core-groupers as well as part-timers, flex-timers, some-timers, telecommuters, temps, independent contractors, and outsourcing. The best mix you can pull together is the best team for the project, no matter how ad hoc it may be. Indeed, the more ad hoc the better. Stanford University professor Harold Leavitt's research reveals that ad hoc teams, or what he calls "hot groups," thrive when they come together to meet an immediate need and then disband, but falter when managers seek to put rigid organization structures around them.[10]

THE NEW ORGANIZATION STRUCTURE

Now you may be asking yourself: With all this flex-time, part-time, here today, gone tomorrow, superfluid talent handling most of the work, who is left minding the store? Who is still going to have what you might recognize as standard jobs? Almost nobody, if they can help it. Of course, it really depends on the organization and the type of work you do. Surely there will be a growing number of employers that will experiment with having virtually nobody in the old-fashioned roles. For many organizations, that will work just fine. Where and when people work (which is all we're talking about here, so far) matters much less in the new economy than what people actually do and how they do it.

MIT professor Thomas Malone, the leading academic researcher on new economy organization structures, heads a major initiative at

MIT's Sloan School of Business Research Center for "Inventing the Organizations of the 21st Century" that is fueled by two massive research projects—the Interesting Organization Database and the Process Handbook. Professor Malone is the guy who coined the term *e-lance* to describe independent contractors who join together in temporary electronic networks to tackle projects. He argues that work is no longer best managed by a stable chain of command but should be carried out by very small subunits of internal and external talent that are formed as needs occur and are then disbanded.[11] Recently Professor Malone and I served together on a panel at the Harvard Business School's "Burning Questions 2000" conference, and he kept vexing the audience of assembled corporate CEOs with the question, "Why do you even *have* a company anymore?"

> "Why do you even have a company anymore?"

I won't go that far. But you can count on this: Successful organizations in the new economy will have very strong and very lean core groups, while they get more and more of the work done by tapping large, robust pools of fluid talent. The key to making this work is the balance and relationship between an organization's core group and its fluid-talent pool.

Where does your core group come from? Well, in the workplace of the past, just about everybody was destined for your core group. That was the only group worth being in. Now it's less clear. You can still recruit every new employee as if they'll serve your organization for long uninterrupted periods full-time, on-site, and on an exclusive basis. But you'll just be pretending. Some will leave and some will stay. The longer a person stays, the closer to the core of the organization the person tends to be. This is merely a descriptive point: Those with long periods of service tend to have the most organization-specific knowledge and have relationships with the most employees, leaders, vendors, and customers. They tend to feel the most committed to the general mission and direction and culture of the organization. For that reason, they often attempt to control such factors, and often they are the best qualified to do so, precisely due to their longevity and psychological (at least) stake in the enterprise.

To a large extent those who stay and those who go, in the free-talent market environment, will be self-selecting. The trick for organization leaders is having some impact on that self-selection process. What are the most effective steps organization leaders can take? Remove obstacles to remaining in the organization and make it easy for good people to go back and forth between the core group and the fluid-talent pool.

Imagine that somebody on your team whom you really value tells you he or she is thinking about leaving the organization. You might ask, "Is there anything we can do to keep you?" "Well," the person might say, "I no longer want to work in this city, or state, or country, or hemisphere." Or, "I no longer want to work with my boss, or coworkers, or vendors, or customers." Or, "I no longer want to work on Thursdays, or during the day, or during the night." Or, "I need to learn new things, or gain new experiences, or take a break." Why lose that person altogether? Retain this person in your fluid-talent pool— in your reserve army, your SWAT team, or, if he or she is planning to hang out a shingle, as an outsource, or as a flex-timer or telecommuter. Whatever you do, don't end the employment relationship. Keep employing that person wherever, whenever, and however he is willing to work for you. Just think, you have so much work to get done and he can probably help you, at least now and then. Sometime down the road he may return to your core group, as long as the relationship is strong and the culture of your organization or team welcomes people who come and go and come back again.

"Wait," you may be thinking, "it's not that easy. I'm going to have to fill that position with somebody else. There may not be a place in the organization for this person when he decides to return." There is always a place for a valuable person in your fluid-talent pool, but your core group is another matter altogether.

First, don't rush to "fill that position" when you lose somebody from your core group. Instead, start from scratch. Remember? Approach every staffing challenge with a clear assessment of the work: Exactly what needs to be done anyway? What can you outsource? What can be reassigned to other core-groupers? Which tasks, responsibilities, and projects are only temporary and can be assigned to someone in your reserve army or SWAT team? Is there any work that was being done that doesn't need to be done at all

anymore? Is there any work that was being done that can be streamlined, combined with other work to save time and energy, or made
more efficient using technology? Is there any work that the person
who is leaving would be willing to continue handling in a more flexible capacity?

If you start every staffing problem with a clear assessment of the
work, you will find that your core group gets smaller and smaller and
your fluid-talent pool gets larger and larger, because that new model
fits the constantly shifting staffing needs of most organizations in the
new economy. You'll find yourself saying, "Why did we have a full-
time person in that role anyway?" Why, indeed?

So what does this mean for recruiting, the point from which most
managers approach their staffing needs? Well, look at what's already
happening.

You go through a long selection process to identify people who fit
positions in your organization chart, bring them in with sweetheart
deals (nowadays), spend lots of time, energy, and money training
them. Then what happens? Sometimes they stay and sometimes they
go. Often it's the best who go because they can and because they don't
have to work in a one-size-fits-all environment. They're able to
demand their own conditions.

If you accede to those demands, they end up in your fluid-talent
pool anyway, despite the fact that you recruited them for the core
group. Many organizations make matters worse: Very often, those
who step off the one-size-fits-all path are no longer treated as fast-
trackers or future leaders simply because of outdated expectations
about employment relationships and career paths. Of course, since it
is often the best people whose demands you are willing to meet, they
are the ones who should be getting the fast-track assignments (wherever, whenever, and however they can do the work) and they should
also be the leaders in waiting. Over time, some of the best people will
move into core group roles where they focus their talents on main-
taining the organization's culture, keeping the overall mission clear
for everybody, assigning work, setting goals, and holding people
accountable for results. In other words, they will come back and
enrich your core.

On the other hand, you hire a temp or an independent contractor or outsource some work to a small niche firm, with no intention of bringing in a core-grouper. And what very often happens? "This person is great," you and your colleagues say to each other. "Let's try to bring her in full-time." When you can test-drive talent, you get a very good sense of where the person might (or might not) fit in your organization or team. At the same time, the talent gets to test-drive the employment relationship too—the people, culture, work, schedule, and rewards. When the managers and the talent both decide, after working together for a period of time, that the fit and the deal are good, it is a rare case that you hire the wrong person. As long as the person stays in your core group, she is going to do a great job. Once you've built a relationship of mutual trust, confidence, and success, you have the basis for real long-term employment, new economy style. If she decides to leave the core group, you'll retain as much of her as you can in your fluid-talent pool, until she decides (or doesn't) to return to the core group again.

Would you buy a car before test-driving it? Talent is the most valuable resource you have. Why buy it without a test-drive?

In the new organizational structure, smart managers are not recruiting anyone they don't know into their core groups. If they do, it's just a pretend game. Who has time for that in business? The fact is, nobody is really part of the core group of an organization until he or she has been there for some period of time (it's different in every organization). So recruit people into your fluid-talent pool. Decide, mutually, over time, on a case-by-case basis if you want to draw individuals closer to the core of the organization.

If you let people flow back and forth between your core group and your fluid-talent pool, both will become stronger. Over time, more and more of those in your fluid-talent pool will have the experience and depth and connectedness of former core-groupers. Those in your core group will have the kind of loyalty that comes from being part of something by choice. Let me paraphrase another nuclear scientist friend of mine: "Structures that are airtight are very unstable because they can be destroyed with just the prick of a pin. But fluid structures are almost impossible to destabilize because they naturally adjust as their environment changes." I cannot say it better.

BE A CHANGE LEADER

You may or may not be the one to transform your organization's staffing strategy, but you can transform your own strategy. Ignore the dinosaurs. Break some rules if you have to. Say it with me: "How am I going to get all this work done? Staff the work, not the jobs." Build your own broad network of talent and keep it together with digital glue. Keep good lists and stay in touch with your talent. Even if your organization doesn't have a reserve army, you need one. Even if your organization doesn't have a SWAT team, you need one. Even if your organization is no good at outsourcing, you can be great at it. Be the person who always pulls together the team to get the work done. People will ask, "How did you do that?" Whether or not you tell them is up to you. I can say this much: If you do it once, people will notice; twice, and they'll start asking questions; three times, some of them will get nervous; by the fourth time, you'll have a reputation and people will want you to help when they need to pull together a team. Create your own pocket of change. If it works, change catches on. Soon your way will become a "best practice" and you'll be the "best-practice leader." Whatever. You've got a bunch of work to get done. Get it done.

Chapter 4

PAY FOR PERFORMANCE, AND NOTHING ELSE

One question that leaders and managers are still asking is this: "How do I get people to put in their time in today's short-term environment?" The question you should be asking is: "How do I get people to deliver the results I need when I need them?"

If you want to get the work done very well and very fast on favorable terms, whatever the work may be, you have to be very good at negotiating. Paul Applegate can tell you that from his decades of experience as a purchasing agent at the Portland General Electric Company (PGE), a major utility serving more than 625,000 customers in the Pacific Northwest. Over the years, Mr. Applegate, like his fellow purchasing agents, has negotiated contracts with hundreds and hundreds of independent contractors ranging from technical writers to chemical engineers. Often the contractors are outside experts, but sometimes they are former employees coming back to PGE on a consulting basis. Of course, the goal is always to get the most qualified person available.

Once you have the right person, the most important factor in negotiating a successful purchasing contract, says Mr. Applegate, is "defining the scope of work. First, I have to know exactly what we are expecting when the project is done. What are the deliverables? You need to spell it out up front in enough detail so there is no misunderstanding." Then you start negotiating the terms—schedule, location, resources, and compensation. Is the deadline going to be March 1, or March 15? Will there be bonuses for early delivery or exceptional quality? Penalties for late delivery or work that fails to meet expectations? Is the contractor going to work in your office, or work from home? Are you going to provide a laptop computer, or will the contractor provide her own? Will the contractor be paid in a lump sum on delivery, or at milestones along the way? "Actually, just about everything is negotiable," says Mr. Applegate. "You can make any kind of deal you want as long as both parties can agree on the terms."

From the standpoint of the purchasing agent, the ideal bargain is one that clearly defines the contractor's deliverables and a concrete deadline, with specific milestones along the way. Every penny of compensation—financial and nonfinancial—is tied either to a specific milestone in the project or to the ultimate delivery by the agreed-upon deadline. If at any point the vendor fails to deliver, she doesn't get paid.

❏ ❏ ❏

If you are really serious about moving into the new economy and winning the talent wars, stop paying people right away. You heard me. Stop paying people and start buying their results. Bring in your purchasing agents to run seminars for the compensation team. Start reworking the compensation system, fast. More important, have the purchasing agents teach every supervisory manager the basics of purchasing results in the free market. To survive in the new economy, every manager is going to have to get very good at negotiating with employees as if they were outside vendors. Managers simply must start establishing clear deliverables and deadlines

> **Bring in your purchasing agents to run seminars for the compensation team.**

with every employee every step of the way, agree on fair prices in financial and nonfinancial compensation for every milestone, and then start paying vendors of talent (formerly known as employees) when they deliver, and only when they deliver. This is also going to short-circuit your performance-evaluation system—the only evaluation necessary will be the ongoing review of deliverables at every milestone and the daily performance coaching along the way.

It's a simple idea: Employment relationships are transactional by nature. They always have been. But instead of being slow-moving, long-term camouflaged transactions, as they were in the workplace of the past, now the transactions are fast-moving, short-term, and fully exposed. Free agents are negotiating with managers every day and they drive a hard bargain. If you keep trying to draw your management power from your position on the organization chart, you are going to be played for a fool by free agents in the new economy. Here's why: You will be constrained by trying to make a long-term deal according to the norms of a limited system (your company's compensation system), while the free agent has all the options available every day in the free market.

Remember, markets are efficient. But only if they are free, fluid, and if the actors deal on good current information. The financial bidding contest only undermines the interests of employers if the seller (talent) is free, fluid, and acting on good current information and the buyer (management) is stuck in an old, rigid system. Paying people the market value of their work—whatever the value is today—is precisely how you can get yourself and your company out of bidding contests that don't work and into bidding contests that do.

The emerging trend of online talent-auction Web sites—which include Monster.com's talent market, elance.com, brainbid.com, icplanet.com, freeagent.com, ework.com, and the much heralded but little-used bid4geeks.com—presents a virtual laboratory that promises to put the free market for talent to the test. In these auction environments, employers create project profiles with key information such as project guidelines, skills needed, anticipated time frames, location (if on-site work is necessary), reporting relationships, potential compensation, and background information about the employer.

For their part, independent contractors complete a profile including their skills and experience, the range of pay they seek, a schedule of availability, and preferred work location. Once the auction "goes live" (has been posted), there is an auction period during which independent contractors and potential employers consider each other's bids; usually employers are bidding on the talent, rather than the reverse. At the end of the auction period, all the bids are evaluated, contact information is exchanged, and terms are negotiated. The beauty of this system is that it contains all the features of a potentially efficient—if still fledgling—marketplace: Free and fluid exchange (liquidity), abundant information (transparency), open access, and opportunity for continual adjustment on the basis of new information.

Short-term, pay-for-performance contracts will be the natural culmination of the free market for talent, and therefore, the norm of employment in the new economy. They are also the best way to give free agents exactly what they want most—to be paid what they are worth when they deliver—without breaking the bank. An ongoing research study at the Wharton School of Business demonstrates that short-term, results-based work relationships often create a higher level of commitment than long-term relationships. The researchers believe this is because the short-term contracts give participants a very clear idea of what's expected of them, what they'll gain from delivering, the time limits of the job, and the work load necessary to complete it successfully within that time period. Not only does this create a different kind of commitment (the kind you get with a short-term contract), but the positive work experience also adds to the employer's word-of-mouth reputation among the workers' peers.[1]

Start negotiating with the people you manage as if they are vendors, regardless of whether they are independent contractors or full-time employees, and you'll start getting your power back in your day-to-day relationships with talent. The fastest way to change your organization is to change the way you pay people. Behavior follows the trail of rewards.

WHEN PAY FOR PERFORMANCE ISN'T

In all my work with people in companies throughout the world, I have found that just about everybody agrees with this basic axiom: You get the performance you reward. That's why most employers wrestle with blending some form of performance-based pay into their compensation systems.[2] Usually ease of administration wins in those wrestling matches. That's why so many pay-for-performance systems fail to accurately measure and reward performance. When that happens, supposedly performance-based compensation plans actually disincentivise high performers. That's a big problem.

One time our research team was interviewing a random sample of the roughly two thousand employees of a telecommunications company in the Midwest before I went there to conduct a problem-solving session with senior executives. Here's what our team found: Everybody in the company hated the compensation system. Why? It was a hybrid between an old-fashioned seniority system and a (sort of) performance-based system that yielded pernicious results.

The system was based on a typical ladder, with the rungs on the ladder called "grades." Within each grade, there were relatively narrow pay ranges. The pay range is where the performance-based compensation comes in. So let's say you are "grade 3" and you start out at the middle of the range (because that's how it works). If you do a great job over the course of an entire year (in the judgment of your supervisor), your pay goes to the top of the range within grade 3 for the next year. Are you with me? Your pay is fixed for the next year. That means no matter how hard you work, no matter how great a job you do, you are stuck at that pay level. And, if you just show up, do a decent job, but don't knock yourself out, you are stuck at that pay level too.

Indeed, you are stuck, until you get a promotion in grade. But in a grade system, of course, there are fewer positions available in each grade as you go up the ladder, like a pyramid. So promotions are far and few between. No matter how many high performers there are at grade 3, only a handful will get promoted (when a handful at grade 4 either leave the company or get promoted themselves). Once people reach the top of their pay ranges, the only financial leverage available to their managers is punitive (the manager can knock a person down in the pay range, but that almost never happens). As one person after another told us in interviews, "The thing is, you do a great job for one year. Then, once you get to the top of your pay range, there is no incentive to keep doing a great job because you are stuck. You just have to do a decent job."

Now get this: If you do a terrible job over the course of a year (in the judgment of your supervisor), your pay goes down to the bottom of the range within grade 3 for the next year. So now you have all the incentive in the world to do a great job, which sounds good, but think about it for a minute. For one thing, the low performers one year have all the incentives the next year, while the high performers have virtually no incentive. Does anyone really think that the low performers one year are all of a sudden going to become high performers the next year? In short, the only way to get a really big raise in this company, without getting a promotion up the ladder, is to do a really bad job one year (go on probation, get knocked down on the pay range so you make less money for a year), and then do a really great job the next year. Then in year three, in theory, you could enjoy a raise from the bottom of the range to the top.

I'm not making this up. What is more, this compensation model is used in a lot of companies in a lot of industries. And it's not crazy. The rationale is simple: Preserve the payoffs of the hierarchy and seniority, and within that system create some kind of variable performance-based pay. The best of those who stay with the company long enough will keep moving up the ladder. For everybody else, it's a good job and it pays pretty well. Get back to work.

So I went to this company's headquarters and gave a presentation followed by a problem-solving session. The CEO was in the room, along with his senior management team, including the CFO, and about fifty managers from the "next level down." We didn't talk long before I ran by the group what we had found in our interviews. Everybody wanted to talk about it. People kept saying the same things, "This system punishes high performers." "It promotes mediocrity." "There are no low performers around here, so you start at the middle of your range, you move to the top of the range, and that's that. There really is no financial incentive to perform here." The more we talked about it, the more heads were nodding (or shaking in bemusement).

Finally somebody said, "If everybody agrees, why doesn't somebody change this ridiculous system?" Then I got a little carried away and said, "Yeah, where's the clown who came up with this system anyway?" And the CFO raised his hand and said, "I came up with this system and, by the way, I'm also the guy who's going to sign the check for your fee." Oops.

Later on somebody explained to me that the CFO had been hearing about the problems with the compensation system for some time from just about everybody and he was damned sick of it. When he designed this compensation plan, it was considered the cutting-edge approach. He had a strong personal belief that the way one should succeed in this company and be compensated is to pay your dues, please your boss, don't leave, be patient, and climb the ladder. Hey, if you stay long enough for it to vest (twenty years), you're going to get a generous pension.

There will always be people who are deeply attached to the compensation system as it is, and it usually won't just be the guy who designed it. Those who have paid their dues and climbed the ladder tend to be pretty attached to those payoffs. And they also tend to be the people in the organization with the most power. It's never easy to make changes in a long-standing system, but it's always hardest to change a rewards structure because those getting the rewards are going to fight hard not to change the system. It's like telling the prince that you think the monarchy is obsolete.

> **Changing a rewards structure is like telling the prince that you think the monarchy is obsolete.**

What are you supposed to do in a situation like this? You have to work around the dinosaurs, or under them, or over them, or straight through them. While you are lobbying for change and building your change coalition, get your hands on discretionary resources and buy results from your direct reports in defiance of the system. Buy the company and fire the CFO. Go work somewhere else. What else can I recommend?

This is the kind of so-called "performance-based pay" system that gives performance-based pay a bad name. So many people in this company and others will tell you that performance-based pay has been tried unsuccessfully, that they've experienced it and it didn't work. But almost always, if you get into the details, you find that the key elements of a genuine performance-based system are missing, and that, in fact, performance per se is not the basis of the compensation system at all. No wonder everybody hates it.

THE GOOD GUYS OF THE PAST VS. THE GOOD GUYS OF THE FUTURE

Another, less common objection to performance-based compensation stems from a set of philosophical beliefs about the very nature of work and the fundamental relationship between employers and employees. I found this out personally with a man I'll call Gerry, a senior executive with a community-owned, integrated health care system of physicians, hospitals, and health plans with roughly 4,200 employees. One morning, I spoke to about a hundred people from the management of this health care company over breakfast at a country club near the company headquarters. As usual, one of the hottest topics of discussion was performance-based compensation. By the time we arrived at the headquarters for a problem-solving session with a much smaller team from human resources, it was apparent that my remarks had caused quite a stir. "That guy said what we've all been saying." The buzz was buzzing. "People should get paid what they're worth. High performers should get paid more than low performers. People shouldn't get penalized for working faster and rewarded for working slower. I shouldn't have to wait around for years on end to get paid what I can get out there on the open market." And so on.

Gerry was part of the human resources problem-solving session I was going to lead and, when he heard the buzz from my presentation, he wasn't happy about it. For some time he had been a strong and vocal opponent of performance-based compensation at his company or anywhere else for that matter.

Throughout our session, Gerry kept coming back to the relationship between compensation and performance. "Surely," he would say, "there must be more than money at stake for people. Do we really want employees who are only motivated by tangible rewards? What about their commitment to our healing mission?" And throughout the session, I tried to respond as best I could, but Gerry was obviously troubled by my message. At one point he said, "Now everybody has heard you say that performance-based compensation is the only fair way to reward people, and they are all going to come back and say, 'we told you so, and this outside expert agrees with us.'" In other words, in Gerry's view, I had poisoned the internal discourse.

Well, I left that company figuring I hadn't made lots of friends among the leadership. Indeed, I didn't think I'd ever hear from them again. However, shortly thereafter, I had a brief exchange of correspondence with Gerry. First, I received a package in the mail with an article by Alfie Kohn, the author of a well-known book, *Punished by*

Rewards.[3] Stuck to the article was a Post-it with the note, "If you still think pay for performance is the magic bullet, I want to talk with you about it." I thought to myself, "This guy really wants me to change my mind."

I read Kohn's article, which contained many familiar arguments, the main point being simply that tangible incentives don't create an enduring commitment to any value or action, rather they *temporarily* influence the actions people take. "Well, of course," I thought, and that's what I told Gerry in an e-mail: "We live in an immediate world. And incentives do, as Kohn points out, temporarily change what we do. . . . It is the job of a good manager to temporarily change what employees do, one day at a time, day after day."

Not satisfied, Gerry sent me a lengthy response in which he asked me if I have read "the work of Maslow, McGregor, Hertzberg, Vroom, and others." Indeed, I have read the work of all of these humanist theorists,[4] and because I have, I immediately thought to myself, "Ohhhhh, now I see what's bothering him." I felt my interpretation was confirmed when I got to this point in Gerry's e-mail: "Perhaps there is another factor to consider here, that comes out of the body of knowledge related to human development."[5] Finally, Gerry repeated his concern that "focus on extrinsic rewards undermines the long-term efforts of both the individual and the organization."

"The focus on extrinsic reward," I thought, "that's what's really bothering him."

What I realized was that Gerry is on the "good-guy" side of a long-standing debate from the workplace of the past. In short, the debate is about whether workers are best motivated from sources internal to themselves such as desire, belief, and self-actualization (Theory Y) or by external sources such as fear, coercion, and financial incentive (Theory X). All the literature Gerry cites is from theorists who argue in one form or another that trying to motivate workers by external means is dehumanizing, and that, in fact, people are not only happier but also perform much better when they are motivated by internal means.

So, the good guy manager from the workplace of the past (like Gerry) tries to follow the humanistic Theory Y religiously. He believes that the role of the manager is to get the worker involved in formu-

Long-term commitment? Free agents have a long-term commitment to their own success, by their own devices. They may have a long-term commitment to your mission too, but that warm feeling isn't going to be enough to convince them to pursue your mission for their livelihood unless you pay them what they are worth, one day at a time.

START MANAGING RESULTS INSTEAD OF TIME

I f I've convinced you that pay for performance is absolutely necessary in a free-market environment, then ask yourself this: Why are most of the rewards in the workplace still allocated to those who put in the most face-time every day and those who stay with the organization long enough to pay their dues and earn seniority? After all, time served is hardly the same thing as results achieved.

It's tempting to say that the focus on time served is just a bad habit left over from the pay-your-dues, climb-the-ladder model from the workplace of the past, but there is more to it. First, time is a great equalizer. People tend to think there is a basic fairness when everybody is rewarded by the same measure: The more hours (or years) you work, the more you get paid. Second, most organizations know very well—from years of experience—how to pay people for their time. Hourly wages and set salaries are very easy to administer, whereas pay for performance is variable and, thus, not so easy. Third, for managers on the front lines, managing results takes a lot more time and energy than managing time. Time served is the most immediately visible element of performance, so managers can monitor it with ease and, indeed, have a hard time ignoring it.

"What's more important to you as a manager: the amount of time your employees put in, or the results they achieve?"

I know what your answer would be if I asked, "What's more important to you as a manager: the amount of time your employees put in, or the results they achieve?" Results win, hands down. Right?

But I'll bet if I came into your office some morning at 9:30 A.M. and one of your employees wasn't at work yet, you might be checking your watch and shaking your head. If I could be a fly on your wall when one of your employees takes two hours for lunch, or disappears from the office at 4:00 P.M., I might just hear you mumble, "What does he think this is, a country club?"

Why is that?

The crux of the problem is opportunity cost. Even if you don't think it consciously, you feel it, almost like an instinct: If a person can get that much work done in, say, five hours, just imagine how much she could do in eight hours. No matter how much a person gets done, no matter how good the person's work may be, it's hard not to think about the opportunity cost.

One time I was speaking to a district managers' meeting of a small coffee company based in the southwestern United States, and of course, I was talking about the importance of paying people for results achieved instead of time served. After the seminar, one of the district managers took me aside and told me the following story.

Her team of seven sales representatives was the highest-performing team in the company. She told me that was really due to the work of three superstars on the team. In each case, these superstars had taken over a sales territory and had doubled or tripled the numbers in a matter of months. One guy in particular had increased the orders of existing customers by 40 percent, while at the same time nearly doubling the number of customers in his territory. The other two were nearly as successful. As the district manager whispered this story to me, she leaned closer and said, "To my mind, these guys could do whatever they wanted, as long as they kept hitting numbers like that." But not everybody in the company felt the same way.

These sales reps carry with them handheld computers on which their customers' orders are recorded and signed for with a graphic-imaging pencil (like the one your UPS driver uses). The customer orders are marked with a particular date and time. At the end of each day (or every two or three days), the sales reps upload the information from the handheld computer to company headquarters.

Whoever was keeping track of the sales reports at the corporate headquarters began to notice a pattern. The superstar sales reps in this particular district almost never recorded orders after 3:00 P.M. In fact, there were plenty of days on which their last orders were recorded before 2:00 P.M. But the standard hours for the sales reps were supposed to be 8:00 A.M. to 5:00 P.M. minimum. Obviously three of the sales reps in this particular district were working half-days, just about. "We can't allow this," somebody at corporate headquarters must have thought.

Well, this district manager told me, she caught lots of flack from her boss: "Why should these guys only be working until 2:00 or 3:00 P.M. when everybody else is working until 5:00 P.M. minimum?" What do you think she said? "These guys are selling twice as much as any other sales reps in the company. They are amazing. Any one of these guys could sell anything to anybody. Every one of them has more than doubled the sales in his territory." What do you think her boss said? "But if they can sell that much by 2:00 or 3:00 P.M., just think how much they could sell in an additional ten or fifteen hours a week."

That's opportunity-cost thinking. It's not crazy. Especially if you are talking about a machine. But these guys are people. Supervaluable people. People who can sell anything to anybody. And they know it.

So, this district manager tells me, she went back to her superstars and broke the news: "You guys can't keep knocking off at 2:00 or 3:00 P.M. I'm getting a lot of heat. You know how I feel about it, but there's nothing I can do." And so on. What do you think these guys said? "Yeah, right. Whatever. We can sell anything to anybody. If the company isn't willing to let us get the results our way, we'll go sell for some other company."

But what about opportunity cost? You see, in a case like this, there is no opportunity cost, because the talent isn't willing to work the extra ten or fifteen hours, certainly not at the same level of performance. "The whole reason I work so hard and sell so much so fast is to buy myself time," one of the guys explained. "I figure if I'm that good, I can work wherever I want, whenever I want. If you just want me to put in my time, what incentive do I have to hit the ball out of the park? I want to hit the home run and go home."

Now put yourself in the shoes of this district manager. She is telling her star sales reps that they have to put in more time. They are telling her, "OK, then we quit." Or at the very least, "If you just want us to put in our time, we are going to downshift our performance considerably."

Here's what she did, she told me, in a very low whisper: She told these guys to start recording dummy orders at 3:45, 4:15, 4:50, 5:05 P.M., and so on, before they sent in their sales records. And then every couple of weeks, she told them, they could go back and void out the transactions, along with the other orders that were canceled. "Is that fraud?" I asked her. "I don't know what it is," she said, "But I couldn't afford to lose these guys, and I thought any shareholder with half a brain would agree with me. These guys are so good, they most definitely should not be treated like everybody else. They should be rewarded for their performance. The reward they choose is more control over their schedules."

This manager understood very well that the opportunity cost of time is turned on its head in the free market for talent. Why? Because of the intersection of two factors: First, speed matters more than ever before in the new economy. People who work faster get products and services to market faster. So, in contrast to the era of face-time, the longer you take to get your work done, the less valuable you are to your employer. Second, the people who can get more work done faster than the rest are valuable enough to command their own terms. In more cases than not, the speed demons are only going to sell their speedy work to employers willing to give them more control over their own schedules.

What is the moral of this story? Forget about time served and focus on results achieved. Do whatever it takes to reward high performers in time, money, and any other currency you can muster. I am not recommending fraud, but if the compensation system is out of alignment, you may have to bend the rules to get the best work out of the best people.

EVERY MANAGER MUST BE A COMPENSATION OFFICER

I know that this is going to require retooling your approach to compensation and, more important, a radical rethinking of your daily role as a manager. Quite simply, if you are in the results business, you need to be in the rewards business as well. Rewards and results go hand in hand in a free market.

Years ago, Gary Jones made all of his frontline managers into de facto compensation officers, and it worked like a charm. Mr. Jones is the inventor and founder of HammerStrength, the plate-loaded exercise equipment maker based in Kentucky and owned by Life Fitness, a division of the Brunswick Corporation, a $4-billion-a-year recreational goods company. He ran HammerStrength from 1987 to 1998 and grew the company from six employees and one product to more than one hundred employees producing a steady stream of more than sixty different exercise machines (that's less than two workers per product in the marketplace!).

How did Mr. Jones' HammerStrength operation get so much work done? Well, part of the answer is that they developed a brilliantly simple and efficient manufacturing process, but the real answer is to be found in human productivity driven by rewards.

The first thing Mr. Jones did was to make sure that working for his company would be the best-paying job available to his potential workforce. According to Mr. Jones: "We only did business in rural towns where people really wanted to live, but wages tended to be lower on average. The goal was that working for us would be the best gig in town. It always was." Anybody working for HammerStrength had a lot to lose, simply because the job paid so well compared to other opportunities.

But Mr. Jones's real innovation was creating a culture in which managers were all about rewarding performance. Mr. Jones continues: "I really believe in spot bonuses. Every supervisor had authority to give bonuses to high performers, anywhere from a few hours' pay to a week's pay. We had a regular supervisors' meeting and I would go around the table and ask the supervisors, 'How many people did you give a bonus to last week?' If they hadn't given anybody a bonus, I'd say to them, 'Do you mean to tell me, you are managing forty people every week, and you couldn't find any reason to give somebody a bonus? What is the matter with you?' So, you know, those guys were always looking for reasons to give the guys on their crew spot bonuses." And you

> "You are managing forty people every week, and you couldn't find any reason to give somebody a bonus?"

can be sure that the guys on the crew were doing backflips to be the ones who would earn those bonuses. It worked. Mr. Jones reports: "In any given year, HammerStrength was outproducing every other company in the industry with half the number of factory workers."

When managers become de facto compensation officers, productivity explodes. Of course, not every CEO is onboard like Gary Jones. So managers sometimes have to go out on a limb and appoint themselves to the compensation team, if you know what I mean. But you don't always have to do this covertly (like the district manager in the coffee company example above). Instead, you could do it like Kambiz Hayat-Dawoodi, another true hero of the new economy. Faced with insufficient rewards to motivate his team, Mr. Hayat-Dawoodi went to senior management and negotiated for the necessary resources.

Born in Iran and educated in England, Mr. Hayat-Dawoodi found himself in the early nineties in Austria working for Austria Mikro Systeme International AG, a leader in the European market of custom-specific circuits for communications, automotive, and industrial electronics, at the time a $200 million company with about seven hundred employees. Mr. Hayat-Dawoodi was there to lead a team project focused on developing a microchip for telephony competitive with the solutions from companies that at the time dominated the wired-telephony market. After a quick feasibility study, he proposed a revolutionary approach that would change the landscape of the marketplace and put his company's competition on the ropes. (In the end, the device his team created was used in a matchbox-size telephone that made it into the *Guinness Book of World Records* as the smallest telephone in the world.) He knew full well that speed to market of the new technology would be everything with this project, as with most high-tech projects.

"To focus the whole team on the time schedules," says Mr. Hayat-Dawoodi, "I requested a bonus scheme which included everyone involved with the product from marketing to test and product engineer." After some serious lobbying, top management agreed to the bonus scheme, but they added a clause that every week of delay on the transfer to production would mean a 10 percent reduction in the proposed bonus. That was fine with Mr. Hayat-Dawoodi, but if the market value of time on this project was 10 percent of the bonus per week, he figured, then for every week the team came in ahead of schedule, that market value should also be reflected in the deal. So Mr. Hayat-Dawoodi cajoled the top management until they agreed to match the potential 10-percent-per-week bonus reductions on the late side of the deal with 10-percent-per-week increases on the early side. What do you think happened?

Mr. Hayat-Dawoodi continues, "The project transferred to production eight weeks ahead of schedule to the delight of all those involved." Did you hear that? Eight weeks ahead of schedule. Speed to market was worth a fortune to the company. And it was worth an 80 percent premium on the bonus for every member of the team. "Having seen the results, the management was keen for me to educate others to use the same techniques in carrying through projects. Soon after, I was given my own section with five engineers, but I quickly expanded it to fifteen by using seven external engineers." To Mr. Hayat-Dawoodi, it didn't matter whether his engineers were internal or external, he treated them all like independent contractors, with short-term, pay-for-performance agreements on every project. When necessary, he negotiated with senior management for institutional support. He has since applied his "record time" approach to project completion with every team in every company smart enough to hire him.

Team-based performance bonuses can be very powerful, particularly in a battlefield environment where everybody is in up to their eyeballs for the duration of the project.

An architect, Mark Bartolone, tells our interviewers this story from his days at a major architectural firm in New York City: A well-known $2-billion-a-year clothing retail chain retained the firm to create plans for a four-story limestone building in Chicago to house one of the company's largest retail stores, as well as a restaurant, salon, and spa. The project had already gone through two other architectural firms over the course of two years, and the firm was given four months to complete a ten-month job. The client knew just how to do business with its vendor—they offered the firm a huge cash premium and said, "just get it done." So this architect gets the assignment, and the firm was smart enough to pass along some of the cash premium in the form of bonuses—huge bonuses totaling 4 percent of the entire fee—tied to the completion of each phase of the project.

The only problem is that there was no way this guy was going to complete the job on time . . . at least not alone. What was he going to do? Hire five subcontractors to help him, that's what. He negotiated with his firm to get more money in his bonus pool and then he split it among the team. "We worked like dogs," he recalls. "About half the nights we worked straight until midnight, one and even two o'clock in the morning to get the work done." Without those bonuses, he insists, none of the people on that team would have been "so dedicated," and they never would have met the deadlines.

REWARD THE MOST VALUABLE PLAYERS THE MOST

By now, of course, there are plenty of adherents to team-based rewards. How such a plan is administered, of course, depends on what performance a company is trying to incentivize.

If you are trying to incentivize profitability, share profits: Asea Brown Boveri (ABB), the innovative power-engineering company based in Zurich, Switzerland, that employs more than two hundred thousand people, is split into twelve hundred different companies with roughly two hundred employees each. Each company within ABB is accountable for its own profit and loss and keeps a third of its net profits.[6] If you want alacrity, pay for it: Continental Airlines CEO Gordon Bethune got a lot of press for turning the company around from bankruptcy largely using a company-wide pay-for-performance initiative. Because the company was losing $6 million a month due to late arrivals, Bethune set up a bonus system where every employee got $65 (half the $6 million divided by the number of employees) for every month Continental was in the top five airlines for on-time arrivals. Within three months, Continental rose from number seven to the number-one spot. Now the $65 is awarded to every employee every month that at least 80 percent of flights are on time. As of April 2000, forty-one on-time bonus payments have been made to Continental staff, with total bonus payments reaching $124 million.[7]

OK, how do you reward something intangible like "good customer service"? Ask your customers if they are happy: Metamor Technologies, the $600-million-a-year IT company based in Texas has 450 software consultants working in Chicago. The company regularly surveys a random sample of clients. Riding on the answers: 10 percent of consultants' salaries and 40 percent of bonuses.[8]

Great stories. Right? But you have to be very careful with team-based rewards. What about the ABB engineer who works twice as hard as the next guy? And the Continental Airlines pilot who shows up early for every flight and works closely with the maintenance crew to check out the plane before it is time to go, while the other pilots don't? And the Metamor Technologies consultant who is so much smarter and more effective than the others, she makes up for the less impressive consultants, resulting in satisfied client reports in the phone survey? What about the star performers? Imagine a team of five people on which two members do 80 percent of the work, one member does 20 percent, and two just show up for meetings. People in my seminars often describe this scenario. And they are absolutely right to complain that it is profoundly unfair to reward everybody on such a team equally. If this happens, your superstars will feel burned, while your low performers are rewarded for work they didn't do.

Those who perform the best work at the fastest pace should get the most rewards. In a recent survey of 770 major North American companies, researchers at Towers Perrin, a leading human resources consulting firm, found that the best-performing companies (those in the upper quartile of shareholder returns) pay their high performers significantly more—in financial and nonfinancial rewards—than other employees.[9] Even Cisco Systems, so well known for its "one company" culture, makes employee stock options[10] contingent upon individual performance measures. Given the skyrocketing success of Cisco, the leading developer of "network plumbing for the Internet" and currently the world's most valuable company in terms of market capitalization, the approach is obviously working. Ultimately, if a reward system is fair, in market terms, it will provide real incentives for performance and create the kind of cohesiveness that comes from a team of high performers playing their individual roles to the best of their abilities.

GIVE PEOPLE THE POWER TO CONTROL THEIR OWN REWARDS

T he critical element in any real performance-based system is that rewards must actually be tied to actions within the direct control of individuals. Perhaps the most common example of this is piecework, where individuals are paid an agreed-upon amount for each defined unit of work they produce. This approach is widely used in manufacturing and farming and should be easy to picture, but let me give you a slightly counterintuitive example. Theraldson Enterprises, based in Fargo, North Dakota, and operator of more than three hundred hotels (including Courtyards and Comfort Inns) across the United States, pays chambermaids by the room instead of by the hour. The result is a higher rate of hourly compensation and a shorter workday for the maids and a savings of $2 million a year to the company.[11]

Stanford University professor Edward Lazear has conducted extensive research on what he calls "personnel economics." His research on piecework in middle- and low-tier jobs demonstrates that productivity increases substantially when pay is directly tied to performance.[12] Why can't the same approach be used with professionals? Accountants could be paid per audit (many are). Programmers could be paid per line of code (many are). Writers could be paid by the word (many are). And so on.

Commission-based sales is another example of real performance-based pay that springs to mind for many. But often a commission-based system only looks as if it is based on actions within the control of the salesperson. Take this composite of a problem I run across frequently in telemarketing organizations.

Say telephone salespeople in company X are paid by commission (10 percent of the actual revenue from their sales), which is very common. OK. Now let's say salesperson number one does a great job (she makes tons of calls, listens carefully, and says just the right things in response). But she is selling a product that has no market reputation and, on top of that, she is working from a list of unqualified customers (there is nothing about the list that makes them likely buyers of the particular product). Whereas, salesperson number two is mediocre at selling (he makes fewer calls than he could, doesn't listen carefully all the time, and says the right things in response sometimes and the wrong things just as often). But he is selling a product with a great market reputation, and also he is working from a qualified list (people who are likely buyers of the particular product). There is a strong likelihood, in this scenario, that salesperson number two will outperform salesperson number one, strictly on sales revenue. So a reward system based purely on sales revenue would be unfair. Salesperson one would suffer and salesperson two would benefit for reasons that are beyond their control.

The dilemma presented to managers in this situation, as is often the case, is this: It is very easy, although terribly ineffective and unfair, to administer a reward system based on sales revenue. But it is very difficult to administer a system based on actual performance. As you can see, in order to reward salespersons one and two on the basis of their actual performance, it would be necessary to measure not only the number of calls each person is making every day, but also to evaluate the technique each person uses on the phone. Is she listening carefully and saying the right things in response? This latter evaluation is probably the most important in terms of really differentiating high performers from low performers. It is also critical to the process of helping low performers improve. But it takes time and energy on the part of managers.

Exercising your own subjective judgment is often the only fair and accurate way to evaluate performance, so you'd better get good at it.

Really and truly measuring and rewarding individual performance takes a lot of time and energy on the part of managers. Think about the purchasing agent, Paul Applegate. Do you think he negotiates a contract with a vendor and forgets about it? Of course not. He has to monitor the vendor's performance at predetermined project milestones, or if there are no natural milestones, then at regular intervals. Any manager supervising the performance of any individual or any team will have to do the same thing. And that's not all. Evaluating performance is often highly subjective and will require you to exercise your own judgment about the quality of an individual contributor's work (in the example above, is the salesperson listening carefully and saying the right things?). But exercising your own subjective judgment is often the only fair and accurate way to evaluate performance, so you'd better get good at it.

Your key to success will be establishing clear performance standards for individual contributors and measuring their performance closely and regularly against those standards. One of the best examples of this pure market system comes from an unlikely source, a private nonprofit agency that serves developmentally disabled children and adults called the Spectrum Center, based in San Francisco. The Spectrum Center, which employs 150 people, has been refining their pay-for-performance system since 1979. Now they've got it right. At least once every six months, every single employee negotiates an individual performance contract of goals and deadlines. As soon as a goal is achieved, the individual is cashed out in the amount agreed upon in his or her performance contract. These bonus payments range from $1,200 to $10,000 per employee per year. Supervisors have the considerable burden of reviewing, evaluating, and documenting that goals have been completed. While the organization doesn't have the same kind of financial bottom line as a for-profit business, turnover at the agency is at an all-time low and productivity is at an all-time high.[13]

USE NONFINANCIAL REWARDS FOR ADDITIONAL LEVERAGE

Don't limit your repertoire of rewards to money. Also use every nonfinancial reward at your disposal to reward performance. Throughout the store system of my client J.C. Penney, the fourth-largest retailer in the United States with $32.5 billion a year in revenue and 260,000 employees, it is common practice to reward store employees with an extra paid day off for maintaining perfect attendance over the course of a year. During the 1999 holiday season, J.C. Penney's Outlet division awarded both temporary and regular store employees with perfect attendance for the thirteen-week holiday season with $200 gift certificates good for store merchandise. Another client, Motorola, Inc., the $31-billion-a-year electronics company that employs 150,000 people and is based in Schaumburg, Illinois, has for many years given managers discretion to reward factory workers for meeting goals with dinners at four-star restaurants and weekend trips to first-class hotels. And food-product maker Thomas J. Lipton Company, the subsidiary of London-based Unilever, has had a long tradition of rewarding workers for meeting specific manufacturing goals with free access to the vending machines.[14]

But don't wait for your company to adopt a policy. Just start doing it. Almost every manager I know has substantial discretion over nonfinancial rewards such as time off, office space, training opportunities, exposure to decision makers, and other less common perks. Use that discretion wisely. Leverage it for everything it's worth. I don't think you'll be surprised to learn that our research shows that the number-one nonfinancial reward sought by employees is time, that is, more control over their own schedules. Position time, and every other discretionary resource, as a reward in the day-to-day, pay-for-performance negotiation process.

How often do you complain that your employees nowadays are too demanding?

> *"This one wants Thursdays off."*
> *"That one wants her own office."*
> *"This one wants to bring his dog to work."*
> *"That one wants to go to every training class we offer."*
> *"This one wants to have dinner with the senior VP."*

And so on. Don't complain. When you discover the wants and needs of demanding employees, you've found the needle in a haystack.

Managers who have learned to negotiate aggressively with their employees tell me every day in my seminars that they use those needles as bargaining chips and exchange them for performance:

> *"You want Thursdays off? I'm glad to know that. Here's what I need from you."*

> *"You want your own office? OK. Here's what I need from you."*
>
> *"You want to bring your dog to work? Great. Here's what I need from you."*
>
> *"You want to have dinner with the senior VP? Here's what I need from you."*

Expand your repertoire of rewards and start using every resource you have to drive performance.

REWARDS ON THE LINE ALL THE TIME

Focus your rewards strategy on three critical questions: (1) Who is in control of the lion's share of each person's compensation? The answer should be: each person. Individuals should never be made to feel that they are competing against each other, but rather that they are competing with themselves against concrete goals, deadlines, and guidelines and parameters.[15] (2) When do people get compensated? The answer should be: when they deliver. The closer in time the reward comes to the performance in question, the more powerful the incentive. (3) In what form do people get compensated? The answer should be: in whatever rewards they value the most that are in your power to offer. It is very important to be 100 percent clear about which organizational resources are included in the pay-for-performance scheme and which ones are available to people regardless of performance. (Please note, I've included an appendix to cover nonperformance-based life resources being offered in companies all over the world in the competition for the status of "employer of choice.")

Some or all of every person's compensation should be on the line all the time and tied directly to his or her performance.

In the end, the key to performance-based rewards is simple: Every individual contributor needs to know that what counts at the end of the day is his or her performance. Some or all of every person's compensation should be on the line all the time and tied directly to his or her performance.

In practical terms, you may not be able to abandon fixed pay right away. So pay as little base pay as you possibly can and make the rest contingent on performance. I call this kind of contingent compensation "available pay." Let's say Mary comes to work for you and she is looking for a salary of $30,000 annually. You tell her, "Mary, we're going to do better than that. We are going to make $40,000 available to you annually. But half of that is going to be on the line all the time. So you get paid $20,000 as long as you are doing good enough work to keep your job. The other $20,000 you get paid as long as you are meeting all your goals and deadlines, as measured at project milestones or at regular intervals." To make it work, you need a manager in there measuring clear and concrete goals, ambitious goals, stretch goals.

Whatever base you offer to get somebody in the door, the bonus is where the real compensation comes in. Remember, if Mary performs, she makes 33 percent more than she was hoping at the outset. That's a great deal for her *and* for you. Here's an added twist: Never give people raises in their base pay. But be very generous about increasing the additional compensation "available" to people in their bonus. Mary could end up with compensation of $100,000 in a few years. But if it were up to me, her base would still be $20,000.

Do you want to see people never have "off days" on the job? Do you want to see people work steadily all the time? Put their compensation on the line and in their own control.

Never forget, an effective pay-for-performance[16] approach requires all the elements of a well-negotiated purchasing contract:

> (1) Measurable individual performance benchmarks. Every step of the way, clear deliverables should be explicitly defined for every contributor and concrete rewards tied directly to those deliverables.
> (2) Clear expectations (among managers and workers alike) about the relationship between specific individual behaviors and specific rewards.
> (3) Regular and close monitoring by managers of individual performance and the keeping of good contemporaneous

records (once again, this is high maintenance) and ongoing communication about the process between managers
and individual contributors.

BE A CHANGE LEADER

Please don't tell me, "But that's not how our compensation system
works." Of course it's not how your compensation system works
. . . yet. So you'll have to work around it, or under it, or drive right
through it, until it changes. It's going to change when cutting-edge
managers like you start proving that when managers drive a hard
bargain, more work gets done, better work gets done, and the work
gets done faster.

Buy results from your talented contributors, one day (or week, or
the life of the project) at a time. Make formal or informal purchasing
agreements every step of the way—short-term, pay-for-performance
agreements. Set goals, deadlines, guidelines, and parameters up
front, and agree, up front, on the market value of the work and on
terms of payment (financial and nonfinancial).

Pay them in whatever currencies you can get your arms around.
Cash them out for what they've delivered, when they deliver. If they
don't deliver, don't pay—if you can help it. That way, you have more
resources to use for rewarding the vendors (inside or out) who *do*
deliver.

Cold? Hard? Whatever. This is business. Talent is driving a hard
bargain. You'd better learn to do the same.

But it is high maintenance. It takes time and energy every day. It
takes incredibly resourceful managers on the front lines who hoard
discretionary resources and then dole them out to high performers in
exchange for agreed-upon results. Even without institutional support,
managers who embrace the philosophy of paying for performance
always find a way. You can do that.

Chapter 5

TURN MANAGERS
INTO COACHES

One question that leaders and managers are still asking is this: "How can we get employees to do our bidding when they have so much negotiating power?" The question you should be asking is: "How do we change the role of managers so they will motivate and inspire performance?"

When my research team interviewed several dozen of the five hundred advertising sales representatives at Comcast Cable Communications, one of the largest cable companies in the world with eleven thousand employees and owned by the $6-billion-a-year Comcast Corporation, the same name came up over and over again: Filemon Lopez.

One person after another told us that Mr. Lopez was the reason they worked so hard every day. His example was an inspiration. His energy was irresistible. Every single person we interviewed seemed to know Mr. Lopez on a personal basis, regardless of where the person was based or how long he had been with Comcast. When I read the interview transcripts, I thought to myself, "Who is this guy?" Now that I've met him myself, I know just what all the sales reps were talking about. Filemon Lopez has that brand of charisma you can't forget.

When he was senior VP of advertising sales, Mr. Lopez was in charge of all five hundred sales representatives at Comcast. (Now he is president of Comcast's internal university.) He once told me that his entire job is to inspire and energize every individual in the sales organization to exceed performance goals. He does it nonstop. "I stay in touch one-on-one with as many people as I can either by e-mail, phone or as I travel," Mr. Lopez explained during a more recent interview. "Although I am maybe one hundred or five hundred or one thousand miles away . . . they feel like they have a personal relationship with me." The only way that happens, he insists, is when a manager is "out there spending time with people."

Mr. Lopez offers this formula for his success: Let people know what's expected of them and coach them every day through continuous, informal communication. Sometimes, he acknowledges, "You have to exercise a bit of tough love. . . . You go and confront somebody and be as direct and as clear as you can." But the key to effective coaching, according to Mr. Lopez, is to stay tuned in to what each person needs to do his job better every day. As often as not, the only resource a person lacks is passion and Mr. Lopez has a passion that is contagious. "People see how much I love the business and they are inspired by it," he says. "People just don't want to let me down."

❏ ❏ ❏

Mr. Lopez goes to great effort to teach his brand of leadership to all of the sales managers throughout the Comcast organization. Why? Coaching is the only way to keep free agents motivated and inspired in the free market for talent. No longer can managers lead by fear—nobody's afraid anymore. Nor can managers throw people into sink-or-swim environments without any support—they just get out of the pool and go home. Managers who are no good at managing people are a luxury that no business can afford in the new economy. You have to be great at managing people and so does everybody else in your organization.

> **No longer can managers lead by fear—nobody's afraid anymore.**

Here's your situation: You are committed to employing people in a whole new way. You are focused on getting the work done today, tomorrow, and next week. You bring in the right person and put her in the right place at the right time. You negotiate a killer pay-for-performance deal—purchasing agent style. You're just getting started.

Now you must drive every person's performance toward the deliverables and deadlines you've negotiated. You will need to monitor performance very closely, holding everyone accountable, advising them every step along the way, routinely adjusting goals and guidelines, making tough calls, and keeping the whole team motivated, inspired, and moving forward all the time. That tall order requires a highly engaged approach to managing people—an approach that looks less like traditional managing and more like coaching.

Remember, in the new economy, managing people is more important than ever before, and it's going to be high maintenance. Once you engage a person's skills, how do you keep that person focused and performing at his highest level every day . . . for you? How do you get him to work harder, faster, and smarter . . . for you? What if he's distracted? What if he just doesn't feel like it?

At the same time, the nature of work itself is more complicated, less predictable, faster moving, and requires greater skill. Instead of static responsibilities being carried out in stable departments by long-term employees, more and more of the work being done—today—is brand new to long-termers and short-termers alike. The work, it seems, is always a moving target. And, of course, a growing number of your people are short-term, or relatively new anyway, so you are always spending time getting somebody up to speed. When people leave—often unexpectedly—you have to make sure the rest of the team remains on task, while you figure out how to fill in the gaps. Meanwhile, periodically, your department (or the whole organization) reorganizes (again) and you need to reassess, realign, and get back on track.

Like everybody else nowadays, you are in a hurry. As is your boss. And her boss. That's why one of the cherished competencies in your organization is demonstrating a sense of urgency. Even more important, creating a sense of urgency in your team. Right?

MANAGING PEOPLE IN THE WORKPLACE OF THE PAST

It used to be that once you got to a certain point on the organization chart, you were in charge of a bunch of people. "How many people do you have under you?" went the saw. If you happened to be good at managing the people "under you," they were very grateful. If not, basically it was too bad for them because you were the one with the institutional power.

Of course, even in the workplace of the past, any manager worth her salt would try to set a good example. Sure, sometimes you'd let people scramble around on their own, making mistakes until they figured it out, whatever it was. That was fine. Everybody had plenty of time. They weren't going anywhere anytime soon, and neither were you. In fact, the promise of close proximity for the foreseeable future in a clearly defined food chain caused most employees to have at least some fear of their boss (sometimes just a very healthy sense of respect). For their part, most bosses lost their temper just often enough (sometimes way too often) to keep that fear alive and well.

Yes, the best managers would sprinkle in plenty of encouragement, praise for good performers, rewards in due course, and support for high-performing employees' own efforts to climb the corporate ladder. In other words, the best managers deployed feudal benevolence hand in hand with feudal power.

But the feudal power is gone, so benevolent management is for suckers. The transactional nature of employment relationships is transparent in the free market for talent. All parties to every employment transaction will get whatever they can through day-to-day negotiations—pay for performance. And that will get a lot of the work done, at a steady pace and a sufficient level of quality. But face it, if that's all you can get out of people in the new economy, you are dead. Performance in the new economy must be dazzling. Nothing less will do.

So how do you achieve that level of performance in a company which still has a traditional approach to managing people? Turn the managers into coaches.

John Madigan, like Filemon Lopez, is a supercoach in the business world. He is vice president of human resources for information technology at the Hartford, one of the oldest, most traditional insurance companies in the world, and also one of the largest at $13.5 billion a year with more than twenty-five thousand employees. I met him when he stood up in the middle of a speech I was delivering at the Hartford, walked up the center aisle, and hugged me. (It's a long story.) Very cool guy. People-centered. Highly intelligent. Insightful. Energetic. Demanding. Not subtle. Everybody who works for him loves him. Exactly the kind of guy you want coaching hot talent in your organization.

Says Mr. Madigan, "I've had lots of high potentials working for me and they can be a real pain in the neck. They are smart, challenging, always have a better way to do something, often challenge the status quo openly. To old-fashioned types, this seems like a lack of control on the manager's part. Channeling talented people in the right direction can be extremely rewarding but can also be tiring, like having a gifted child who keeps you, as a parent, hopping." To cope with that challenge, Mr. Madigan coaches people throughout his organization every single day in one-on-one meetings and also by "seizing the moment whenever it presents itself."

Unfortunately, this is the exception in many old-fashioned companies. "Most managers say they would love to have a bunch of high potentials working for them," says Mr. Madigan. "However, they don't have a clue about how to manage really good people. . . . The traditional approach centered on the position and its level in the organization which brought with it power over resources. . . . Also, people were socialized to expect consistency and stability at work and to work at the same job or employer for a long time. . . . The old-fashioned style of management worked OK even a decade ago when organizations were still more hierarchical and bureaucratic, less networked and reliant on relationships and influence than they are today.

"Those days are gone," says Mr. Madigan. "The problem now is whole organizations can change overnight. Some people find themselves working for three different companies in the course of eighteen months, never having left the office they occupied before (due to mergers, acquisitions, buyouts). We definitely have to change the culture around managing people."

Mr. Madigan and his team surveyed the IT organization at the Hartford and asked people to describe the best leader for whom they worked. "Many either specifically referred to that leader as a good coach or described good coaching behavior." At a subsequent leadership conference, the managers in the organization "asked for a way to get better at coaching." Under Mr. Madigan's leadership, the IT organization at the Hartford has made a commitment to coaching, and now trainers are busy teaching coaching skills to hundreds of managers throughout the ranks.

"We believe that developing a coaching style in our leaders will help us maximize peoples' contributions to the organization and help us reduce turnover. . . . The challenge [we] face is keeping the momentum. It's too easy to lapse back into old behavior." The other big challenge according to Mr. Madigan? Making coaching skill a key selection criterion for choosing new leaders at the Hartford.

It is a formidable task to change even one leader's style of interacting with direct reports. But transforming the management culture of an entire organization is monumental. It requires a strong coalition of change leaders who can demonstrate one success after another, build momentum, and then keep pushing until the groundswell is unstoppable.

THE POWER OF COACHING

It takes time to build an unstoppable groundswell, but the need for coaching is immediate. That's why so many organizations are now bringing in outside professionals, or dedicating insiders, to be personal coaches to employees throughout the ranks. I have met and interviewed numerous coaching professionals, and my company has interviewed hundreds of people who have worked with personal coaches. The practice is so widespread in the corporate world (in North America) that it is almost old news, except for the wonderful lessons to be learned from this incredible trend. Borrow the techniques of personal coaching and adapt them to help you coach people in achieving their daily tasks and responsibilities.

What is personal coaching? Picture Tony Robbins,[1] the startlingly enthusiastic all-purpose success guru from infomercial-land who has coached presidents of the United States, professional athletes, CEOs, and literally millions of people through his books, tapes, and seminars. Mr. Robbins is surely the most recognizable icon of a phenomenon discursively underwritten by the self-esteem movement in psychology and driven as a business by the growing self-help industry. In the business world the trend took off as "executive coaching" for very high-level people whose talents simply had to be maximized and whose salaries justified the expense of a hands-on coach. With so many senior people coached and converted, the movement has grown steadily.

How does it work? Individuals are matched up with professional coaches (often at company expense, sometimes at their own), and the coach's job is to help that individual reach his or her full potential as a human being and for the company. Why is it catching on? Quite simply, coaching works. It actually brings people to higher levels of performance.

People who have worked with personal coaches tell me the experience is profound. If a coach is good, she will spend enough time with you to be an objective third party with no agenda other than your personal growth who can tell it like it is. The coach pulls no punches. "Your body is too fat, that's why you have no energy," the coach might say. "You must get in shape. You are going to start having oatmeal for breakfast and cantaloupe for lunch, and you are going to start working out. I am going to come to your office at 10:30 A.M., take you to the company gym, and then we are going to have lunch together, every day for two weeks."

But it's usually not physical. The coach might tell you, "Do you know why people don't work hard for you, undermine your authority, and quit on you? Because you act like a jerk. You yell and scream. You are self-indulgent. You never even say thank you. Now here's what we are going to do: We are going to practice assigning a task in a calm tone and asking the right questions to make sure the assignment has been understood. Then we are going to practice saying thank you and being very specific about why you are saying it."

> "Do you know why people don't work hard for you, undermine your authority, and quit on you?"

Personal coaches are not there to berate their clients, but to be acutely observant and honest. Coaches are there to say the right things, negative and also positive. One person who has worked closely with a personal coach told me, "The first week, all this guy did was tell me how great I am. 'You are so smart, you are so capable, you work so much, everybody likes you.'" That's what some people need.

This same person's story takes a turn, however: "For the next year that we worked together, once a week, it was, 'You are so great, why are you not living up to your potential? You have to get focused. You try to do too many things at once. Focus your resources on one thing at a time, get it done, and then move on to the next thing.' My problem was partly time management and partly an issue of follow-through. This guy taught me that, for me, the thing I needed to do was not put something down until it was finished. Or else I'd never finish it."

Personal coaches will often recommend tools as well. The most common of these are goal-setting and time-management tools. Goal-setting tools seem obvious on the surface, but they are very powerful if they are tied directly to time-management tools. For example, when people seem to be working like crazy but not getting anything done, a time log is very useful not just to see where all their time is going, but to show them where their time is *not* going. In a time log, you write down everything you do all day:

> 8:00 A.M., arrived, turned on computer, checked e-mail
> 8:30 A.M., went to get coffee
> 10:15 A.M., went to team meeting

And so on. Of course, a good personal coach will look at this and say, "Wait a second here. You spent an hour and forty-five minutes getting coffee?" "Well, no. I stopped and talked to Mary. Then I went to the rest room . . . and read the paper. Then I had to call the auto repair shop." And so on. The coach might say, "Look, if you want to start earning your monthly sales bonus, you've got to be closing thirty sales a week. That means you need to be making three hundred calls a week, which is sixty per day. Right now you are only making fifty calls per day. Between 8:30 A.M. and 10:15 A.M., you have time to make ten or fifteen calls. That's the missing link."

Personal coaches are personal advocates for their clients, but the advocacy is aimed at the client. What great personal coaches are great at is helping people help themselves. They offer penetrating insights to people about themselves. They give them the good news and the bad. They help people believe that they can do better. They give people concrete solutions to help them improve. And coaches are right there with the people they coach, encouraging them, scolding (but not berating) them when necessary, praising them when it's appropriate, and constantly helping their clients move in the right direction. Being coached can be a deeply personal experience.

"My coach could see right through me," one person told me. "She was totally honest with me about my weaknesses. She would say, 'You are fooling yourself. You have to stop sitting there staring at your computer screen all afternoon not getting anything done. It's just draining you. You get more done from six to nine in the morning than you do during the rest of the day. What's going on?' That caused me to take a good look at how I was working. We were testing out all kinds of things to do after nine o'clock to be more productive. But it also got me looking at some other issues that were much deeper. I realized that I prefer to work when nobody else is around, almost in secret. There was something deep within me that made me feel ashamed about my work. I really had to work that out."

As many people have said about personal coaching, it is sort of like therapy. It is so deeply personal, time consuming, and expensive that as many followers as this movement has in the workplace, it also has detractors. One personal coach, who is very, very good at what he does, told me this: "The truth is, very often it's great for the company because people who go through it are so moved by the experience. It's always great for the people who go through it. They get healthier, their attitude improves, they become much more effective, they usually are much better to work with and to be around. It can have the effect of a complete overhaul, like putting a new engine in a car." That's the upside.

But there is a downside: "Sometimes it's not in the company's best interests because people decide they are in the wrong company, or in the wrong town, or in the wrong line of work altogether." Indeed, I've interviewed people who have gone through personal coaching and, as a result, quit their jobs. In one case a computer programmer quit her job and opened a flower shop; in another, a lawyer quit his job and became a high school teacher.

There is much to be learned and applied from the techniques of personal coaching if you are going to motivate and inspire the people on your team to do extraordinary work. However, as I often tell managers in my seminars, if your day-to-day coaching of employees starts looking like personal therapy, stop what you are doing. Send those people to a psychologist and get back to work. The whole reason I advocate coaching-style management is that work is short term, every day, urgent. Coaching is the way to maintain that energy level and keep people focused on what matters: What results are getting done right now . . . very well and very fast?

"THE ONLY THING THAT MATTERS IS WHAT WE ARE DOING HERE TODAY"

The most powerful approach to coaching is one that focuses urgently on day-to-day, high-quality results. Basketball great Michael Jordan says, "I approach everything step by step using short-term goals. When I meet one goal, I set another reasonable goal I can achieve if I work hard. Each success leads to the next one."[2] This kind of focus on short-term goals produces extraordinary short-term performance, and for those who stick with it long enough, it produces long-term transformational growth . . . one day at a time.

I cite the example of Frank Gorman, who is the greatest coach I have ever known and has been my karate teacher for more than twenty-five years. As long as I've known him, Frank Gorman has been intensely focused on one thing, karate. He is a master at getting a room full of people to share his focus and work intensely on one short-term goal for hours on end without even considering a break in the action. How does he do that?

"The only thing that matters is your thumbs," Frank would say over and over for weeks. "Pull in your thumbs, press them hard against your palms, so hard the tendons in your forearms raise up." Here would be thirty people in a crowded training hall sweating and straining from physical exhaustion, trying to keep their eyes straight ahead, chins down, shoulders back, elbows in, backs straight, hips square, feet pressed into the floor and twisting to tighten the leg muscles. And Frank Gorman would be yelling, somehow in a whisper, "Your thumbs, pull in your thumbs. . . . The only thing that matters is your thumbs."

Then one day, the only thing that mattered was . . . something else. Your eyes. Your chin. Your shoulders. And on and on, for twenty-five years. The amazing thing is that the impact of the mantra never wore off. Somehow, "it" really was all that mattered, whatever "it" happened to be on any given day.

Finally one day I had to ask, "How can anything be the only thing that matters, when that thing always changes?" Frank told me, "Nobody can learn karate in one day or even one year. But all we have is today. What can I teach you today? What can you achieve today? I don't think we should waste each other's time. I really believe it when I say, 'the only thing that matters is' whatever it is today. That's why you believe it. Because it's true. The only thing that matters is *what we are doing here today.*"

The lesson: From the standpoint of the coach, the unyielding force of your own will leaves those on your team with no choice other than to focus acutely on the work at hand (otherwise they are not on the team). For those being coached this way, the demands are great, but the payoff is incredible: First, one builds a repertoire of abilities one at a time. Second, by practicing focus, one learns the incredible skill and habit of focus itself. Third, and perhaps most important, through acute focus on one detail at a time, one is distracted from the seeming precariousness of balancing so many tasks at once. Distracted from the precariousness, everything seems to come into focus, and somehow the whole balancing act is easier.

STOKE THE FIRE IN YOUR OWN HEART FIRST

Maybe you are thinking, "That's just not me. I am a ____, not a coach." Fill in the blank. Are you a programmer? An engineer? Doctor, plumber, lawyer, landscaper, accountant, merchandiser, architect, welder, teacher? I don't care what you do for a living. Unless you want your productive capacity to be limited to your own time and energy forevermore, you are going to have to manage people.

Tell me this: Who's going to manage a programmer but a programmer? Who's going to manage an engineer but an engineer? Who's going to manage a plumber but a plumber? Just about all work today requires esoteric skills. In order to manage somebody with those skills, one must have those skills too (or similar ones) and have a real understanding of the work that person is doing. That's why it's not enough to say, "Just have the 'people-people' do the managing and let me go ahead and do what I do best," be it accounting, welding, landscaping, or teaching.

Indeed, this reality—that people doing esoteric work must be managed by people who share their skill set—is behind another business truth: In every organization, in every industry, there are lots of people who move into positions of supervisory responsibility because they are very good at something, but often they are not good at managing people. So there are lots and lots of skilled people in the workplace who find themselves in charge of other people but without the skills to manage those people effectively (I really hope you are not one of them).

When I go into a company, I'll start asking around, "Tell me about the people here who are really good at managing people." And of course, everybody names the same names: Mark, Carolyn, and Joe. Then I'll ask, "Are there people who are not so good at managing people?" Just as fast, people start ticking off names (usually in a careful whisper): Betsy, Peter, and Harold. "Oh," I usually continue, just for fun, "so Betsy, Peter, and Harold aren't allowed to manage people?" After a confused silence, somebody says, "Oh, they manage people. In fact, I have to deal with Peter all the time and . . ." Even though they are not so good at managing people, they do it anyhow. And everybody knows it.

How could this be allowed to go on?

What would happen if the accountants were great at math but not so good at financial statements? If the surgeons knew anatomy inside and out but were not so good with a scalpel? If the landscaper was great at flowers but not so good with shrubs? Everybody would say, "But that's an important part of your job. You have to be good at that too." And the accountant and the surgeon and the landscaper might respond, "Well, that part of the job just doesn't come naturally to me." Everybody would say, "Then you'd better learn how to do it and practice, practice, practice."

Once you reach the point in your career where you are given enough institutional authority that you are asked to supervise people, you must take that part of your job as seriously (or more seriously) than any other part of your job. Failing to do so is nothing but an act of personal indulgence that comes at a great cost. Human talent is the most critical resource in your organization. Don't squander it. Leverage it. And remember, no matter how much institutional power you have, you can no longer rely on that power to drive performance. You must motivate and inspire people, get them "into" the work, and help them make the connection between the work and their own greatness.

Sometimes when I say this to managers on the front lines of the workplace, they will say something along these lines: "How can I get somebody 'into' the work we are doing here. It is really just grunt work. I mean, the people here are actually digging ditches." Frank Gorman once said to me, "Karate is art. But everything is art, if you are artful. How do you sit? How do you tie your shoes? How do you brush your teeth? It doesn't matter what you are doing. If every single detail is purposeful, then what you are doing is art." Be like Frank Gorman. Stoke the fire in your own heart first. Make your own work of coaching into art by making every single detail of your interactions with the individuals on your team purposeful. Then you can help those on your team be artful about the details of their work.

Make your work of coaching into art.

Don't let anyone (including yourself) in a position of supervisory responsibility off the hook. Hold yourself and others accountable for managing people as well as you do every other part of your job. If you don't know how, learn. If it doesn't come naturally, practice. I promise you, if you work hard at it, you will be great.

CAN COACHING-STYLE LEADERSHIP BE LEARNED?

You are probably asking the same question leaders and managers ask me almost daily, "Is coaching-style management something that can be boiled down into a methodology and taught to any person, regardless of natural ability?"

That's a problem that one of my clients, the United States Marine Corps, tackles on an ongoing basis. With a one-to-nine ratio of officers to enlisted people, the Marine Corps depends a great deal on leadership throughout the enlisted ranks. People move up and out of the Marine Corps very quickly; only 25 percent are allowed to remain after their first term of enlistment. If a marine is on track, within two years, he will find himself in the role of corporal, the lowest level of leadership in the corps. At any given time, there are nearly 23,000 corporals out of a total force of 174,000 marines. In the Marine Corps, "everybody has a chance to be a leader," says Sergeant Major William Whaley. Why? There is no other option. The Marine Corps simply must be able to transform an ordinary person into an effective leader.

Sergeant Major Whaley is an extraordinary person and a great marine who has been decorated many times for his courageous service. Among the many roles he has played in his career, Sgt. Maj. Whaley has been a leader in the training of enlisted Marines. "The product I am giving the corps is better, more capable enlisted leaders," says Sgt. Maj. Whaley. Like everything else they do, the marines are painfully methodical about building leaders: Each corporal is in charge of a "fire team" of three marines. At each new level, an enlisted leader's sphere of supervisory authority is expanded, and he is trained aggressively to take on that role.

The competencies stressed most in that ongoing leadership training look a lot like coaching. According to Sgt. Maj. Whaley, "We teach them: Get out of the office twice a day minimum, and talk to people. It doesn't have to be a lot of time. Your marines don't want to see you forever, but they do want to see you every day. Make your presence felt. Take the pulse of your marines. Get to know them. Gather information. See how things are working firsthand. Carry the message down to the lowest levels yourself. Your marines want to be an important part of something special. It's that back-and-forth exchange, coaching, and persuasion a leader has to use to get the best out of people."

Isn't it true still, at least in the Marine Corps, that people will obey you because of your rank and position? Yes. But, according to Sgt. Maj. Whaley, "people will only respect you and give you their best because of who you are as a person and how you treat them. . . . That's how we turn ordinary people into leaders in the Marine Corps."

THE CORE COMPETENCY OF EVERY GREAT COACH: GIVING FEEDBACK

From all of our work and all of our research, I have studied, as closely as I know how, what the best coaching-style managers actually do. How do they keep people focused on the work at hand every day? Help people build repertoires of ability and skill every day? Make the connection between everyday work and every person's greatness?

Here's the most important thing I have learned: Responsive communication, or feedback, is the key. The person being coached performs and the coach responds, over and over. As much as it is a technique, giving constant feedback is a habit. Every instance of performance gets a response. For most managers, that's a hard habit to get into. You are just so busy. It takes time and energy to stop what you are doing regularly, tune in to each person's performance, think carefully, say something to evaluate each person's work so far, and then keep each person moving in the right direction. But it will transform your relationship with every person you manage.

"Great job on that. This is what you can do better. And here's exactly what I want you to do next." That is feedback—the constant dialogue of coaching.

But feedback is not aimless repartee. It is the banter of acute focus, ongoing improvement, and constant accountability. The only thing that matters is what we are doing here today. So that's what we talk about. And we talk about it all the time. Nobody gets chewed out, but nobody can hide. Everybody gets reminded all the time, so everybody is always on notice. Standards are high. There are no excuses, only performance. If somebody is failing to perform, their only choice is to improve or else leave the team: "Good riddance."

This is what Filemon Lopez meant when he said that sometimes you have to "exercise a bit of tough love." Mr. Lopez tells a story about one of his sales representatives who was failing to meet her performance goals. After examining the situation, Mr. Lopez determined that this sales rep's activity level was simply not high enough to achieve her numbers—she just wasn't making enough calls. So he intervened, like a ton of bricks. He recalls, "Initially she was taken aback and felt threatened, thinking that this was one step before being kicked out." Indeed, if she failed to improve, she would be off the team ("good riddance"), but that was the last thing Mr. Lopez wanted to see happen. "I said to her, 'You should consider this a real honor that we think so much of you that we are going to make sure your performance improves.'" In the wake of this intervention, Mr. Lopez made sure that this sales rep's immediate supervisor met with her every morning and every afternoon, coaching her on goals and deadlines, until her performance was back on track.

When you coach people to success in this manner, they have no choice but to get "into" their work because you, like few others in their lives, require them to be great. Their work becomes art because you remind them to be purposeful about every single detail. They build their repertoires of ability, one day at a time. From focusing, they learn focus itself. The whole balancing act becomes less and less precarious. They become black belts at whatever they do. Perhaps long after they work for you, they will carry your voice of constant feedback in their heads: "The only thing that matters is what we are doing today."

THE FINER POINTS OF COACHING

Whenever I teach coaching to leaders and managers, regardless of the industry, the company, or their level in the company, I emphasize four best practices. Our research shows that the best coaching-style managers consistently do the following things:

> (1) They customize their approach with every person because every person is different. This is what I call tuning in to each person's unique *frequency*.
>
> (2) They choose their words carefully to make sure they get the facts right, balance criticism with praise, and try hard to strike an appropriate tone. This is what I call *accuracy*.
>
> (3) They set concrete goals with clear parameters and dead-

lines every step of the way. This feature tells you exactly how *specific* your feedback must be.

(4) They make time regularly to give feedback. Effective feedback is *timely*.

Remember the acronym *FAST—frequent, accurate, specific,* and *timely.* If you add this acronym to the core competency of coaching—feedback—you get a simple model that is easy to learn and easy to teach to other managers: *FAST Feedback.*

I'll bet you are thinking: "This is a great approach. But all I have is demands on my time. I'm sure I can learn the basic techniques. I just don't think I can make time to do this." If you think you don't have time to manage people well, you are fooling yourself.

> **If you think you don't have time to manage people well, you are fooling yourself.**

Think about Filemon Lopez, who was responsible for five hundred sales representatives and knew almost every single one of them by name. Or take the example of Howard Schultz, the CEO of Starbucks, the nearly $1.7-billion-a-year coffee roaster and retailer with roughly thirty-two thousand employees in more than twenty-four hundred stores. Mr. Schultz says, "I spend a significant portion of my time in trying to touch as many people as I possibly can during the work week. That means visiting lots of stores, walking the halls of the company, communicating via e-mail, communicating in every way possible. I want our people to know how much they are appreciated and to know why the contribution they make every day is so valuable." And Mr. Schultz insists that managers throughout the Starbucks system spend time coaching people every day too. Why? He says, "There is no replacement for being in front of people face-to-face, eyeball-to-eyeball."[3]

Mr. Schultz and Mr. Lopez give new meaning to the question, "How many individuals can one person possibly manage?"[4] However, beneath the surface of that question is a difficult reality. In all of the downsizing, restructuring, and reengineering, one of the most common things that happened in organizations is that whole levels of management were simply eliminated. Otherwise, the organization chart was left intact. You still have the same pyramid structure, with all reporting relationships going up and down. So now an individual who, in the old org chart may have been responsible for six people (each of whom was responsible for six people), is responsible for forty-two.

How can you be a coaching-style manager for forty-two people? You can't. But you don't have to be. In most organizations where managers have found themselves in charge of that many employees, one or both of the following is what actually happens: First, it doesn't really matter, because those reporting relationships only exist on paper. In reality, everybody is moving around from one project team to another, and the person on the team who knows the most about the project is de facto in charge. Second, managers with too many people to manage simply deputize others, and these others either formally or informally do the managing.

Who do you answer to? Really, it depends on what you are working on today. Almost everybody will find themselves managing people at one point or another. Most people will find themselves managing others earlier in their careers than they would have in the workplace of the past, because it's not organizational authority that puts you in charge of people anymore. Who is in charge depends a lot on the work that needs to be done on any given day and the people assembled to do it on today's ad hoc team. The person in charge is whoever knows the most about what we are doing and has the gumption to take charge. So everybody at all levels must develop the basic competencies of coaching because everybody at all levels is a de facto manager.

When you first get started, coaching will take more time because you and the people you are coaching will be easing into it. As you get better at coaching, though, you will find that brevity and simplicity are not only time savers but also make the coaching process more effective. If you keep people focused on the details of the work at hand, the investment of time will return great dividends. Timeliness pays off.

If you have trouble figuring out what to say during coaching interactions, remember this: "Great job on that. This you can do better. Here's exactly what I want you to do next." That's accurate and specific rolled up into one brief script. Stick to the script. The details will come in each encounter. Just don't say anything you're not sure about. And when you are taking corrective action, be sure to focus on only one element of performance at a time until it is corrected.

So then how do you customize the approach for each person you are managing? Everyone is different. Some people need more feedback. Some need less. Some people need more feedback on Mondays and less on Thursdays. Often there are those who need more feedback in the early stages of assuming a new responsibility and less over time. But it really varies. Sometimes people need more feedback when they are feeling depressed and less when they are feeling upbeat, or vice versa. Some respond better to enthusiastic feedback, others respond to feedback that is more businesslike.

Tuning in to each person's unique frequency is by far the subtlest aspect of coaching, the hardest part to learn, the most daunting to teach. The problem is that asking people how much feedback they need is usually not much help. Sorry. Those who truly know how much feedback they require are likely to be so self-aware they are also primarily self-motivated. That doesn't mean they won't need any feedback—they do—but they are not the ones who leave you scratching your head. Those who do leave you scratching your head are probably less self-aware, so they won't be a good source of information. For example, most low performers want to be left alone.

The only effective way to tune in is to start giving feedback and then fine-tune your approach with each person through trial and error. Experiment. Pay close attention. Experiment some more. Whatever brings out the best performance is the winning frequency. Says Sgt. Maj. Whaley, who has coached thousands and taught coaching—Marine style—to tens of thousands, "You can write down the steps to riding a bicycle, but that doesn't mean you know how to ride a bicycle."

If you start coaching the people you manage, you will learn to be a coaching-style leader. You really have no choice. In the new high-speed, high-productivity workplace, virtually every new economy management practice depends on intense personal engagement from managers at every level. According to study after study, including the exhaustive research of the Gallup Organization, which interviewed more than one hundred thousand employees in twelve different industries, coaching-style management is the single greatest factor in improving productivity, morale, and retention.[5] Day-to-day coaching creates the kind of trust and confidence, the genuine bond between managers and individual contributors, that cuts through everything.

BE A CHANGE LEADER

Even in companies that make a top-down commitment to turning managers into coaches, it takes time to change the organization. Plenty of people just dig in their heels and resist, especially when it comes to their relationships with direct reports. They have the institutional power, and they figure that should be enough to get things done. Some of them wonder why their employees no longer seem to be afraid. Others haven't even noticed, despite the fact that their teams are not getting the work done very well or very fast anymore.

Leave them all behind. Forget authority for the sake of authority, rules for the sake of rules. Change your role as a manager. Be a coaching-style manager. Make the time every day to give people *FAST Feedback*. Help them make the connection between their work and their greatness, one detail at a time, one day at a time. Be Filemon Lopez. Be Howard Schultz. Be William Whaley. Be John Madigan. Be Frank Gorman. Tell your best people every day, in your words *and* actions, "All that matters is what we are doing here today."

Chapter 6

TRAIN FOR THE MISSION, NOT THE LONG HAUL

One question that leaders and managers are still asking is this: "How are we going to get a return on our training investment if people won't stay for the long haul?" The question you should be asking is: "How can we redesign our training program to get an immediate return on our investment?"

Samantha, one of several thousand new employees every year at Enterprise Rent-A-Car, walks into one of the company's branch offices for her first day of work. She's had just three days of formal training, albeit nine hours a day at the hands of two trainers assisted by computer-based training tools.

On her first day at the branch, Samantha finds herself out in the parking lot washing cars. As soon as she comes inside, she is given a set of training materials by a fellow employee who has been assigned to sit down with her once a week for half an hour to help her along in her self-directed study. And study she will, because each week she must demonstrate proficiency in a range of subjects including the company's computer system, details about the company's fleet, insurance, reservations, sales, marketing, customer service, billing, administration, problem solving in everyday situations, corporate philosophy, and on and on. The training materials spell out everything she must learn from week to week. Samantha is studying at night, though, because from the outset she is expected to work during the day.

The more she learns through her own efforts and the weekly coaching sessions with her fellow employee, the more skill and knowledge she has to apply on the job. At regular intervals, Samantha will be given computer-based exams on everything she has been learning, and her progress will be reviewed by her manager along the way. Assuming she succeeds up to this point, she will soon take a three-hour written exam called the RSET (rental skills evaluation test). She will be moved along in the training process and in her corresponding responsibilities as fast as she can learn.

When she is ready, probably somewhere between eight and twelve months after her first day, Samantha will take "the Grill," a lengthy oral and computer-based exam that will qualify her for the position of assistant manager. After she passes the Grill, she can go just about anywhere in this fast-growing king of the car rental world. Every step of the way, she'll be working like crazy by day and, by night, learning the prescribed curriculum for the next opportunity. The company views Samantha, like every one of its roughly fifty thousand employees, as an entrepreneur and a leader-in-training, even though so many of them turn over every year. According to the company, every day is meant to be "like an MBA crash course" because "we've hired you to run our business."[1]

❑ ❑ ❑

Fast-paced, superintense, mission-driven training from day one is the only way to get people into meaningful roles immediately and move them along to greater and greater responsibility as fast as they can possibly learn. It is also critical if you are going to get a decent return on your training investment.

> **The more you train people, the more valuable they become, and the more likely they are to leave.**

You have to train your employees. That much is obvious. But the more you train people, the more valuable they are, and, therefore, the more options they have in the free market for talent. In other words, the more you train people nowadays, the more likely they are to leave . . . with your training investment in hand. This frustrating reality is what I call the "training investment paradox."

Let me give you an example. I've done

some work with a supermarket chain that has roughly 125 stores throughout the northeastern United States and more than seventeen thousand employees. Like most supermarket chains, they are experiencing a real shortage of industrial bakers (people who know how to make hundreds and hundreds of cookies, bagels, French breads, muffins, etc., every single day). If you can't recruit talent with the skills you need, your only alternative may be to recruit raw talent and help them build those skills.

This is just what my client did. Faced with the industrial baker shortage, the company made a huge investment in planning, developing, building, and operating an industrial baking school. This way, they can hire people without industrial baking skills or experience, just the ability and desire to learn, and train them. Putting people through industrial baking school takes seven to eight weeks. The problem is that this massive investment is going to produce just forty industrial bakers every year and every newly minted baker will have a skill that is valuable to every supermarket in the world. Remember? There is a shortage of skilled industrial bakers.

To my mind, this investment is very, very vulnerable in the free market for talent. When I told this to the president of the company, he replied, "They have to promise to repay the cost of training if they leave within a certain time. But we think they'll be very grateful for the training and loyal to the company because of that." I think they will be very grateful for the training. And to a point, they might be loyal because of that—just like pet lovers will be loyal to IAMS Pet Food and those committed to the healing arts will be loyal to the hospitals they work for—but only up to a point. As soon as the employment relationship isn't working for them, whether it's because they don't like their hours, their pay, or their boss, they are going to look for other options in the free market for talent. With their new industrial baking skills, those options will be readily available.

Could my client sue departing bakers to recoup their investment? Sure. But, even if the repayment contracts are enforceable, does it make sense for the company to incur the legal costs? And even if it does win judgments against bakers, one at a time, of course, these judgments will have to be enforced. The likelihood is that they would be enforced, if at all, on a payment plan. That means the bakers would be, in effect, paying back a student loan over time, while benefiting at their new jobs from a higher salary, a better boss, a better schedule, or whatever.

Surely the solution to this brainteaser can't be that employers shouldn't invest in training their employees. That's why the problem is a paradox. Again: You have to train people. The more you train them, the more options they have, and so the more likely they are to leave, with your training investment in hand.

To me, the training investment paradox is probably the very best argument for getting good at fluid and flexible staffing as described in Chapter 3. It is better to get a return on the training investment part-time, flex-time, or sometimes, than not at all. That's something one of my clients, the Central Intelligence Agency of the United States, has known for a long time. At the CIA, the learning curve is unavoidably very steep—one year minimum of intensive training for operatives. On top of that, operatives come into contact with highly sensitive proprietary information. True, it is a crime for operatives to use that knowledge in ways not permitted by the agency, just as it may be a contract violation for employees of many private employers to share proprietary information with individuals outside the organization where they work.

But the CIA is smart enough to rely on much more than legal constraints. When an operative considers leaving the agency, she is offered a one-year sabbatical. After that year, she may return without any interruption in her career. If she doesn't return as a full-time officer, she may well be utilized as needed on a flexible basis. Indeed, it is common practice for the CIA to keep the security clearance of former agents active long after they leave the agency so they can accept missions on an occasional basis. Why? In order to maximize their massive training investment and, even more critical, to give the individual a strong personal incentive to maintain the integrity of the proprietary information in her brain. The more you have invested in an employee's skills and the more proprietary information that person has access to, the greater your incentive to keep the person on his own terms if that's what it takes.

But flexible staffing is only part of the solution to the training investment paradox. The rest of the solution is to retool your approach to training.

GET PEOPLE INTO MEANINGFUL ROLES AS SOON AS THEY WALK IN THE DOOR

Here's what every experienced manager and leader in every organization in every industry will tell you: "In our industry, it's different. It just takes a lot of time to prepare people for a meaningful role in a company like ours. There is so much you really have to know to be able to do the job." I promise you, I've been told that by people who run supermarkets and nuclear weapons labs, as well as everybody in between.

If it takes your organization months on end or years to get people up to speed and into a meaningful role, you've got a serious problem in today's short-term environment. Don't tell me you have a staffing crisis and then tell me it's going to take years to train new people to do the work. No wonder you have a staffing problem.

As unique as your field of work may be, it is exactly the same as every other in that there is tons to know if one is to do the job, whatever the job may be, as it is currently conceived. This simply cannot be the end of the discussion. It is only the first consideration. Of course, nobody can develop overnight the kind of depth and breadth of knowledge that we used to expect from people who were taking "career positions" on the old-fashioned organization chart. It remains the case, however, that neither individuals nor the organizations that employ them have time any more for traditional long-term knowledge acquisition.

> It's going to take years to train new people to do the work? No wonder you have a staffing problem.

Still, one thing hasn't changed. The only depth and breadth of knowledge people are going to acquire in the new economy, just as in the old economy, will come from experience over time. But it will have to be the long-term experience of moving from one short-term role to another.

For most employers, the logistical challenge will be creating valuable bundles of tasks and responsibilities for employees—meaningful roles—at much earlier points in the employment relationship than their current development processes support. Creating meaningful roles earlier usually requires unbundling the elements of more complex existing roles and creating new, more narrow roles that people can learn and assume in short order. This approach very quickly gives individuals a great sense of ownership in their work and thus a greater commitment to its quality because their reputations are tied directly to observable results within their control.[2] As a person gets up to speed on each set of tasks and begins performing them ably, the goal is to keep adding new responsibilities, training the person in stages for each new bundle of work—like Samantha at Enterprise Rent-A-Car. Every new bundle of work is like a proving ground, which enables her to earn more responsibility right away.

The good news is that you can put important work in the hands of people who don't yet have depth and wisdom. But you won't be able to do that and just walk away. Like every management strategy for the short-term flexible workforce, this approach to training requires a high degree of engagement—ongoing negotiation, coaching, and measuring—on the part of managers.

MAKE EVERY PERSON A KNOWLEDGE WORKER

In my discussions with business leaders and managers, I find that most have come this far in their view of corporate training: "We know that we are operating in a world of constant change—new technology, shifting markets, vanishing complexity in one sphere and new complexity in another. With new information coming at us all in an ever-growing tidal wave, old information becomes obsolete more quickly than ever before. It is no longer sufficient for anybody to receive their education up front through formal schooling and expect that education to last them very long. It is the job of everybody now to be a lifelong learner."

MIT researcher Professor Peter Senge has been singing the gospel of the learning organization for more than a decade.[3] And just about everybody agrees with him by now, I think. The open question is this: How should employers be allocating limited training resources when the need is universal?

One time I was conducting a problem-solving session with a small group of senior human resources people in a nine-thousand-employee division of a multibillion-dollar-a-year company that manufactures and distributes several well-known brands of packaged foods. I was there to talk with them about two key issues: employee retention and employee training. One of the first things I was told when I got there was this: "We are very concerned because we are losing so many of our best people. Turnover is up to about 25 percent. And we think, based on employee surveys, that the best way to retain our best people is to accelerate the training we provide."

One of the HR people went on to explain: "We are planning to create a fast-track, twelve-week executive-development program and start putting people through the program in groups of several hundred. This way, we can get maybe a thousand people through the program in the course of a year. Once we get rolling, we'll accelerate the program so that by the end of two years we'll have put almost three thousand people through." I was hired to give advice about what kind of career-skills training (networking skills? negotiating skills? and so on) would help the company retain its best and brightest. But all I could see was a giant can of worms.

With this brainchild, the HR team was planning to take hundreds of people at a time (presumably the best people) out of circulation in the company—out of the pool of talent available to do the work every day—even though the organization was short-staffed due to its high turnover. Those passed over for this executive training and left behind would be working that much harder to make up for the missing staff. Meanwhile, the best and brightest are going to be armed with an additional twelve weeks of executive training, making them even more valuable in the free market for talent than they were already. How long will they stay? At 25 percent turnover, the average is less than four years altogether. Will the company be able to get a sufficient return on its twelve-week training investment in each person before she leaves?

I shared my concerns with my client, but they tried to assure me that their strategy would work. Here's what they told me: "We came up with this development program precisely because we want to get our knowledge workers on a longer-term career path." You can imagine all that I wanted to say in response. But my curiosity got the better of me, so I asked, "Who exactly are your 'knowledge workers'?" They told me they were focusing only on the two or three thousand professionals in the division.

Now I saw their problem had an additional, profound dimension. No matter what I said to try to change their minds, they were convinced they had only two or three thousand knowledge workers in that division, which meant there were another six or seven thousand people who were not considered knowledge workers. That's a monumental problem.

Everybody today, in a successful organization, must be a knowledge worker. Knowledge work is not about what you do, but how you do whatever it is you do. If you leverage skill and knowledge in your work to do a better job, you are a knowledge worker. If you don't leverage skill and knowledge in your work to do a better job, you are useless to any organization with a prayer of survival in the new economy. That's true whether you are digging a ditch or designing the foundation of the building that is going to be built in that ditch.

The real challenge for every organization is creating an environment in which everybody is a knowledge worker. That means creating an approach to training that focuses on training everybody, not for the long haul that never will be, but one day at a time.

TRAIN PEOPLE ONE MISSION AT A TIME

I'm sure you remember the classic query of the high school student, "Is this going to be on the test?" To me, this information-savvy question is a critical guidepost for training in the new economy. It takes fully into account the information-rich environment that keeps us struggling desperately to stay ahead of the accelerating obsolescence curve of knowledge and skills. More information is produced in a day, on almost any subject, than a small army of people could possibly master in a lifetime. So how do you learn effectively in a world like that?

Let's start with this basic proposition: People learn best when they have a skill or knowledge gap that is preventing them from achieving a tangible result. Every day people go to their managers with skill and knowledge gaps and are told, "There is a training program available in four months for that. We'll sign you up for it." This is very frustrating to most people. And of course, these people don't show up for the training when it is finally offered because, more likely than not, they found a way to learn what they needed to learn when they needed to learn it, in order to complete work on a tangible result. Or else they didn't find a way and completed the tangible result without ever filling the skill or knowledge gap.

Then again, if they do show up to the training, four months too late to fill their need, the strong likelihood is they will be forced to sit through *a, b, c, d, e, f, g, h,* and so on, even though they might only need to learn *g.* "I wanted to learn *g,*" they'll be thinking, "but they made me sit through all this other stuff. All I needed was *g.*" By the time they have a chance to use *a, b, c, d, e, f,* and *h,* much of the information may well be obsolete.

Most people today want to learn what they need to learn when they need to learn it, not because they are lazy and not because they have short attention spans. Learning just in time is simply in sync with the tidal wave of information in which we are all living and working every day. The only way to learn effectively in a tidal wave of information is to learn strategically—"Is this going to be on the test? Tomorrow?"

I once discussed this phenomenon at length with an experienced training professional at one of the world's leading beverage-manufacturing-and-marketing companies. She said to me, "What you are saying is no doubt true, but isn't there something terribly important that is lost in all of this? Where is the patient, methodical, penetrating learning? When do people have time to get really deep in their understanding?" My too-glib response was this: "There were plenty of very smart people in the early twentieth century who were absolutely convinced that if you didn't read and write Latin and Greek you couldn't possibly be well educated. But as we all know, Latin and Greek didn't come in too handy for most people throughout the twentieth century."

But I was wrong. She was right. Something very valuable is lost in today's information environment—the kind of patient, methodical, penetrating learning that is necessary for people to get really deep in their understanding. And that loss is sad indeed. The fact is that patient, methodical, penetrating learning is a luxury in today's world. It is the luxury of academics, and that luxury is fast disappearing, especially when it comes to business learning. Robert Hamada, dean of the University of Chicago School of Business, predicts that corporate training and distance learning will eventually "wipe out" many, if not most, of the graduate business programs in existence today.[4] He is undoubtedly right.

Currently there are more than sixteen hundred corporate universities in the United States at companies ranging from Intel to McDonald's (including more than 40 percent of the Fortune 500 companies) and the number of students enrolled in them is rising by 30 percent a year.[5] I've visited dozens of them and I can report that they range from the paltry to the truly magnificent. Companies in the United States collectively spend more than $56 billion dollars a year on training (a number that just keeps rising).[6] General Electric alone— with its stunning college campus–like facility in Crotonville, New York—spends $500 million a year on training and education, ten times more than the total annual tuition paid by Harvard's MBA student body in a typical year.[7]

Meanwhile, more and more hybrid educational institutions are being launched to partner with business in the lifelong education of employees. The University of Phoenix, a private university that is the flagship institution of the Apollo Group, Inc., a $500 million publicly traded company in the professional training business, educates more than 114,000 degree and nondegree students a year at fifty-one campuses and eighty learning centers all over North America. When the University of Phoenix first pioneered the business of partnering with companies to provide customized and accredited degree programs that coordinate with work schedules and work responsibilities, the credibility of its approach was questioned. The University of Phoenix is now the largest private accredited institution for business and management in the world. Faculty members at the University of Phoenix are mostly working business people who are experts in their field, and courses combine classroom training with distance learning and self-directed study. Students may take one course in each five-to-eight-week academic period, and programs run through the calendar year. This approach is convenient for students and promotes maximum learning immersion.

Corporate training is dissolving the boundaries between education and the workplace. It must. And you cannot afford to wallow in feelings of despair over the loss of depth and wisdom in today's information environment. Nor can you afford to be stubborn and insist that the only way to train people is for the long haul, mimicking the obsolete pedagogy of yesteryear. Yes, many valuable traditions will be lost in the new economy. But there is much to be gained. Learning one mission at a time as needed cultivates a different kind of deep knowledge—diversity of exposure, multiple skill sets across disciplines, and perhaps most important, the ability to learn new things very quickly.

Whether you create your own internal university, partner with outside institutions, or take a third path, you must realign your approach to training so it fits with the new, fluid realities of work. The pragmatic answer is training in short-term stages that correspond directly with adjustments in day-to-day responsibilities. What does that look like? You should keep in mind that there is no one-size-fits-all approach to corporate training. Harvard Business School professor Morten Hansen has studied the whole range of approaches to corporate training—from what he calls "codification" of stored knowledge in databases to the other end of the spectrum, completely personalized learning on a case-by-case basis. Professor Hansen argues persuasively that, in order to be effective, an organization's knowledge-management and learning system must be aligned with the tasks and responsibilities actually being carried out by its workers.[8] So you'll need to design a system that fits your particular business requirements, mixing and matching elements of the emerging best practices in training.

THE BOOT CAMP APPROACH

My company has been honored to work on occasion with the United States Marine Corps, and, as you may know, they have a little training program called "boot camp." In just eleven weeks, they take an ordinary person and transform that person into a marine, a person with a unique set of values and a unique set of skills, a person ready to walk into the line of fire, literally, and win battles. Through the boot camp process, the corps builds forty thousand marines every year.

Of course, the marines' training program includes rigorous physical and mental training, as well as training in firearms and so on. But far more important than the curriculum is the philosophy. My friend Sgt. Maj. Whaley, whom I introduced in Chapter 5, has been a boot camp drill instructor himself, an instructor at Drill Instructor School, and at this writing, he is director of the Staff Noncommissioned Officer Academy based in Quantico, Virginia.

Sgt. Maj. Whaley described for me the Marine Corps's training philosophy: "We have ordinary people. But we get extraordinary performance out of those people. What matters in the Marine Corps is what we do with the talent we have. You have to identify quickly what a person is capable of, choose the right role for that person, teach that person exactly what he needs to know to play that role, and then require that he gives his all."

> "We have ordinary people. But we get extraordinary performance out of those people."

That's the boot camp approach: Identify what a person is capable of, choose the right role for that person, teach him exactly what he needs to know to play that role, and then require that he gives his all.

What makes the marine boot camp different from the industrial bakery school described earlier in this chapter? Yes, the marines have invested a lot, but they produce forty thousand Marines every year, as opposed to forty bakers. True, the marine boot camp takes eleven weeks, but the transformation of an ordinary person into a marine is wholesale—far beyond the acquisition of a skill set. It is also worth noting that, while industrial baking skill can be marketed easily to any supermarket in the world, what marines learn in boot camp is not immediately transferable to other employers. The most important difference is this: There are many ways to hire industrial bakers, but the only way to hire a marine is to build one. The essence of the boot camp approach to training is maximum impact in the least amount of time possible.

That's why more and more companies are taking the boot camp approach in order to get people up to speed very quickly so they can start adding value right away. Like the marines, every organization needs its own formula for teaching trainees the specific skills necessary to do the job they've been hired to do. One example is Texas Instruments, the $9.5 billion global semiconductor company that employs thirty-eight thousand people in more than twenty-five countries. Texas Instruments runs a two-day technical boot camp for teaching high-level technicians to work in the wafer-fabrication facility where the company prepares the fragile and all-important wafers that go into microchips.

As much skill as a technician may bring to the table, the boot camp is necessary to teach her how to use those skills in the very sensitive wafer-fabrication environment—the slightest irregularity or contamination will ruin a wafer. (By the way, if you want to see a bunch of grown men, Texans no less, dressed in baby blue operating room–style jumpsuits and booties, go check out the wafer-fab plant in Dallas.) By keeping the technical boot camp fast and furious, the company also ensures that if and when their staffing needs shift, the technicians can be redeployed quickly and efficiently. Because the approach is so effective, Texas Instruments has also used it to teach management skills in a hurry (three days) when a large number of people are promoted at the same time into positions of supervisory responsibility.

Another example I have seen firsthand is at Deloitte Consulting, one of the world's leading firms with offices in 34 countries and the largest segment of the $5-billion-a-year Deloitte Touche Tohmatsu, which employs ninety thousand people in more than 130 countries. There, brand-new consultants are rushed through a ten-day, twelve-hour-per-day boot camp in which they learn the basics of the consulting-engagement cycle—opportunity development, analysis, diagnosis, recommendations, implementation. Using a case-study method (like business school), the consultants are actually taught both the basic consulting skills required of any consultant regardless of the service line to which they are assigned as well as skills specific to that service line.

Katie Weiser was director of education at Deloitte Consulting from 1995 to 2000. When she took over, consultants received little more than a three-day orientation, heavy on indoctrinating people to the firm culture, and light on specific skill building. She and her team fundamentally redesigned the program. Again, more important than the particular curriculum they put in place is the philosophy: very quickly building a "job-ready consultant."

Job ready. That should be the goal of any boot camp–style, quick, up-to-speed training. Get people ready, very quickly, to do the job you hired them to do. But maybe you are thinking, "Well, that's great for Deloitte Consulting, Texas Instruments, and the United States Marines. I just don't have the resources to set up a training facility, develop a curriculum, hire a faculty, and run that kind of program." Maybe your organization hasn't made a commitment to boot camp–style training (or isn't likely to), or you work for a small organization in which resources are limited. If that is the case, it is even more urgent that *you* adopt the philosophy and approach of boot camp–style training right away. There is no time to lose.

In one software consulting firm I know with fewer than one hundred employees and limited resources, one of the design teams—on their own initiative—does it this way: When a new person joins the team, he or she has already been carefully chosen. New hires are chosen, not only for the specific technical skills they bring to the table, but also for showing a proven ability to learn quickly. As soon as a new person is hired, she is matched with an initial, relatively simple mission. She will be trained initially around one concern: Exactly what does she need to know to be job ready . . . tomorrow or next week? Then one experienced person spends as much time as necessary to teach the new person how to accomplish her first mission.

This design team's approach differs from the typical "buddy" or "peer mentor" approach so common in small organizations where just one person is hired at a time. The new person is not following around the more experienced person taking notes, expected to learn somehow by osmosis. Nor is she ever told, "You'll get the hang of it after a while." This is a low-cost, low-tech, one-on-one boot camp—maximum impact in the least amount of time possible.

One experienced person puts aside her own work for the better part of a week (more or less) and teaches the new hire step by step until the person is capable of accomplishing a small bundle of work. Because the teacher's work is delayed as a result of this approach, the design team catches flack from other people in the company from time to time. But it works so well, they remain committed to making the up-front investment in people because it allows them to move new hires into meaningful roles almost immediately. Whenever new responsibilities are added to anybody's job, somebody more experienced stops what they are doing and provides hands-on instruction—for several hours a day if necessary—until the new responsibilities are understood. Then it's back to work for everybody involved.

JUST-IN-TIME TRAINING

Online learning is the rage now throughout the corporate training world. I talk with training professionals every day and, trust me, just-in-time is what they are all talking about. Pick up one of the leading industry publications—*Training & Development* or *TRAINING*—and you'll see articles with titles like "E-Learning," "An Open-Door Discussion on Learning Portals" and "Getting Started With E-Learning."[9] Attend the industry conferences, as I do, and you will find keynotes and workshops with similar titles. The spotlight is shining on high-tech delivery. But just-in-time training need not be high tech. Training is just-in-time, in my view, if it meets one very simple test: Does it provide learners with the information they need when they need it to fill skill and knowledge gaps preventing them from achieving tangible results?

In order to meet that test, you need to put in place an easy-to-access information infrastructure. Such an infrastructure can be high tech, low tech, or somewhere in between. A very well-indexed set of files in a filing cabinet, for example, is a powerful learning resource as long as those who will be expected to use the files have a good road map to find what they need when they need it. Equally valuable is a well-organized resource library with books, periodicals, videotapes, audiotapes, and self-assessment tools to help people figure out what learning they need most. You can go one step further, even, and create libraries of finished work product.

Imagine that filing cabinet and resource library, now, on a shared computer server or on a corporate intranet and it becomes an incredibly sophisticated system. All of the work product done throughout the company (by inside talent and outsiders), including PowerPoint presentations, lines and lines of computer code, articles, drawings, client files, case studies, and on and on, can be stored and indexed, for mission-driven learning—as well as for copying and pasting into new projects.

One example is Microsoft's intranet-based library of all the source code ever produced by its programmers. One of my clients, Dow Chemical, the $19-billion-a-year science and technology company, links all of its 39,000 employees to a comprehensive knowledge base. The company provides workers across its 14 different businesses in 32 countries with critical best-practices information on safety, customer service, technical specifications for its more than 2,400 products, and even designs from the best of its 123 manufacturing plants for guidance in building new ones. Meanwhile, Intel Corporation, the $30-billion-a-year computer-chip maker with 73,000 employees, must guarantee that its chips will work in PCs of every shape and size. Because every assembly is just a little bit different, Intel has created an assembly test manufacturing information system that technicians can access on the company's intranet. Using visualization technology, the technicians actually plug in final product specifications and look at a virtual assembly on the screen, along with a step-by-step breakdown of how best to put it together.

With mission-specific learning resources available on an as-needed basis, employees can access training from their desktop at work or at home, and they can, in effect, fast-forward to the parts they want and *only* those parts. They can go over the material at their own pace, as many times as they want, without anybody else ever knowing . . . or caring. One of the hidden points of value of just-in-time learning systems is that they are dynamic assets owned by the company—they may be built up over time and cannot walk out the door, the way the brains of experienced people can.

Computer learning systems cannot walk out the door, the way experienced people can.

THE MOST-FREQUENTLY-ASKED-QUESTIONS APPROACH

Here's an approach I learned from a group of line managers in one of the large manufacturing facilities of a multibillion-dollar-a-year global agriculture-and-nutrition-products company that employs tens of thousands of people. The plant was experiencing very high turnover. I was asking these managers what they do all day, a question I ask virtually everybody I meet at one time or another. "You arrive at work, get a cup of coffee . . . and then what do you do? Then what?" And so on. As it turned out, most of these managers spent lots (maybe half) of their time every day answering the same questions over and over from people working on the production line.

"If we had a PC on the floor in the plant, with the most frequently asked questions displayed on the screen," one of the managers suggested, "people could either scroll down or type in a few keywords until they hit their particular questions. Then they could get the standard answer. Maybe there could be a link to related questions. We could even include a list of recommended resources if they want more information." Everybody thought this was a great idea. And it was.

You can create the same kind of resource. The key steps in the process are simple:

- First, you need to pull together all the interested parties (usually the managers who are answering the same questions over and over) for a brainstorming session to identify the most frequently asked questions. Or this brainstorming can be done through a series of e-mails with someone to collect and assimilate the responses.
- Second, each question must be assigned to the one or two people most knowledgeable on the particular subject, and the responses must be collected and edited.
- Third, the questions and answers must be indexed in an easy-to-use manner.
- Fourth, the managers on the front lines who are spending so much time answering questions must be very disciplined

about pointing people to this just-in-time learning resource instead. The resource is no good unless it's used.

The most-frequently-asked-questions resource dramatically reduced the impact of employee turnover on the line managers because they no longer had to spend so much of their time answering questions. In fact, this story has kind of an odd ending because the approach freed up so much of the line managers' time that nearly a third of them were downsized over the course of the following year.

From a business standpoint, however, the solution worked like a charm. And once again, one of the most valuable aspects of this approach is that the knowledge captured by the system becomes an asset of the company. Indeed, systems like the most-frequently-asked-questions resource help solve one of the most important problems with just-in-time training, namely the loss of tacit knowledge. A great deal of academic research is being dedicated to studying proprietary information systems. Researchers at Stanford University and the University of Delaware confirm one of the common findings: That such systems are usually great for conveying explicit knowledge, but often fail to support the transfer of more informal, experience-based knowledge.[10] That's why systems that capture tacit-knowledge transactions—such as common questions and answers—are so important.

THE ONE-MINUTE MENTOR APPROACH

An idealized twist on the real-life question-and-answer approach to training came to me from a very smart woman I once met, but whose name I have never since learned. I was at Cornell University doing a management seminar for a group of HR people from TRW, the Cleveland-based $17-billion-a-year automotive, aerospace, and information systems giant with more than seventy thousand employees. We were all talking about just-in-time learning and the fact that it can be done without interactive video streaming and so on. One woman raised her hand and proposed what she called a "one-minute mentor" approach to training, an idea beautiful in its simplicity.

First she would create a database of subjects within each area of work, and then subcategories within each subject. For automotive engineers, for example, maybe there would be a list of subjects that would include things like transmissions, electrical systems, exhaust systems, suspension systems, and so on. Then within each subject, there might be a list of subcategories that would include things like previous designs, new design process, production planning, and so on.

This database would be searchable. So you could type in, for example, "new design process for electrical systems" within "automotive engineering." What would pop up as a result of this search, according to this ingenious idea? Names of people who would know a lot about the subcategory within the subject within the particular area of work, along with current contact information for that person. People could also volunteer to add a few notes to their contact information detailing their personal experience and expertise, so it would be really easy for users of the database to identify the best experts for the particular question at hand.

Ideally, this type of system would allow somebody working hard on a project who comes across a skill or knowledge gap preventing him or her from achieving the next tangible result to get help from the most qualified person in the company available to answer the question. E-mail could make this extremely efficient, assuming the expert has a ready answer and a free moment to respond. The great thing about the e-mail twist on this solution, of course, is that the best experts can answer, in effect, at their own convenience. With any luck, the best experts can answer most quickly because they understand the question well enough to get to the real point of the matter and the answer is probably at the tip of their fingers.[11]

Of course, people informally do this sort of thing all the time, but the well-indexed database of experts would allow anybody in the company to access internal talent they probably didn't even know existed. In large, diversely skilled companies with huge employee populations, this sort of system is critical for really getting the most leverage out of the organization's collective knowledge. Everybody can potentially have, on the other end of an e-mail, a one-minute mentor. The key, however, is to capture and store all those wonderful knowledge transactions.

KNOWLEDGE-SHARING NETWORKS

Capturing, storing, and making available explicit and tacit exchanges of knowledge are the essence of a powerful resource that is used now by a growing number of large companies—this resource is known as a knowledge-sharing network (or "k-net"). Most of the major consulting firms—Deloitte, Ernst & Young, Arthur Andersen, PriceWaterhouseCoopers, KPMG, and so on— have been successfully using some form of k-net since the mid-nineties or earlier.

Here's how it works: When a person runs across a skill or knowledge gap, he sends an e-mail to everybody in the organization or to a selected group, narrowed by criteria such as what kind of work the recipients do, maybe clients they've worked with, or geography. If your question is a legal one, for example, you might ask the legal department. If your question regards a particular company (or a company within a particular industry), you might ask people who have worked with that company before or with similar companies in the same industry. If you are doing a job in Japan for the first time, you might talk to people who have worked there. And so on.

So you send a message to everybody or some selected group of recipients and you ask the question: "Here is my situation. This is my question. Does anybody know what to do?" Then in real time multiple people respond. The really good systems make all this dialogue transparent, displaying the dialogue in bulletin board format, so it is a chance for knowledgeable people to show off . . . and they do. But more important, it is a chance for people throughout the organization to learn from the work done by their colleagues. Sometimes people are working on similar projects but one of them doesn't even know he has a knowledge gap. I've heard the same thing from dozens of people: While viewing questions and answers posted on a k-net, they found themselves realizing, "Hmmm. . . . I never thought of this. I better go back and fix that [whatever 'that' may be]." K-nets also provide opportunities for people at all levels to see what kinds of work others are doing, what the common gaps are in people's knowledge, and which gaps could be filled in the knowledge archive.

The "knowledge archive"? Yes.

You see, the brilliance of the knowledge-sharing network approach, what makes it so sophisticated, is that it combines the benefits

What are the common gaps in employee knowledge?

of real-life questions being posed to real experts in real time, with the benefits of a searchable knowledge repository. A dedicated knowledge manager keeps track of all the questions being asked and answered, sorts and assimilates information by subject matter emphasizing the best entries, adds them to a knowledge archive, and indexes them. Once again, a dynamic asset is always under construction that captures knowledge on an ongoing basis. In practice, then, a user with a skill or knowledge gap always stops first at the knowledge archive. If the question has been asked and answered in the past, the gap is filled from the archive and traffic on the system is reduced. But if the question has not already been asked and answered, the user goes out to the network with the new question. There he gets an answer for himself and new material for the archive.

THE J.C. PENNEY LEARNING SYSTEM

The first time I was invited to speak at the Plano, Texas, headquarters of the J.C. Penney Company, Deborah Masten—director of training at the time—gave me a tour of the company's training facility. It consisted of two television studios, a distance-learning viewing room, and some offices occupied by a team of instructors/developers.

A large majority of J.C. Penney's training is delivered to more than eleven hundred geographically dispersed stores via distance-learning broadcasts. It's an all-training, all-the-time internal television network: Maybe Thursday morning at 10:00 A.M. there is a program on a new line of perfumes that will be sold in the store, for those people who will be selling the perfumes. Thursday afternoon at 3:00 P.M., perhaps there will be a program on supervisory skills for managers. Thursday at 5:00 P.M., maybe a rerun about store safety. And so on.

These are live interactive broadcasts that allow J.C. Penney to provide material to store associates at the time it's most needed. Store participants can log into the teleclass via keypads to ask questions or share success stories with others who perform the same job across the country. Training professionals can respond immediately to the needs of those in the field. In one instance, during a broadcast on a new catalog process, over three hundred of the one thousand store associates who were logged on pressed the call button on their keypads to ask questions. To meet the instant training demand, the teleclass instructor asked participants to e-mail their questions to him and then rescheduled the class for the next day.

J.C. Penney does not rely on distance learning alone, and is committed to providing training that Ms. Masten calls "just in time, just enough, and just down the hall." In addition to distance-learning teleclasses for example, management trainees will find their weekly training objectives, the support materials, and weekly activities on their FirstClass desktop. FirstClass, J.C. Penney's proprietary knowledge-management system, is a collaborative conferencing software that supports online open forums for people doing similar work, as well as access to a knowledge archive and a case-studies library. Trainees can also access online self-assessments and, based on the results, seek appropriate learning resources through the FirstClass system, the company's intranet, or in their next teleclass. Training histories are maintained for every employee.

This whole system is the brainchild of Ms. Masten, who has become well recognized as a leader in the field and is now in charge of all communications, internal and external, for the company. J.C. Penney has what I would call the Cadillac of training systems, and, as you can imagine, it required a huge up-front investment. However, it pays off in the company's culture of constant learning. Training initiatives large and small can be rolled out instantly throughout the entire store system. Everybody in the organization is on the fast track when it comes to learning and development. And since adopting this innovative approach, J.C. Penney has trained many more people with less overall expense and in much less time than ever before.

Perhaps the most important point, once again: With this system, J.C. Penney has created an asset that captures knowledge so it can be used and reused on an ongoing basis to train and retrain employees regardless of how long they are in the company.

Remember: The human factor can never be fully supplanted by technology, no matter how good your organization becomes at capturing knowledge. You still need people to put their knowledge into the system. Too often, in fact, people refuse to share what they know because they fear losing their primary source of value to their employer. Think about the line managers who came up with the most-frequently-asked-questions resource—they're probably not going to be suggesting that approach when I meet them at a seminar with their next employer. But getting people to share what they know is absolutely critical. That's why it is so important to reward people with real premiums—financial and otherwise—for transferring knowledge.

I've seen this work at Sandia National Laboratory, one of the nuclear weapons labs I've worked with (referred to earlier in the book). Sandia's human resources director Don Blanton explains, "A very real concern for us is the loss of critical skills and knowledge due to retirement. Our workforce is aging with an average age of forty-six and sixteen years of service." Unlike most employers, when knowledge and skill walks out the door at Sandia, it is not just a business problem but rather a problem of national security. So they've embarked on an extensive program to reward senior scientists for documenting what they know in thorough, methodical interviews, in order to capture what could otherwise be lost forever. Of course, the content of these interviews is top secret, but the strategy is laudable and is not a secret. It is a best practice and very simple.

Until recently most organizational information was trapped in the brains of knowledgeable people, people who could walk out the door at any moment. Don't let it. Create a corporate culture of efficient training, promote knowledge sharing, and provide supporting technologies to capture that knowledge transfer.

BE A CHANGE LEADER

Maybe you can't redesign the company's orientation-and-training program for new employees (or maybe you can). And maybe you can't decide to install a television network throughout the organization (J.C. Penney style), or to put in place a one-minute-mentor system, or a knowledge-sharing network. Some of these training initiatives, of course, would require a huge investment. At the very least, they might require a substantial investment and a company-wide commitment.

Here's what you can do: Change your philosophy about work-related learning, for yourself and for anyone you manage. By all means be sad about the loss of patient, methodical, penetrating learning that leads to deep understanding. But then get on with the show.

No matter what the work at hand may be (never forget, it's all about the work), carve it up so there is a small meaningful bundle of tasks and responsibilities that can be attacked by whoever is available almost instantly. Remember, everybody is a knowledge worker. Train every person up to speed very quickly so he or she can get to work. Yes, you'll have to monitor people closely, because they'll be doing work with less experience and wisdom than people did in the past: So hold people accountable for goals and deadlines, and coach them to success every day.

With whatever resources you can get your hands on, create a just-in-time learning infrastructure to support your own ongoing, as-needed learning as well as the learning needs of anyone you manage. Remember, low tech or high tech or somewhere in the middle, if it anticipates skill and knowledge gaps and makes the right information available to fill those gaps as needed, it's just-in-time learning. Not only that, but capture the knowledge as it's being shared, and you will create a fixed asset that contains all the knowledge that passes through the organization.

Chapter 7

CREATE AS MANY CAREER PATHS AS YOU HAVE PEOPLE

One question that leaders and managers are still asking is this: "How can we move people up the ladder if they aren't willing to pay their dues and follow the career path we have set out for them?" The question you should be asking is: "How do we design career paths that lead to the work situations people want and which maximize the long-term value they can add?"

I was delivering a career-success seminar for about one hundred summer interns (undergrads and MBA students) who were working in offices in the Mid-Atlantic region of Arthur Andersen, the giant accounting and consulting firm. After a while, I asked if people had questions, and one young man raised his hand and said, "What I want is to do work that is really interesting and meaningful and I don't mind working hard, but I want to do it on my own time, you know? I want to work, when I'm feeling inspired. . . . And I also need to work with really smart people that I like a lot . . . in a great company in a location that's a fun place to live. . . . Where I'm learning every day. . . . And I also want to make a lot of money, I mean a lot of money . . . really fast. How do I make that happen for myself?"

He was dead serious. For a moment, I couldn't help myself and I started laughing. Nobody else in the room did. They were all nodding their heads. That's what everybody wants.

❏ ❏ ❏

Of course, that's what people have always wanted. Who wouldn't? But now people expect it.

Please bear in mind, this was not a group that I had selected. Arthur Andersen selected them. And Arthur Andersen wasn't looking for a bunch of mediocre twenty-somethings who were going to attend success seminars by day, go to cocktail parties by night, slack off the rest of the time, then go work somewhere else. No, no. These are the best and the brightest. It's not easy to get this internship—people compete for it. The powers that be at Arthur Andersen selected the people they thought had the most promise as young stars—people who had garnered good credentials and could demonstrate a proven ability to work hard and achieve valuable results. This is the new crop of corporate stars. Count on it.

These people should be at the beginning of the long, hard climb. They should be planning to work like dogs around the clock. Do the grunt work. Be miserable. Travel. Do what they're told. Sacrifice everything in their personal lives for as long as it takes to reap the rewards of the internal hierarchy of the organization. They should be worried that they might not make it. Thinking about how to prove themselves so they're not among the mediocre ones who drop off along the way. They should believe: Only the best will stick with it long enough, ten years maybe, to become partners, to move into the power positions with the great rewards (when, little do they know, they'll work even harder). Climbing the ladder was the career goal of every ambitious person starting out and it was worth waiting for. Not anymore.

This reality is the centerpiece of the paradigm shift that is free agency: The very best people are the least likely to follow the old-fashioned career path in the new economy because they simply don't have to. Their options in the free talent market are endless. And they know it.

Well, that's what I was thinking as I looked over this room of incredibly talented and ambitious young people who, just about every one of them, were going to be immensely successful in their careers. No doubt about it. They were all nodding their heads along with this young man's question, nodding right through the uncomfortable silence when my laughter stopped and I was deciding how to respond. Are these young people going to grow up and get realistic?

Nonsense. They were being realistic, far more realistic than those who had hired them expecting they would play an obsolete career game when they obviously have no need or desire to do so. On the contrary, these people, and their peers everywhere throughout the world, were destined to reinvent success. They were not going after it the old-fashioned way because to them, paying your dues, climbing the ladder, and wrapping your whole life around a one-size-fits-all career path was not only failure, but anathema. There was no way they were going to do that, and they had the market muscle in their talent to resist it and chart their own course. And what I thought to myself was how often the king turns out to be the fool.

I realized that this attitude was not so much a career issue for all the young people in the room as a serious business problem for companies like Arthur Andersen and every other company that will try to squeeze them into the old career path. So here's what I said to this young man and his peers: "That is an ambitious career goal. And you are going to achieve it. And so will everybody in this room. And here's how: You are going to be so valuable that you can customize your career path to your exact specifications. You are going to be able to do that as long as you have marketable skills and the ability to get a lot of very valuable work done very well and very fast. You will be able to work wherever you want, whenever you want, doing whatever you want, with whomever you want, and you are going to make a lot of money, very fast. You are going to do that because you won't have it any other way."

> **You will be able to work wherever you want, whenever you want, doing whatever you want, with whomever you want, and you are going to make a lot of money, very fast.**

NOBODY QUITS A DREAM JOB

If you learn to negotiate seemingly outrageous terms with the likes of these Arthur Andersen rising stars, you will have a huge strategic advantage in battles for talent. But maybe you are worried that if you start accommodating one request after another from individuals seeking to customize their work arrangements, you will find yourself on a slippery slope. "Pretty soon, everybody will be asking for it. Then what are we supposed to do?"

Say yes. That's exactly the point. Jump on that slippery slope and slide down, one person at a time, as fast as you can. If you are going to win the talent wars, you will need to create as many career paths as you have people.

When a valuable person goes to the trouble to customize his work situation, negotiating special arrangements with the organization, his manager, and his coworkers, his stake in the position grows tremendously. His investment in the organization, his commitment, his willingness to deliver results grows.

Why? "This is my dream job," he will say. That's a job worth keeping.

Money is, by its nature, interchangeable. Custom work conditions most certainly are not. If money is the primary currency you have for negotiating with talent, it is very easy for your employees to quantify the value of the job you are offering and measure it against deals being offered by other employers. Just so you know, other employers tend to pay people in money too. More is always better. Any substantial differential in financial opportunity is hard to resist because there is nothing special about your currency. Do you really want to lubricate the escape hatch from your company so much that the only currency you wish to offer is money?

Make your currency special so you can make a deal that is very difficult to match anywhere else. Based on our research, these are the five nonfinancial factors of an employment relationship that people care the most about:

(1) when they work (schedule),
(2) where they work (location),
(3) what they do (tasks and responsibilities),
(4) who they work with, and
(5) what they are (or are not) learning on the job.

If you let people customize these factors, they will design dream jobs. The dream-job factors are the most valuable currency you can possibly offer as an employer.

So often managers think that they are losing their best people over money, or to dot coms with perk-filled work environments. But people almost always leave in search of the dream-job factors. If you are willing and able to negotiate on these factors, you can help people wrap the work you need them to do around the kind of life they want to have. You can often turn the reasons why people leave into reasons why they will stay for the foreseeable future and work harder than ever before.

IN THE NEW ECONOMY, WORK–LIFE BALANCE IS MISSION CRITICAL

I had a very interesting conversation in the backseat of a Chicago taxicab one time with a woman named Elizabeth Perle. Ms. Perle wrote a book called *When Work Doesn't Work Anymore*[1] about women who opt out of the one-size-fits-all career path for work–life balance reasons. We had each just spoken at the same senior leadership meeting at Ernst & Young, yet another of the big accounting and consulting firms (this one also earns billions of dollars a year)—I spoke about Generation X and she spoke about women. Her point was an interesting one: "Twenty years ago, women were the outsiders in the workplace, challenging all the established norms. Women could see that the workplace was not organized around the realities of people's lives."

The workplace of the past depended on an equally well-organized and well-run homeplace and family. Until women entered the workplace in sufficient numbers, especially the white-collar workplace, they were largely the hidden workforce, keeping the homeplace and family organized and operating smoothly enough that employers could run the workplace without regard to these personal needs of employees.

What Ms. Perle told me provided the context of what many baby boomer women have said to me after my seminars, with regard to work–life balance. "We've been saying this for twenty years. But we had to bend to the norms of the workplace and work where and when and how and with whom we were told, like men always had. If we were going to fit in and make it in the workplace, we had to do what men had always done." While gradually, women have chipped away at many of the boundaries separating work and life, many of the same gender biases remain regarding work–life balance.

The fact is, valuable women in the workplace were the first to make employers think about family leave, telecommuting, flexible schedules, sabbaticals, day care at work, and on and on. Women brought life into the workplace. Particularly as women became less and less available to singlehandedly keep the homeplace running smoothly. As gender roles have blurred and parenting standards have evolved (especially for men), the need for women and men alike to balance their working lives with their personal lives has grown. Indeed, a recent study conducted by the Radcliffe Public Policy Center shows that having a job schedule that allows for family time has become more important to men—especially those born after 1960—than money, power, or prestige.[2]

As the demand for work–life balance accelerates, the pressure on employers continues to grow. The one-size-fits-all career path is now the single greatest obstacle to reliable staffing because the best people simply won't work for you if they can't get their personal needs met. Break free from the mold.

HIRE FOR TALENT, NOT CONFORMITY

One senior executive in a midsized advertising firm owned by the $5-billion-a-year holding company the Omnicom Group told me this story: He and his colleagues had interviewed dozens of people for a senior account-executive position. They needed somebody with fantastic people skills. Somebody who was a supercreative type and could dazzle their clients on a consistent basis. Ideally, they wanted someone with great experience both in spearheading focused product research, interpreting it, and spinning it into a great creative message. But they also wanted somebody who had great experience with print and broadcast media. And who had the strength of personality to handle accounts from the pitching-new-business stage all the way through the final execution of a high-level multimedia advertising campaign.

This is exactly how this guy described his firm's staffing need to me. I thought, that's going to be one valuable person.

Then he tells me, "We felt like we were looking for a needle in the haystack, so we interviewed more than thirty people. And we got it down to two finalists, but one was clearly the best candidate for the job. She was exactly what we were looking for. She was perfect. But she insisted that she wanted to work only three days a week in the office. Thursdays she wanted to work at home. And Fridays not at all." I said, "Yeah, . . . so? She sounds perfect. Does she know what's expected of her?" He said, "We made our expectations very clear. We tried to tell her how demanding the job was, that we didn't think it was a part-time job. And she said she didn't want a part-time job, either. She expected a full-time position, with full-time pay, all the accoutrements of a full-time position, and she expected to be on the fast track to partnership. But she wanted to work at home on Thursdays and not at all on Fridays." I said, "Hmmm, . . . she sounds perfect. So, what did you do?" He said, "Well, she insisted she would do more in four days a week than most very good people would do in five, but we just couldn't go there. So we offered the job to our second choice. Do you think we made a mistake?"

Big mistake.

I said, "You were looking for a needle in the haystack, and you found it. And you offered the job to somebody else? What were you thinking?" He said, "We just thought that she probably wouldn't ultimately be our kind of person if she wasn't prepared to work five days a week in the office."

Big mistake. What is their kind of person? Willing to work in a certain building during certain hours? Or extremely talented?

> **What is your kind of person? Willing to work in a certain building during certain hours? Or extremely talented?**

This woman could have done the job standing on her head. She was phenomenally valuable and she knew it. She could demand whatever she wanted, obviously, or she wouldn't have been so demanding. When I said that to this senior partner, he said, "Well, we kind of thought that, but we weren't sure. We really agonized over the decision. She was the right person. But we just thought her work style and her expectations were obviously so different from ours. It would be too much of a clash." In fact, I later learned, she went to work for a competing firm that allowed her to design her ideal job and there she remains an absolute star in her field. Will she leave that firm anytime soon? Not likely.

The imperative of negotiating terms and conditions with the best talent applies not only to the ranks of very high-level talent, but across the board. Free-market principles apply to everybody worth employing. That's why, in the new economy, career customization will be the norm, not the exception. Will this be true for everybody? More or less. So then how much will a nursing home orderly be able to customize his career? The answer: exactly as much as he can negotiate.

In fact, one orderly whom I have interviewed tells me this: He was the guy who could empty twice as many bedpans as the next guy. He was the guy who could do it without disturbing the patients. He cared enough not to disturb the patients. And he cared enough to show those with whom he worked some of his tricks. He had a trick for everything. His work was art because he was artful. He cleaned up after sick people and he didn't mind. He felt what he did was important. He was underpaid and he knew it. He wanted to work days, no nights; weekdays, no weekends. His boss wouldn't hear of it. He had to work his nights and weekends like anybody else. So he quit. He knew a doctor, just a little bit, from his work in the nursing home. The doctor could see that he was special and got this gentleman a job working (weekdays only) in the hospital across town. You can be sure it is the nursing home's loss.

A person's willingness to conform to arbitrary parameters is not a good criterion for selecting talent or allocating rewards. The best people are worth accommodating. I saw this fact in action when I was in rural Minnesota conducting seminars for Minnesota Technologies, a state agency that provides consulting services to more than four thousand small to midsized manufacturing and high-tech companies throughout the state. When I was there, I met some of the most high-level, sophisticated, and valuable production engineers and managers anywhere. These people could make a lot of money working for their pick of manufacturing organizations. But instead they are working in smaller, much less sophisticated facilities for much less money. Why? Because the manufacturing companies that employ them have been willing to negotiate some pretty unusual scheduling arrangements.

These high-level production engineers and managers I met all have something in common. They love farming, and each wanted to pursue the dream of having a small farm of a scale befitting an elaborate hobby. It turns out that if you have a farm—even a small one— you need several weeks off both in the spring and fall (planting and harvest times). As I talked with these people, I learned that their farming was so important to them they were willing to walk away from superhigh-level manufacturing jobs to pursue that dream. The beneficiaries are their employers—small to midsize manufacturing companies in rural Minnesota. I asked some of the senior executives at these companies how they feel about the arrangement. Each said the same thing: "It's a big pain in the neck to have these guys disappear for weeks at a time. When they go, it drives everybody nuts. And we suffer. But on the other hand, our willingness to accommodate them means that forty-plus weeks out of the year we have the talents and the energies of a person who we would never in a million years be able to afford otherwise. So it's worth the hassle."

It's worth the hassle.

Every person at every level in every organization is trying to negotiate custom work conditions to fit his life needs. The question is, Will employers have the mind-set and the organizational flexibility to negotiate as effectively as their best employees? Will you? Never be content to end a negotiation by saying your hands are tied. If your hands are tied, you lose.

OFFER SOME RELIEF FROM THE GRUELING SCHEDULE

When I first started getting to know the people at Deloitte Consulting, they were considered leaders in the work–life balance arena, certainly when it came to the high-level consulting world. You see, consultants work like crazy. Hundred-hour weeks are not unusual. And they travel. Weeks on end away from home, again, are not unusual. For years at a time. Until they become partners. And then they work even harder. But they make a fortune, do gratifying work, have considerable prestige, and retire young.

"Can you cut it?" That's the big question in front of anybody who goes to work for a major consulting firm. Traditionally, they have prided themselves on an "up or out" mentality. If you can't keep moving up, you're out. Deloitte Consulting, in particular, had adjusted this internal slogan in the early nineties so that instead of "up or out" they were fond of saying "grow or go." The problem was that a lot of their best people were turning the challenge on its head: Growing as much as they could, as fast as they could, and then . . . going. While the firm was saying "grow or go," the best talent was thinking "grow and go." My best advice to them: Forget the "us and them" challenge. Instead, create a career path that challenges people to "just grow." Grow yourself. Grow your value. Grow your career in any direction you want. As long as you are willing to add value here in our firm, we will compensate you appropriately.

In fact, Deloitte Consulting certainly led the consulting industry when it came to work–life balance, trying earlier than most to make it more palatable for people to work for the organization without expiring. The leaders there realized that people were simply not willing to make the kinds of sacrifices that people had made traditionally, because they simply didn't have to. There were other ways to look at success. And there were other options in the marketplace of success. From a business standpoint, Deloitte made such a great stepping stone (the same goes for any high-level organization with a great name) that they were in great danger of becoming a training ground (at considerable expense) for the employees of their clients, vendors, and competition.

The leadership figured that if they could become known as leaders in work–life balance, maybe people would go to the other consulting firms, soak up the training resources and client contacts at those other firms, and then come work for Deloitte, which would offer a more sustainable career path. It worked to a large extent: Deloitte adopted a "3-4-5" travel policy, meaning the standard week for consultants would be three nights away from home, four days at client sites, and the fifth day at the office working on client projects. (That's a relative vacation compared to the normal life of consultants. Of course, it wouldn't always come true, but it marked a new standard.) Deloitte also implemented a number of flexible work arrangements—less than full-time schedules for some people, short-term personal leave policies, longer-term sabbaticals, and so on.

All great progress. And as a result, Deloitte benefited from a 5 percent differential in turnover with their competitors for several years, proving that recognition as a leader in work–life balance has significant business value. Of course, like anything that works, Deloitte's strategy was soon adopted by virtually all of its competitors.

Indeed, more and more employers in every industry are now going to great lengths to give employees more control over their own schedules. At one customer service center owned and operated by Xerox, the $19-billion-a-year document company with 94,600 employees worldwide, managers turned over scheduling to the center's employees and the result was a 30 percent reduction in absenteeism. Meanwhile, leaders at Johnson & Johnson have found that workers who worked flex-time averaged 50 percent less absenteeism than others.[3]

And at Microsoft's Redmond, Washington, headquarters, every employee is encouraged to design her own schedule. (A Microsoft employee once told me, "Microsoft has a flexible scheduling policy for everybody: You can work any eighty hours a week you want.") In a fashion similar to Microsoft, Cisco Systems is well known for offering its employees flex-time, telecommuting, and even part-time work schedules. When employers give more scheduling freedom to employees—regardless of how many hours the employees must work—the result is greater productivity and increased morale, according to the research of Wharton School of Business professor Stewart Friedman and others.[4] Scheduling flexibility is the single greatest nonfinancial tool—and the number-one

> **Scheduling flexibility is the number-one dream-job factor at your disposal for winning battles in the talent wars.**

dream-job factor—at your disposal for winning battles in the talent wars. Use it.

LOCATION, LOCATION, LOCATION

I have always had a strong mental image of the power employers can wield in the lives of their employees. There was a substantial factory in my hometown owned by General Electric, the $110-billion-a-year highly diversified corporate giant that employs more than 340,000 people throughout the world. Next door to my parents' house (the house in which I grew up) was a house owned by GE (the house that Jack [Welch] built). Over the years we had one family after another living next door. Why? Families lived in that house for only two, three, or four years at a time before they were transferred by GE to some other place, wherever the company told them to move. "You're moving to Pittsfield," someone must have said one day to every GE employee whose family lived in that house for a while. Then, one day, two or three or four years later, when the family had finally settled in, the kids had made some friends, and so on, someone must have said to that employee, "Now you're moving to __." Fill in the blank.

Wow. What power over people's lives. And people would do it. Go wherever the company told them. Why? Because that's how you paid your dues and climbed the ladder in a great company like GE . . . in the workplace of the past.

Of course, many employers still try to tell people where to live. It's just that more and more people, especially the best ones, with lots of career options, say, "No thanks. My family is settled here. My kids have friends. My spouse has a good job in town too. So I can't very well move." I can't tell you how many people I've interviewed over the years who have gotten to that point in their career with a great company and then left because the only way to keep moving up the ranks was to relocate wherever the company told them to. People are simply not willing anymore to make those kinds of personal sacrifices in their lives just so they can keep working for the same employer.

What's a company to do? The company has a need in a particular place at a particular time. The company needs to be able to move talent where they need it. I have encountered this issue over and over with employers in just about every industry. Once I was having this discussion with a group of leaders at J.C. Penney. At the time, the only way to rise in the company was to let the powers that be move you around wherever they needed you. But this was causing J.C. Penney to lose some of their best people. And it was causing great dissatisfaction among many people who remained with the company.

I urged them to reconsider this policy, for the sole reason that it wasn't serving their best interests. I suggested a matching system: Post geographical opportunities and let people post their geographical preferences. As they coincide, which they so often do, match the opportunities with the preferences. "Good idea," they all said. In this simple way, the company was able to turn a negative into a positive. It turns out that not only were there lots of people who didn't want to move but there were lots of people who did. Instead of a guessing game sure to fail, the company created a matching game with lots of chances to succeed.

Of course, it made great sense. So why didn't they think of it sooner? It just didn't occur to them that anybody but the company should be in the driver's seat. Not anymore. I am fond of using one particularly poignant example to drive this point home to attendees of my seminars. During the war against Serbia, squadrons of U.S. pilots literally commuted five hundred miles every day to war from Aviano, Italy, where their families had taken up residency for the duration of the crisis. If the military can manage to be this flexible with its employees in wartime, surely you can manage it in your organization.[5]

The opportunities are increasing every day for employers to give people more control over where they live and work. With advances in communications and transportation technologies, proximity of location is steadily diminishing as a logistical concern. What is more, an increasing share of the work to be done is information related—"bytes not bits," as the saying goes—and thus more amenable to being done from remote locations.

Because individuals increasingly want and expect more control, smart business leaders are doing everything they can to accommodate flex-place demands. These are among the reasons why telecommuting is so common throughout Silicon Valley's high-tech firms. It's really not because they want to seem cool. Leaders and managers in these companies are simply not constrained by norms from the work-place of the past. Starting from scratch, looking at the business situation alone, flexible work arrangements make a lot of sense. "We don't care where you do the work or when you do the work, we just need you to get it done," one Silicon Valley business leader told me. These firms would rather have somebody writing computer code for them from home—two thousand miles away—than not writing code for them at all.

THE ALTERNATIVE CAREER PATH TREND

Beyond flexible work arrangements such as flex-time and telecommuting, more and more organizations are developing alternative career paths that allow talented people to step outside of the organization chart and still remain within the organization. This option has come to be known as "career downshifting."

The big problem with "career downshifting" is that while it does give talented people new options, these options require a person to opt out of the fast track—the path to the greatest status and rewards. This is easiest to see in professional services firms with partnership structures because they make the choice most explicit. One young lawyer I spoke with told me, "The firm is losing so many people, they are creating an option to work three days a week, but if you do that, you are pretty much saying, 'I don't want to be a partner.'" In a growing number of professional services firms, there is no need to wonder. They have created what they explicitly refer to as "nonpartner" tracks. Typically, those on the nonpartner tracks are required to develop a deep technical expertise in some area and then are asked to manage a specific area of responsibility—usually an assignment that affords the employee greater control over his schedule and location.[6]

These nonpartner track initiatives, like other work–life balance initiatives, represent real progress in the move toward career customization. But they are often precisely the exceptions designed to perpetuate the rule. The underlying message is this: "If you are a real superstar, one of us, the kind of person likely to reach the pinnacle of success here (the top of the ladder), you are going to pay your dues like the rest of us did. Yes there are flexible options . . . for the people who can't cut it the old-fashioned way." Employers with this view are still betting that, faced with the choice, most of the best people will choose the fast track and many others will stay and choose the slower track because it's the best choice available to them. But it won't be for long.

A senior partner at Ernst & Young (now Cap Gemini Ernst & Young Consulting [CGEYC]) told me that his firm now operates on the assumption that all of its employees are volunteers to the enterprise. For that reason, the firm now maintains a database of best practices and success stories regarding alternative career paths that are available to "volunteers" within the firm. Far more ambitious is an effort that I was thrilled to contribute to in telephone consultations with the human resources team—the firm's impressive role-based reconfiguration of its organization structure.[7]

In place of its traditional "up or out" structure—five ascending levels in the consulting hierarchy leading to partner—CGEYC has now put in place a far more flexible structure with fifteen different roles that consultants must apply for specifically on each new consulting engagement. The roles are defined, not by level, but rather by exactly what the person is expected to do during a particular assignment—in other words, the roles are defined by the work, not the job. This structure allows for much more fluid career paths because individuals may apply for any role on any project, moving from one role to another as projects end and new ones begin. By reviewing the detailed role profiles, individuals can see what competencies they will need to be accepted for a particular role and perform successfully in it. Thus a person can focus her professional learning at any given point on the role she aspires to play—in other words, train for the mission. CGEYC now provides role-based learning maps to enable individuals to train for each mission more effectively. The system promotes clear expectations every step of the way and helps managers more accurately evaluate performance against specific work objectives.

Even outside of the new role-based structure, CGEYC provides unique opportunities for very talented people who wish to step off the traditional path but stay on the fast track. One opportunity available to highly skilled consultants is to work in what the firm calls its

"Advanced Development Centers" (ADCs), located throughout the world and dedicated to providing clients high-level technology solutions—Web-based, client-server–based, and so on—to complex business challenges. For the most part, ADC consultants do not travel to client sites, but rather work on high-level assignments within the centers. Another high-level career alternative at the firm is what CGEYC calls "Global Operate" (GO). An innovative combination of traditional outsourcing and consulting, the firm's GO employees take long-term responsibility for one or more of a client's business processes, such as managing a complex integrated database or an e-commerce platform. Consultants working in GO environments typically look more like, and in some cases become, employees of the client organization and are located on site on a relatively permanent basis, eliminating the constant travel element of the traditional consulting role.

By abandoning its obsolete organization chart, CGEYC has opened a world of possibilities for its "volunteers" (employees) and given itself a huge strategic advantage in recruiting and retaining the best consulting talent. Every track at the firm is now a fast track, and, as a result, high-level talent can negotiate custom work arrangements without being forced to downshift. Of course, the competition will follow suit in short order. You should do the same.

Every track at the firm is now a fast track.

ONE GOOD EXAMPLE OF TOTAL CAREER CUSTOMIZATION

I was making this argument as emphatically as I know how, one afternoon in June 1998 in a small conference room at the Wilton, Connecticut, offices of Deloitte Consulting with three of the firm's top leaders (one by teleconference). They had asked me to come in and help them prepare for a long-range strategic planning meeting the senior partners were about to have. How could they stem the tide of good people flowing out of the firm?

"Abandon the up-or-out career path," I said plainly. "Let your best people work wherever they want, whenever they want, however they want. Just negotiate on an ongoing basis a market-based deal that makes sense. Buy their results on a short-term basis, on whatever terms you and they can negotiate. Don't be locked into one rigid way of employing people." When they assured me they already had alternative career paths, I urged them to think about their best people. "It is your best people who want the fast track to authority and compensation, but they are also the people with the most negotiating power. If you are offering people the old fast track or the slow track, that is no option for ambitious, success-minded people. They want to do the fast track their own way. And if you don't let them do it here, they will do it somewhere else."

One of the people in our meeting jokingly said, "To hell with them." But he seemed genuinely troubled.

Then all three of them began having a thinly coded conversation, the upshot of which was the following: This guy has got a point. The best people do have a lot of negotiating power. We can afford a certain amount of attrition, but we need to slow it down. What we really need to focus on is keeping our very best people. No doubt about it. And it's also true that our very best people have the most negotiating power. But, you know what, we are not going to give in to the demands of the best people at the lowest end of the food chain. We will not be coerced (I would say "outnegotiated in the free market"). We all had to pay our dues and climb the ladder. We'll be damned if we are going to start kissing the asses of our youngest best and brightest, the people whom we haven't yet dubbed rich and powerful by virtue of partnership.

Then, as if a lightbulb had turned on over his head, the same person who said, "To hell with them," said, "If we are going to create this kind of flexibility—work wherever, whenever, however you want—we should do that for the senior partners, not for the junior consultants."

This meeting, I believe, was the genesis of a huge and meaningful initiative on the part of Deloitte Consulting. Deloitte's "Senior Leaders Program" has received a lot of attention in the business media. It is a bid to retain some of the firm's best and brightest by allowing them to customize their careers so they can work wherever, whenever, and however they are able to add value in the firm—but only the best and brightest over the age of fifty. It is reserved, like so many other privileges and rewards, for those in the firm who have paid their dues and climbed the ladder in tribute to the rites of the established hierarchy.

Here's the thinking: The typical retirement age for consultants is around fifty (because the work is so grueling). That's when pensions vest and that's when people have usually had just about enough. With the aging of the firm's population (the number of partners reaching fifty is doubling over the next five years) and the general drain of talent afflicting the firm, Deloitte decided to retain some of their best talent the only way possible. "Restructure your job any way you want," they are saying to their top partners. "Create your dream job." And it's working. After all, who would quit a dream job?

Now instead of losing many of their best and most seasoned partners, the firm will keep them indefinitely. They will be called upon when and where they are needed, and they will do the work at hand if they feel like it, negotiating appropriate fees for their services on an ongoing basis. What a great way to stem the tide of talent flowing out of your firm. Smart move.

Many other companies have been tailoring flexible work arrangements to accommodate their best older workers. Monsanto, the massive life sciences company, and Prudential, the gigantic insurance firm, both use retirees as temporary workers to do everything from sophisticated technical jobs to answering phones. GE Global Exchange Services, a subsidiary of GE, hires retired engineers to service older systems still in use. Castle Harlan, the New York–based merchant bank and leveraged buyout firm, recruits retired top executives as board members and advisers for the companies it invests in.[8]

Because the workforce is aging[9] and so much valuable knowledge and experience is held by older workers, retirees are pioneering some of the most successful flexible work programs. Often, people at the tail end of their careers have a lot of negotiating power with potential employers because they don't need to work and they have valuable skills to offer. For their part, employers tend to have a higher degree of trust in older workers—especially older workers who have had successful careers within the organization—and feel they can count on retirees to perform well even in nontraditional arrangements.

What is more, older workers often have important institutional knowledge that must be passed on, and their employers will employ them on any terms in order to get them to transfer that knowledge. Just as women spearheaded the work–life balance movement, the aging of the population and the resulting frequency of semiretired work arrangements is showing employers just how successful custom-work arrangements can be—and how valuable they are when it comes to winning battles in the talent wars.

All of these semiretirement programs are brilliant. But the leaders of these firms are wrong if they believe that they will continue to have a steady stream of people at the tail end of their one-size-fits-all career paths to funnel into these custom-work arrangements. The stream is going to dry up as fewer and fewer of the best people follow the old path. If they are going to work in the long term, semiretirement programs must be applied across the board to people of all ages at every level. Think of it this way: If your company is currently losing one in five people annually, let's say half of those people are worth keeping. Are they as valuable as experienced people with twenty-five years service? Probably not. But they are still worth keeping. Why lose them altogether when you can keep part of them through a semiretirement program? Anybody worth employing should be allowed to semi-retire—early and often. Let people create their dream jobs—on terms you and they negotiate together—and you'll retain just about everybody. Plain and simple: Total career customization is the key to retention in the new economy.

NOT ALL WORK IS AMENABLE TO EVERY CUSTOMIZATION

Of course, not all work is amenable to every customization. Retail stores, for example, must be open certain hours on certain days. A grocery store cashier can't work from home. "Come over to my house and I'll sell you some groceries" is just not feasible. A factory worker must be at the plant in order to use the assembly equipment. And so on.

As always, you must approach every staffing issue by starting with the work that needs to be done. Examine every task and responsibility. Then ask yourself, Does this need to be done in a particular building during certain hours? Sometimes the answer is yes—both time and place are nonnegotiable elements of the work. However, often time or place or both are negotiable. And then there is room to customize—all that is left to do is negotiate the terms.

When managers set about this process, they almost always find that when examining a particular role, some tasks and responsibilities in a person's job are flexible—especially as to time and place—while others are not. The job, therefore, looks as if it cannot be customized. This is often when it is necessary to unbundle the package of tasks and responsibilities that currently make up the job, rearrange the elements, and make a new package—a more flexible role. If a person is willing to continue working for you, for example, but only from home, you may have to adjust that person's role so that it consists only of tasks that can be done from home.

To achieve the desired effect, it is rarely necessary to customize 100 percent of every dimension that may or may not matter to an employee. Almost always, a particular individual has one or two dream-job factors that really matter to him. Perhaps he has a child. It is simply undeniable that the needs of a child sometimes clash with the needs of an employer. What if the child is sick Tuesday morning and neither parent's work schedule is free? Inevitably, work must come second for at least one parent that Tuesday morning. This sort of thing happens every day. The only question is this: Has the parent negotiated enough scheduling flexibility that the parenting doesn't compromise his success at work? Many people—regardless of whether they have children—have just a single scheduling issue that gets in their way. A small adjustment can have a tremendous impact. Sometimes the customization a person wants has to do with the work she is doing: One person hates telephone work, while another loves it. The right match between a person's interests and her work can make the difference between a job that is "just a job" and one that is worthy of her very best efforts.

No doubt, some of your employees will have needs that cannot be met: George Jones loves the company, but he is dying to work in Paris. You don't have a Paris office. You are not going to be able to customize the job to his satisfaction. It's OK. You can't please everybody. But often you can. One person wants to burn incense, another wants to play music, and still another wants to rearrange the furniture in his office. Who cares? To the person who does, the value of those slight accommodations will be immeasurable.

Should people have to earn the custom features of their jobs? Of course. And they should keep earning them. Negotiate whatever terms make sense. When you make a deal, both sides are expected to deliver. And the deal is always open, changing over time along with the organization's needs and the person's availability and circumstances.

I should add this caveat: Sometimes performance problems will occur as you negotiate custom-work situations. That's because people can be wrong in their self-evaluations, just as employers can be wrong in their assumptions. An employee's insistent "I really want to work from home" can turn into a plaintive "I can't concentrate at home . . . I just don't end up getting my work done." That doesn't have to mean the whole deal is off, it just means the deal needs to be renegotiated. If the source of the performance problem is obvious (for example, since the person started working from home, his productivity has diminished substantially), then a smart manager will cut short the arrangement and renegotiate, making a deal that eliminates the problem-causing factors.

But that almost never happens. People are so thrilled, usually, to customize their work arrangements that they become very protective of the deal they've created for themselves. In a results-based relationship, where engagement and accountability are high, that self-protection almost always manifests itself in exceptional performance.[10] Often people perform much better when they have flexible work arrangements because they don't want any question to arise that might compromise their situation. That's the explanation for common findings like those of Aetna, the $26.5-billion-dollar-a-year insurance company based in Hartford, Connecticut, where productivity levels increased by as much as 50 percent among six hundred claims-processing and member-services staffers when they started working from home.[11] When people customize their jobs, they work doubly hard to prove themselves and keep that arrangement in place. And they won't be leaving to work anywhere else anytime soon.

BE A CHANGE LEADER

As long as you have people who can get the work done, very well and very fast, don't lose them. Think about what happens when somebody you really value comes into your office and says, "Thanks for everything, but I'm going to be leaving." What do you say? "Is there anything I can do to keep you?" Isn't that what you say?

Here's the problem: That conversation happens on the last day that person works for you, but it should happen on day one. "Welcome aboard, is there anything I can do to keep you?" And it should continue every single day. When you are about to lose a valued employee, instead of accepting the limitations of the dominant form of long-term employment, create a flexible solution that works for the organization and for the employee you need to keep—this type of solution is what I call a personal retention plan.

Start planning long-term relationships with valued contributors around each individual's unique life plan (not the other way around). Help people play to their strengths and interests and develop along those lines, and continue adding more and more value. Encourage them to "just grow" in their dream jobs—working for you. Forget "that's not the way we do things around here" and start doing things that way. You may have to be the one to break new ground. So what? One day at a time, as you are negotiating short-term, pay-for-performance deals for the results you need, you should be negotiating the conditions of employment as well. Customize a deal for every person—value for value—around the roles they actually play (their tasks, responsibilities, and projects) rather than positions on an organization chart.

At the very least, whenever you can possibly do it, grant people the slight adjustments they request. Even small efforts at customization go a long way. The best people will climb over each other to work for you. Disdain the old-fashioned rites of passage. You are not a feudal lord. You are a free-market manager. Play that role aggressively and you are going to start winning the talent wars.

EPILOGUE

LIFETIME EMPLOYMENT IS DEAD, LONG LIVE LIFETIME EMPLOYMENT

I was sitting in the copilot's seat of a six-seat propeller plane. The pilot was my friend Walt Gislason, who owns and operates two auto-service malls (gas, oil, wash, detailing, convenience) in rural Minnesota. I had just finished doing a seminar for one hundred or so business leaders (including Mr. Gislason), where I had been hammering away at my message, "Let go of your fear. Finish your transition to the new economy. Don't hesitate."

Mr. Gislason had offered to fly me to Minneapolis, and we were now racing down the runway, picking up speed. Through the headphones I heard him say, "When we hit eighty miles an hour, pull back on the wheel." I kind of laughed to myself. He said it again, this time pointing to the speedometer, "When we hit eighty, pull back." Again, I kind of laughed, but this time more nervously. He said, "I'm not kidding. . . . Pull back or the plane won't take off."

As the speedometer approached eighty miles an hour, I was sweating bullets and looking over at him with increasing alarm. He looked back at me with a smile and said, "Let go of your fear. Don't hesitate." I pulled back on the wheel, and sure enough, the plane began to take off. As he coached, "pull back more, pull back more," I did, and the plane gained altitude. And he just kept giving me instructions: "Pull back more. . . . OK, level off. Turn the wheel to the right." I kept waiting for him to take over, but he didn't for more than twenty minutes.

Finally, he took over. And he grabbed my hand, which was soaking wet with my own fear. Though I am not usually a thrill seeker, I was feeling exhilarated and now very relieved. "I've never flown an airplane *before," I said. Mr. Gislason replied, "You'll never be able to say that again."*

❏ ❏ ❏

I think many business leaders and managers feel, right now in the midst of the transition to the new economy, the way I did on that runway. You're used to driving a car, yes. But flying a plane? You are moving in exactly the same direction (forward), doing what you've always done (a bunch of work), toward the same destination (the marketplace). Instead of feeling grounded, however, you feel suddenly like everything is up in the air. There's a whole new dimension to manage.

As I've traveled the world, championing fluid and flexible employment relationships, I've learned that my message can be frightening. The idea of the best employees simply coming and going at will seems unmanageable. How can a company maintain any kind of mission internally or identity externally without long-term employees? Who will be the seasoned professionals in a company without long-term employees? Ultimately, what *is* a company in the new economy, if it has no long-term employees?

I have come to the conclusion that long-term employees are indeed necessary in order for a company to maintain any kind of meaningful continuity. That's why, in many ways, my mission in writing this book has been to rescue lifetime employment from what seems to most people like an all-but-certain death.

Lifetime employment is only on its deathbed for employers irrevocably attached to the old-fashioned, one-size-fits-all employment relationship—full-time, on-site, uninterrupted, exclusive, and made to fit the organization chart. But for those employers ready and willing to reinvent their companies as fluid and flexible organizations, long live lifetime employment.

All of the terms of the new lifetime employment relationship will be routinely adjusted through ongoing negotiation. The norm will be to work for several employers; on again, off again; as an employee one year, as an independent contractor the next year; forty hours one week, twenty hours another; on-site this month, telecommuting the next; and so on. Employers will still get all the work done very well and very fast, but they'll do so using a staffing mix comprised of just a few core-groupers and a majority of individuals pulled in for short-term engagements from the organization's fluid-talent pool.

In-house staffing pros will work with project leaders to identify all the work that needs to be done on every project, outsource whatever they can, and then fill the roles on the team from every source available. They will contract with individuals from the talent pool for specified results at agreed-upon fees and working conditions. The project leader will make sure the team is trained up to speed quickly for the mission and then coach everybody to success until they meet or beat their deadlines. When individuals deliver, they get cashed out. If more work needs to be done, it will be time to renegotiate. If there is no more work to be done right now, then it'll be "See ya next time."

At the front lines of many organizations, this is the way business is being done already. It's just that the systems and competencies of most organizations are still out of alignment with this new reality. Much more important, the expectations of leaders and managers are too frequently out of sync.

You are going down the runway doing eighty miles an hour. If you don't pull back, your plane is not going to take off. Let go of your fear. Finish your transition to the new economy.

MEMO TO MANAGERS

To: Managers
From: Bruce Tulgan
Re: To-do list
Date: Now

This book is full of cutting-edge strategies, the best management practices, and great stories about real managers leading change in organizations all over the world.

So what are *you* going to do about it? Which strategies and best practices are you going to implement?

Here are my top ten recommendations:

1. *Strengthen your core group.*
Identify the best people on your team and invest time, energy, and money in them. Interview every one of them. Get them onboard all over again, on an ongoing basis. But only make promises you know you can keep.

2. *Build your own reserve army.*
Maintain relationships with great independent contractors, temps, consultants, small-niche firms to which you can outsource work, part-timers, flex-timers, some-timers, and past employees. Create a database including key information and learn to employ them on an as-needed basis.

3. *Continue recruiting, in good times and bad alike.*
Keep the supply line of talent full by attracting a large applicant pool all the time. That means you need a world-class employer brand message. What do you have to offer? How are you going to make every employee smarter, faster, and better?

4. *Be very selective when it comes to hiring.*
Do not hire people unless they have the ability, skill, and will to get the work done very well and very fast every day. That means you have to

teach managers how to conduct effective job interviews. Also test applicants rigorously against defined skill and performance criteria. And let them select *you* too—give them the bad news about the job as well as the good news.

5. *Turn orientation into boot camp.*
Don't waste orientation. New employees are excited—stoke that excitement with a fast-paced, intensive learning experience. Excite new employees about the mission of the team. Make the connection between every new employee's role and the mission. Get new employees up to speed quickly with classroom instruction and hands-on simulation so they can start adding value right away.

6. *Train every person for every mission.*
Require employees to learn key skills and knowledge, just in time, before taking over a new task or responsibility. That means you need to make great learning resources available either internally or using outside training vendors.

7. *Develop the best talent only.*
If you want to draw the top performers into your longer-term core group, you'd better save the best development opportunities for them. Meet with each top performer regularly to assess her growth, commitment, and career aspirations. Help her chart her own course: Move her from one team to another. Set her up with role models and mentors. Expose her to a wide range of assignments.

8. *Coach every employee to success.*
Prepare to roll up your sleeves and spend time with every person every day—bargaining, cajoling, inspiring, motivating, and teaching. Every day, set clear goals and firm deadlines for every person. Every day, hold every person accountable. Every day, help every person work smarter, faster, and better.

9. *Reward the high performers, not the low performers.*
Have the guts to make the distinction and act on it. Give the big bonuses and the big raises to the people who work smarter, faster, better, longer, and harder. Don't give bonuses and raises to low per-

formers. Hoard discretionary resources and dole them out in exchange for agreed-upon results. Cash people out when they deliver. If they don't deliver, don't pay them.

10. *Keep the best people longer with personal retention planning.*
From day one, ask every employee, "What can I do to keep you?" And keep the conversation going as long as that person works with you. Whenever possible, grant employees the short-term accommodations they need to balance work and life. Create dream jobs for the best people—custom deals contingent on continued performance.

Appendix 1

"EMPLOYER OF CHOICE" LIFE RESOURCES

Depending on your vantage point, you are probably wondering when you will be getting manicures in your cubicle, your car washed in the office parking lot, your groceries delivered to your home by a corporate concierge, and your heart rate increased in the company gym . . . or else you are wondering when you will have to start offering such extravagances to your employees. There has been so much publicity around all the newfangled perks in the workplace that they have almost become a symbol of the new economy and the increased negotiating power of valuable talent. Pick up the newspaper and you will read not only about stock options and BMW signing bonuses, but also about corporate nap rooms, pet care, desk massages, gourmet lunches, and so on. It seems that the sky is the limit in the new economy.[1]

It is important not to confuse such life resources with nonfinancial and quasi-financial compensation. You should be very clear about which resources in your organization will be treated as compensation—those you will be leveraging for performance—and which are being offered to employees for reasons apart from compensation.

What purpose is served, apart from compensation, by providing valuable resources to your employees? First, by creating a corporate culture that supports the life needs of individuals, you cultivate positive morale and good will among your employees. Second, by making it unusually convenient to work for you, working anywhere else seems inconvenient by contrast. Third, by providing resources that contribute to the physical, psychological, emotional, and even spiritual well-being of individuals in your workplace, you will help your employees be more focused and energetic and, as a result, more effective in their work.

I put employer-provided life resources into three categories: concierge services, family support, and wellness. Because different services are more and less appropriate to different work situations, and different services are more and less feasible for different employers, and there are so many great examples of innovative approaches to providing life services, I have compiled here some of the most common and some of the most unique services being offered.

One caveat: If these programs are going to work, you need to make sure they are well publicized and that your culture not only offers life-support resources but also supports using them.

CONCIERGE SERVICES

To speak of concierge services is to evoke five-star hotels in which well-trained attendants are available to save you time by taking care of your personal business on your behalf. Concierges will make dinner reservations and travel arrangements, they'll mail a letter for you, order flowers, and get your suit dry-cleaned. Well, that's what corporate concierges are doing in organizations all over the land. They are available either in person or via telephone to take care of your employee's personal business, and in the process, save them valuable time. LesConcierges, a corporate concierge firm based in San Francisco, California, includes among its clients Microsoft, Netscape Communications, and Sun Microsystems, to name a few.[2] Another corporate concierge service is Time Unlimited, based in Vancouver, British Columbia. They report that concierges are available by phone, fax, and e-mail twenty-four hours a day. In case your imagination is not exploding with possibilities, Time Unlimited's Web site offers a wonderful list to get you thinking of just "some of the tasks and services" they will handle for your employees:

Personal Services: Personal shopping / Moving services / Decorating services / Landscaping services / Home repair / Courier service / Dry cleaning and laundry / Car wash / Automotive repairs / Party staffing

Travel Arrangements: Hotel reservations / Private home/condo rentals / Airline reservations / Ground transportation / Translation services / Golf, ski, adventure packages / Visa and passport assistance / Personal document library

Meeting Planning: Site selection / Conference registration / Conference materials / Professional speakers / Entertainment / Wine tastings / VIP arrangements / Off-site dining / On-site catering / Audiovisual services / Incentive trips / Public relations

Professional Services: Audiovisual equipment / Cellular phone rentals / Language translation / Computer training/seminars / Computer rental/purchase/repair / Corporate motivational programs / Courier services / Placement services / Complete office-relocation services / Complete small business programs / Trade-show marketing / Meeting materials / Web site design/marketing / Chauffeur services / Focus groups / Photography and videography / Printing / Temporary-staffing services / Public relations / Business associates

Entertainment Services: Concert, theater, and sports tickets / Private club arrangements / Restaurant reservations / Tee times and tennis court bookings / Musicians, bands, orchestras / Fitness trainers / Massage services / Catering services

Visitor Management: Airport meet-and-greets / Transfers / Accommodation arrangements / City tours / Dining arrangements / Visitor gifts / Area maps/information / Complete relocation services

Miscellaneous: Baby-sitters and nannies / Balloons and gift baskets / Dinner theaters / Film developing / Airport pickup/drop-off / Emergency pickup / Floral arrangements and delivery / Haircuts / Kennels and veterinary services / Locksmiths / Shoeshine and repair / Tailoring and alterations / Wedding planning / Grocery and liquor delivery

WELLNESS SERVICES

When people are healthy in mind, body, and spirit, they are happier and more productive. Add that simple fact to the growing interest among people of all ages in self-help of all kinds, physical fitness, therapy, spirituality, and so on, and you have the seeds of corporate wellness programs. Many started with a treadmill, an exercise bike, and maybe a barbell. But corporate wellness programs have given companies some of the most extensive athletic facilities anywhere, facilities in some cases that would put any commercial gym to shame. Meanwhile, employers are investing in services ranging from acupuncture and meditation to on-site health clinics where you can get your teeth cleaned, your psyche shrunk, your blood pressure checked, and even pick up new glasses. Here is a sample of real-world examples:

- Athletic facilities and fitness programs such as aerobics and stretching/toning, basketball, volleyball, in-line skating, golf, soccer, softball, and rock climbing
- Personal wellness budgets for individuals to spend at will
- Massage therapy
- Dedicated time and resources for napping, including nap rooms with mattresses or couches, washable sleeping bags, pillows, blankets, alarm clocks, eye shades, and cassette-tape headphone sets
- Full-service, on-site health clinics
- On-site health care services including tests, screenings and assessments of employees' particular health risks and nurses to discuss the results of the tests, and literature on common disorders and health needs
- Civic involvement and personal wellness through community wellness: paid leave for the time contributed to employee-chosen nonprofit organizations in the community, including hours during the regular work day

FAMILY SUPPORT

The number-one priority for most people is family, whether they have children, parents, siblings, cousins, or puppies to worry about. Family is number one. The first family care support that organizations began offering was flexible scheduling to allow parents some opportunity to balance their children's needs with the requirements of the job. Next came formal workplace-sited day care and informal arrangements in some workplaces allowing parents to bring their kids to work on occasion when there is no other child care option. Close on the heels of the children were pets coming to work. Nowadays one of the most significant family care issues for many people is elder care—care of their parents or other elder relatives.[3] Here are some of the most commonly offered services:

- Toll-free telephone consultation and referral services
- Elder care ranging from advice to facilities offering round-trip transportation, meals, nursing care, exercise, classes, and assistance with daily routines like showering and grooming
- Child care including on-site centers, child care spending accounts, backup child care, school holiday and after-school programs
- Prenatal care and lactation programs
- On-site schooling
- Pet care ranging from bringing pets to work to paying for health insurance for pets

WHAT ABOUT UNIONS?

In my work with leaders and managers, the role of labor unions often comes into question. Here are the two most common questions: (1) If many of my employees are union and subject to collective bargaining agreements, how do I implement the kinds of new-economy management practices you advocate? (2) Are unions in fact gaining power or losing power in the new economy?

To the first question, my primary response is simply: Deal with it. Every management practice for the new economy requires intense personal engagement on the part of the managers. If your employees are subject to a collective bargaining agreement (or if they are public employees whose employment relationship is circumscribed by statutes and regulations), then it's going to be a little harder. So what? I find that often managers in this situation say, "Well, the collective bargaining agreement covers this, so there is nothing I can do." Anytime you find yourself saying "There is nothing I can do," stop. What kind of mantra is that? There is always something you can do. Instead of starting with the collective bargaining agreement and telling yourself you are powerless, always look at the collective bargaining agreement last.

In any management situation, you should first and foremost ask yourself, "What is the most effective action I can take?" Then, if there is a collective bargaining agreement or some other legal constraint, check your action against an outline of the restrictions. Most collective bargaining agreements can be read in terms of what you are prohibited from doing, so you can keep a checklist handy of actions that are prohibited. If your solution isn't prohibited, go ahead and do it. On with the show.

So what about the future of unions? It should be noted that in the United States nearly one in five employees is a member of a union. In some parts of the world, the number is much less, while in other parts, most notably Europe, the number is much greater.

Recently Detroit's "big three" car makers struck the sweetest deal in two decades with the United Auto Workers union. As a result of the new contract, UAW members will see a 25 percent wage increase over the four-year contract period and will garner additional benefits and bonuses—which translates to a whopping $30,000 in pay and benefits for the average UAW worker. And workers in Ford's Visteon Automotive Systems scored lifetime job and wage guarantees, even after the parts unit becomes independent from Ford. In return, the auto makers gained more flexibility in restructuring their workforces and boosting efficiency. Included in these new contracts are provisions outlining rates at which new workers must be hired if employment falls below certain levels, unless jobs are lost due to market-driven reductions in sales volumes. In addition, GM will be able to cut its workforce by about 20 percent through worker attrition.[1]

There have been many high-profile union victories recently, including the UPS drivers' strike and the Los Angeles janitors' strike. This is a stark contrast to the labor actions of the early 1980s, most notably the air traffic controllers' strike, in which unions failed to deliver for members and their failures served as apparent bellwethers of the demise of collective bargaining power in the United States in general.

Here's my view on the rising and falling power of organized labor in the new economy: As individual employees are gaining a tremendous amount of negotiating power in the employer–employee relationship, the potential for collective bargaining power grows too. In a talent shortage, with very low unemployment, labor unions will have more leverage on behalf of their members when it comes to dealing with employers. So labor is gaining power with employers.

The problem is that labor is losing power with employees, the membership base. Why? What labor unions traditionally offer individuals is the chance to work for the same employer for years on end and get treated the same as everybody else. The whole idea of collective bargaining is that everybody is going to get treated better as a result of the collective bargain because all the workers together have more negotiating power than individual workers alone. That's the problem. Increasingly, individuals—especially valuable ones—feel they can negotiate a better deal for themselves than they can get through a collective bargain.

Here's the thing: Most unions, as they are currently conceived, are fundamentally inefficient in economic terms because they are designed for the old economy. They are based on a model of long-term employment relationships in which employers had virtually all the power. Unions were a check to ameliorate the potential tyranny of employer power over employees in the old feudal employment system. With the help of a legal framework, unions prevented the kind of employer–employee coercion and violence that occurred in the early days of labor organization. They also gave legal protection to the practice of employee collective bargaining, and as a result employees were able to get a better deal.

But in a free and fluid market for talent, the traditional role of unions doesn't work. They slow down the free exchange of time, energy, and creativity for money and nonfinancial rewards. They slow down the movement of talent from one employer to another. They are intent on protecting job security when job security is obsolete.

So labor unions must reinvent themselves to be relevant for the new economy. First, they should position themselves as the best anchors for individuals moving around in an otherwise fluid environment. Unions should be the best source of life resources (and smart employers will compete with unions for this honor). Unions should be the best source of health insurance, investment advice and funds, job training and retraining, and job placement.

Indeed, if you look at the very early unions, the trade unions, this is what they offered: mutual aid (in the form of pensions, insurance, and so on) and job placement. Think about the way a building-trades union operates today. Skilled builders who qualify may join the building-trades union. The fact that they qualify to join means their skill level has been ratified by a good source—this is an important credential in the new economy because it says, "This person can do the work very well and very fast." When a building contractor needs builders for a job, she calls the union and they will staff the work for her: "How many people do you need? With what skills? When do you need them? OK, here are the terms of engagement."

Three additional points:

First, those at the lowest end of the skill spectrum will be the most likely casualties in the new economy. Unions can help to mitigate the pain. I surely hope they will play this role because, as I have said many times, while markets are efficient, they do leave casualties.

Second, there are employers who are hopelessly locked in the feudal mind-set and refuse to let go of their rigid employment relationships. In these cases, collective bargaining may be the only way to get the employer to abandon its Dark Ages, apprenticeship approach to employment and move in the direction of the free market.

Third, at the highest end of the skill spectrum, where some labor organization is occurring and making headlines (for example, medical doctors unionizing in the face of huge health care organizations), my view is that this kind of collective bargaining is outside the realm of traditional union activity. These are often individuals who have had so much negotiating power on their own in the old economy that in the face of certain developments they must pull together to maintain their princely power. I think these kinds of organizations are not really unions, but more like cartels. So they are interesting to think about, but really a red herring in discussions about unions, per se.

NOTES

Prologue: Welcome to the Talent Wars

1. I always keep in mind that the great Tom Peters, whose first book, *In Search of Excellence,* was all about "excellent companies," began his second brilliant work, *Thriving on Chaos,* with the words "There are no excellent companies." I should add here an acknowledgment of my intellectual debt to Peters. For me, he was the original new-economy thinker, and he has been a powerful influence on my own thinking.

Chapter 1: The New Economy 101

1. Worker productivity for nonfarm businesses in the United States grew at an annual rate of 2 percent from 1990 to 1999; and from 1995 to 1998, the rate was even higher, 2.6 percent; during the third quarter of 1999, productivity grew by 4.9 percent at an annual rate. Source: Bureau of Labor Statistics. In a report published in March 2000, the Bureau of Labor Statistics of the U.S. Department of Labor reported fourth-quarter and 1999 annual rates of productivity change, as measured by output per hour of all persons. The business sector showed a 6.1 percent increase in fourth-quarter productivity, bringing the annual average to 3.1 percent. As of this writing, the most recent report (summer 2000) shows that average productivity increased 5 percent over the past four quarters.

2. See, for example, David Leonhardt, "Law Firms' Pay Soars to Stem Dot-Com Defections," *New York Times,* 2 February 2000, p. 1. Many of the law firms are tying substantial portions of the increased associate pay to performance targets—for example, billing 2,500 hours in a year. I applaud the effort to tie at least some of the increase in pay to concrete performance targets. The overall point remains, however: This will cause their billings to clients to increase or partners' profit draw to diminish. Either way it is a classic example of wage pressure from the workplace of the past as opposed to productivity pressure of the new economy.

3. See "The Futility of Golden Handcuffs," *Harvard Business Review,* January/February 2000.

4. The following are just a few samples of the ongoing downsizing reports: "Compaq laid off 450 employees . . . most of whom worked in the commercial PC group . . . [as] part of a restructuring announced last fall, which

included plans to eliminate 7,000 positions by the end of the second half. . . . Compaq [will] cut management, engineering and marketing staff" (Joe Wilcox, "Compaq Lays Off Workers from PC Group," CNET News.com, 20 April 2000). "[T]he H. J. Heinz Company said yesterday that over the next four or five years it would revamp its global operations [and] lay off up to 10 percent of its work force" (David Barboza, "Heinz to Shed Units and Jobs in an Overhaul," *New York Times,* 18 February 1999). "Hamilton Sundstrand is planning to restructure, a process that will mean job reductions and plant changes in Connecticut and Illinois. Hamilton Sundstrand, an aerospace company based in Windsor Locks, Conn., is planning to eliminate about 1,000 jobs" ("Aerospace Job Cuts," *New York Times,* 17 September 1999). "Conagra Inc., one of the world's largest food companies, said late today that it would lay off up to 8.4 percent of its work force, or about 7,000 employees, and close dozens of production, distribution and storage sites" (David Barboza, "Conagra Enlisting in the March Toward a Leaner Food Industry," *New York Times,* 13 May 1999). "First Union, the nation's sixth-biggest banking company, plans to cut about 5,850 jobs, or 7 percent of its work force, in a reorganization" ("First Union Plans Job Cuts in a Reorganization," *New York Times,* 20 March 1999).

5. "Employee turnover shot to its highest levels in nearly two decades last year, according to a survey conducted by BNA, Inc. Median rates of permanent separation—excluding layoffs, reductions-in-force, and departures of temporary staff—averaged 1.2 percent of responding employers' workforces per month in 1999, up from 1.1 percent in both 1998 and 1997 and just 0.9 percent in 1996, and the highest 12-month average recorded since 1981" (Bureau of National Affairs, Inc., "Economy Spurs Highest Turnover Rates in Nearly 20 Years, BNA Survey Finds," www.bna.com/press/turnover.htm, 13 March 2000).

6. I am indebted intellectually to William Bridges, whose books have taught me so much. See *Creating You & Co.: Learn to Think Like the CEO Of Your Own Career* (Addison Wesley, 1997), *JobShift®: How to Prosper in a Workplace Without Jobs* (Addison Wesley, 1994), *Managing Transitions: Making the Most of Change* (Addison Wesley, 1991), now in its eighteenth printing, and *Surviving Corporate Transition: Rational Management in a World of Mergers, Start-Ups, Takeovers, Layoffs, Divestitures, Deregulation and New Technologies* (published by, and available only from, William Bridges & Associates, 1990; originally published by Doubleday, 1988). Also see *Organizations in Transition.* This quarterly newsletter contains articles by William Bridges, his associates, and clients of his firm. According to the William Bridges and Associates Web site, it focuses on "how and why to manage organizational transition," and on "understanding the changes taking place in how work gets done, and the strategies that organizations and individuals can use to capitalize on them."

7. Downsizing had such a big impact on the social/cultural mood in America that the *New York Times* even ran a seven-part series in March 1996 called "The Downsizing of America."

8. In March 2000, the Labor Department reported that the unemployment rate had been at or below 4.5 percent for twenty-four months in a row. See also, Yochi J. Dreazen, "March Jobless Rate in U.S. Holds Steady At 4.1%, Despite Sharp Gain in New Jobs," *Wall Street Journal,* 10 April 2000. The rate of unemployment actually hit its thirty-year low in May 2000 at 3.9 percent.

9. See Michael M. Weinstein, "Cream in Labor Market's Churn," *New York Times,* 22 July 1999. See also Robert D. Hershey Jr., "When Downsizing Moves Up the Ladder," *New York Times,* 14 March 1999. Note: Thirteen percent of responding employers expected to cut their production/service ranks in the last three months of 1999, up markedly from projections for the third quarter (5 percent) and two points above the level recorded one year ago. Reports of planned office/clerical cutbacks (8 percent) climbed three points from last quarter. Source: Bureau of National Affairs, Inc., "Dimmer Hiring Prospects, Greater Threat of Job Loss This Fall, BNA Survey Finds, but Employment Outlook Still Is Fairly Strong," www.bna.com/press/out499.htm, 23 September 1999. In January 2000, there were 1,936 substantial downsizings in the United States (still called "mass layoffs" by the U.S. Department of Labor) as measured by new filings for unemployment insurance benefits during the month, according to data from the U.S. Department of Labor's Bureau of Labor Statistics. Each action involved at least fifty persons from a single establishment, and the number of workers involved totaled 223,784. Source: U.S. Bureau of Labor Statistics.

10. The "quit rate"—the number of people who quit their jobs without another job waiting for them, a benchmark measured by the U.S. Department of Labor—reached 14.4 percent in December 1999, up from its 12 percent rate at the end of 1998. The extent to which people are taking responsibility for their own careers in the new economy is also reflected in the plethora of self-reliance–oriented career books published of late: See, for example, Price Pritchett, *The Employee Handbook of New Work Habits for a Radically Changing World,"* (Pritchett Publishing Co., 1994), which has sold more than 2 million copies worldwide and preaches such advice as "Accept ambiguity and uncertainty" and "Behave like you're in business for yourself"; Tom Peters, *The Brand You 50: Or: Fifty Ways to Transform Yourself from an "Employee" into a Brand That Shouts Distinction, Commitment, and Passion!* (Knopf, 1999); William Bridges, *Creating You & Co.: Learn to Think Like the CEO of Your Own Career* (Addison-Wesley, 1997); and even my own: Bruce Tulgan, *Work This Way: How 1000 Young People Designed Their Own Careers in the New Workplace—And How You Can Too* (Hyperion Books, 1998).

11. There are a number of analysts who point to technology as a key impetus of rising productivity. Tristan Mabry writes: "While the slower pace of job creation may prove short-lived, the question [arises: How does] the economy [continue] growing robustly without adding ever more jobs, cutting unemployment even further, and running the risk of exhausting the supply of workers[?] One explanation is that businesses, partly through technology, are continuing to squeeze more productivity out of current workers" (Tristan Mabry, "Jobs Decline but Unemployment Holds," *Wall Street Journal,* 11 October 1999, p. A2). Federal Reserve governor Laurence Myer concurs. He, like a growing number of economists, believes that business investment in new equipment and technologies has increased trend productivity growth. Source: Jacob M. Schlesinger, "Fed Skeptic Bows to Some 'New Economy' Ideas," *Wall Street Journal,* 9 September 1999, p. A2. A 1999 study by Macroeconomic Advisers, a St. Louis forecasting firm that Myer founded, reports that improvements and investment in technology and computer equipment have boosted productivity. In fact, the study estimates that the U.S. economy should be able to grow 3 percent a year during the next decade without causing the nation's unemployment rate to drop further. Source: Jeannine Aversa "Economic Reports Calm Inflation Fears," *Washington Post,* 28 October 1999—syndicated from the Associated Press. Sun Microsystems Inc.'s president Edward Zander recently suggested that the United States was in the third year of a ten-to-fifteen-year high-tech cycle that is just beginning to have an impact on productivity. Source: "Productivity: It Just Keeps Going," *BusinessWeek,* 21 February 2000.

12. For an overview of reengineering, see Michael Hammer, *Beyond Reengineering: How the Process-Centered Organization Is Changing Our Work and Our Lives* (HarperBusiness, 1996); Michael Hammer and Steven A. Stanton, *The Reengineering Revolution: A Handbook* (HarperBusiness, 1995); Michael Hammer and James Champy, *Reengineering the Corporation: A Manifesto for Business Revolution* (HarperBusiness, 1994); David K. Carr and Henry J. Johansson, *Best Practices in Reengineering: What Works and What Doesn't in the Reengineering Process* (McGraw-Hill, 1995); Kelvin F. Cross, John J. Feather, and Richard L. Lynch, *Corporate Renaissance: The Art of Reengineering* (Blackwell Pub, 1994).

13. *BusinessWeek* (10 January 2000) reports on a 1999 survey (authored by Edward Yelin and Laura Trupin of the Institute of Health Policy Studies at the University of California, San Fransisco) of workers in California, where the new economy first took root, and where trends are often established that later sweep across the United States and the rest of the world. According to the survey, 39 percent of workers in California got a promotion or moved on to a better job in 1999; 50 percent had a rise in earnings; 40 percent have been in their current jobs less than three years; 12 percent hold more than one job; almost 33 percent work more than forty-five hours a week; 20 per-

cent have been downsized in "the last three years"; 33 percent have jobs that are "traditional"—meaning permanent, full-time, exclusive (only working for one employer), and paid for by the employer at the employer's site; only 22 percent have held "traditional" jobs for three years or more.

14. See Capelli's book *The New Deal at Work* (Harvard Business School Press, 1999). See also Peter Cappelli, "A Market-Driven Approach to Retaining Talent," *Harvard Business Review* 78, no. 1 (January/February 2000): 103.

15. When it comes to leading organizational change, John Kotter is the leading thinker. See John Kotter, *Leading Change* (Harvard Business School Press, 1996) for an eight-stage model, the highlights of which include forming a strong change coalition with a strong change message, achieving small visible victories early, and then (my words) kicking the door off the hinges. It's all about momentum.

Chapter 2: Talent Is the Show

1. News about the war for talent is ongoing, and the news touches the competition for people at all levels of all kinds of organizations. Here is a selection. June 30, 1999: Robert Frank reports in the *New York Times* that Arcnet, a wireless telecommunications company in Holmdel, N.J., figures to slash its recruiting and training costs by more than half with its recent offer of a "free" BMW sedan to every employee with at least one year of service. Several other companies have reported success with similar offers. Also: The Labor Department estimates that the shortage of high-tech workers will top 1 million by the end of 2005, a 285 percent increase in demand over the next five years. Source: Tom Dworetzky, "Forget 'My Son, the Doctor,'; Mom Wants a Techie," *Investor's Business Daily,* 4 October 1999. Estimates are that there were anywhere from 450 to 1,500 CEO vacancies at Internet companies in October 1999; at the same time the year before, there were only sixty-five openings. This according to Joann Lublin, "To Find CEOs, Web Firms Rev Up Search Engines," *Wall Street Journal,* 26 October 1999. The 24 January 2000 *BusinessWeek* reports in "So Hard to Get Good Help These Days" that strains on the labor supply are the greatest they have been in a generation, and according to the 24 January 2000 issue of *BusinessWeek,* some experts at the Bureau of Labor Statistics believe that the economy will add 20.3 million jobs between 1998 and 2008, mostly in the services-producing industries. Exec-U-Net, an executive career-management center, tracks what they call the "executive talent-demand index," a nationally recognized index based on the number of executive job openings posted with its firm each quarter. It reported that the index rose 35 percent in the fourth quarter of 1999, higher than earlier quarterly gains of 16 to 24 percent. As for the public sector, "[i]n 1999, The Securities and Exchange Commission lost 14 percent of their attorneys and 17 percent of their accountants. The turnover

for Treasury bank examiners was 15 percent to 20 percent." Source: Winston Wood, "Uncle Sam Wants You," *Wall Street Journal,* 11 April 2000.

2. Survey after survey of management concerns show access to talent as one of the top concerns of most managers and leaders. Several more extensive studies reveal the same. See the study by the Saratoga Institute, *Retention Management: Strategies, Practices, Trends* (American Management Association, 1997), and its successors. More than 89 percent of respondents indicated that their organizations viewed employee retention as a critical strategic business issue. See also Corporate Leadership Council, *Employee Retention: New Tools for Managing Workforce Stability and Engagement* (Corporate Executive Board, 1998), which found that disproportionate turnover was occurring in the departure of top performers and in pockets of key talent. See also Mike Johnson, *Building and Retaining Global Talent: Towards 2002* (The Economist Intelligence Unit, 1998), a superb compilation of research showing talent as the number-one strategic resource in the new economy, globally. See also Hewitt Associates's 1998 study of over 150 leading global organizations, which takes a different vantage point. According to Hewitt, 24 percent of respondents anticipated that difficulty in finding and retaining talent would be the greatest obstacle to their company's growth between now and 2002. And see McKinsey & Co.'s year-long study of seventy-seven companies and almost six thousand managers and executives. Ed Michaels, a McKinsey director who helped manage the study, put it very well when he said, "all that matters is talent."

3. The Labor Department estimates that 40 percent of job growth from 1998 to 2008 will be in occupations that require at least an associate's degree, and a third of job growth will be in occupations that require a bachelor's degree or higher. Source: Gene Koretz, "America's Jobs are Changing," *Business-Week,* 24 January 2000.

    Note also that throughout the professional world, there is a dramatic skill upshifting, not just for paraprofessionals, but for the professionals themselves. Here's why: Paraprofessionals increasingly do more and more of the work previously reserved only for the professionals themselves. For example, largely because of cost pressures from HMOs, nonphysician health care professionals are increasingly doing work that only doctors were allowed to perform in the past. What this means is that the only work left for doctors themselves is high-level diagnosis, patient interaction, and invasive and noninvasive procedures. Every health care company we work with reports this trend. But it is true for law firms (maximizing paralegals), accounting firms (maximizing non-CPAs), engineering firms (maximizing draftspeople), and so on. So the upshifting in skills is at play for both paraprofessionals and professionals alike.

4. Roberto Fernandez, "Skill-Biased Technological Change and Wage

Inequality: Evidence from a Plant Retooling," Stanford GSB Research Paper no. 1600, June 1999. See also Kevin M. Murphy, Craig W. Riddell, and Paul Romer, "Wages, Skills, and Technology in the United States and Canada," in Elhanan Helpman, ed., *General Purpose Technologies and Economic Growth* (MIT Press, 1998).

5. See *Executive Excellence,* 12 April 1999.

6. GM, Ford, and DaimlerChrysler recently announced that they will link all their tens of thousands of suppliers into a single, Internet-based network that will encompass hundreds of billions of dollars annually of suppliers' products and eliminate waste in the procurement system. This is the kind of thing people are talking about when they talk about "B2B" (business-to-business) Internet applications.

7. Six Sigma was originally a quality-assurance program, based on a statistical unit of measure that reflects a defect rate of 3.4 parts per million. This has grown into an entire strategy to improve quality, market share, profit margins, and costs reduction through benchmarking tools and statistical methodologies. Six Sigma uses data gathering and statistical analysis to pinpoint sources of error in any part of an organization or product and determines ways to reduce the error. Improvements that have immediate customer impact have top priority. Mario Perez-Wilson, head of the Statistical Methods Department at Motorola from 1987 to 1991, developed the standard methodology for characterizing manufacturing processes and achieving Six Sigma Quality. The program today is used at companies such as GE with great success. The advantages are customer satisfaction in the quality of the product and bottom-line savings. Between $500,000 and $1,000,000 bottom-line benefits can be achieved yearly on the average for dedicated Six Sigma practitioners (often called a Six Sigma Black Belt—a term originated by Motorola). (This description taken largely from www.geharris.com/aboutgeharris/sixsigma.html and www.smartersolutions.com/html/what.htm).

8. Workers in manufacturing have had to increase skills as more sophisticated technologies have diversified each worker's job. But the number of newly trained workers is falling. One reason for this could be that there is still a stigma that only children who exhibit a lack of academic ability are sent to vocational schools. The percentage of high school graduates who go on to college increased from 33.5 percent in 1983 to 44.3 percent in 1997, while the percentage of high school students who took at least three vocational classes in precision production fell from 8 percent in 1982 to 5 percent in 1998. Nowadays, however, machinists and tool-and-die makers must acquire an increasingly more complex set of skills to do their work. For example, "today's machinists need to be able to read a blueprint for a part, make decisions about what tools and steps will best shape it, and then use a comput-

er to program machines to do the task. In order to do all this, machinists must have a solid foundation in trigonometry, computer-aided design, calculus, and geometric design." Source: Sara Natham, "Machine Shops Diligently Looking for a Few Skilled Workers," *USA Today,* 22 February 2000.

9. The fastest growing jobs in the United States projected by the Bureau of Labor Statistics and Employment Policy Foundation tabulations of data from National Center for Education Statistics and National Science Foundation, as reported in the *New York Times,* 26 January 2000: computer engineers, computer support specialists, systems analysts, database administrators, and desktop publishing specialists. The number of these positions together is expected to climb from 1.5 million in 1998 to 2.8 million in 2008. Note that new technology training is affecting nontechies as well as techies. For both, the rapid obsolescence of new technologies constantly replaced with even newer ones means that even after one acquires new technology skills, one will have to be retrained again in short order. That means that one of the new most-valuable and least-visible skills for people operating in the new economy is the ability to learn new skills fast, particularly the ability to learn new technology skills very fast (at least before they become obsolete!).

10. See Richard W. Judy and Carol D'Amico, *Workforce 2020* (Hudson Institute, 1997). In this book, skilled economists, education experts, and policy researchers at the Hudson Institute offer ideas about what lies ahead, including the likely imbalance between the supply and demand of skilled talent for the foreseeable future. See also a great book by my friend Hamish McRae, *The World in 2020: Power, Culture and Prosperity: A Vision of the Future* (HarperCollins, 1994).

11. In September 1999, a report from the federal advisory commission studying national security in the twenty-first century, headed by former senators Gary Hart and Warren B. Rudman, cited recruiting shortfalls as a threat to the military. In that year, only the Marine Corps managed to meet its recruitment goal; the army took the biggest hit, falling 7,000 enlistees short of its 74,500 goal, their worst shortfall since 1979. See Steven Lee Myers, "Drop in Recruits Pushes Pentagon to New Strategy," *New York Times,* 27 September 1999, p. A1.

12. In the 17 May 1999 issue of *Newsweek,* a workplace story, "MBA: Managed by Agent," reports on a new trend that has corporate executives represented by agents, in much the same fashion as athletes and actors are: "[T]he much ballyhooed talent shortage has created tremendous demand for capable executives. . . . [A]s executives become more like free agents, agents of their own could come in handy." In *FutureWealth* (HBSP, 2000), by Stan Davis, who is the senior research fellow at the Ernst & Young Center for

Business Innovation in Cambridge, Massachusetts, and Christopher Meyer, a partner at Ernst & Young and director of the Center for Business Innovation, the authors argue persuasively that efficient markets for human talent are emerging. They go this far: As the market becomes increasingly efficient, there will be human capital markets with talent-backed securities. The example they cite is David Bowie, the rock star, who has issued fifteen-year bonds ($55 million worth) that got a Single-A rating from Moody's and which Prudential Insurance Company of America promptly bought in its entirety. The Pullman Group, a New York investment bank, led the deal. Pullman is trying to do the same thing with other celebrities as well now. Free agency began with celebrities and cascaded through the entire work-force—could this be next?

13. See www.people.hbs.edu/mhiggins for a quick sketch of Professor Higgins's research.

14. James N. Baron, Diane M. Burton, and Michael T. Hannan, "The Road Taken: Origins and Evolution of Employment Systems in Emerging Companies," in *Industrial and Corporate Change,* forthcoming. Michael T. Hannan, Diane M. Burton, and James N. Baron, "Inertia and Change in the Early Years: Employment Relations in Young, High-Technology Firms," in *Industrial and Corporate Change,* forthcoming.

15. This according to the University of Michigan's Customer Satisfaction Index (published 22 February 2000), which rated Publix the number-one company among all the companies it measures, with a score of 82 out of a possible 100. Also see *Consumer Reports,* which has rated Publix the number-one supermarket in 1999 and 2000.

Chapter 3: Staff the Work, Not the Jobs

1. The best exposition of the cliché is still the classic: See William H. Whyte, Jr., *The Organization Man* (Simon & Schuster, 1956). Also worth reading: Alfred Sloan, *My Years with General Motors* (Doubleday, 1996 [current edition]). For more analysis, see Paul Leinberger and Bruce Tucker, *The New Individualists: The Generation after the Organization Man* (HarperCollins, 1991).

2. The leading thinker on core competencies, in my opinion, is Gary Hamel, and he has been a huge influence on my own thinking. See Yves L. Doz and Gary Hamel, *Alliance Advantage: The Art of Creating Value through Partnering* (Harvard Business School Press, 1998); Gary Hamel and Aime Heene, ed., *Competence-Based Competition* (John Wiley & Sons, Inc., 1994); Gary Hamel and C. K. Prahalad, *Competing for the Future* (Harvard Business School Press, 1994); Gary Hamel, C. K. Prahalad, Howard Thomas, and Don

Oneal, eds., *Strategic Flexibility: Managing in a Turbulent Environment* (John Wiley & Sons, Inc., 1999); Gary Hamel, *Leading the Revolution* (Harvard Business School Press, 2000).

3. Michael Greaver, *Strategic Outsourcing: A Structured Approach to Outsourcing Decisions and Initiatives* (AMACOM, 1999).

4. See *BusinessWeek e.biz,* 13 December 1999.

5. Michael L. Tushman and Charles A. O'Reilly III, *Winning through Innovation: A Practical Guide to Leading Organizational Change and Renewal* (Harvard Business School Press, 1997).

6. See the *New York Times* report by Steven Lee Myers, "New Role of Guard Transforming Military" 24 January 2000. See also Steven Komarow, "National Guard Facing Mission Impossible?," *USA Today,* 13 September 1999, p. 24A.

7. There are literally thousands of Web sites dedicated to providing job-search (for applicants) and recruitment (for employers) services. By 1999, online recruiting accounted for one out of every eight new hires in the United States, and most companies are planning to expand their online efforts in this area. Source: *Wall Street Journal,* 20 March 2000, p. 1. An American Management Association survey of 134 member companies showed that 59 percent used e-cruiting in 1998, up from 13 percent in 1997. Another survey of 200 human resources people by JWT Specialized Communications demonstrated that 70 percent of respondents used e-cruiting methods in 1998, up from 21 percent in 1996—and, more important, of the 81 percent who had Web sites, 73 percent used them to post jobs. See Marlene Piturro, "The Power of E-Cruiting," *Management Review,* January 2000, 33. See also Stephen H. Wildstrom, "Wanted: Better Job Listings," *BusinessWeek,* 20 September 1999, 19. See also "Internet Recruiting Results," *HR News,* February 2000, 3.

8. The number of temp workers has tripled in the last ten years. In 1997, the temporary help industry employed 2 percent of the nation's workers but accounted for 10 percent of employment growth from 1991 to 1997. The sectors in which temp use is rising is in manufacturing, where it has tripled to 30 percent of the temp workforce, and in the service sector, which now accounts for 45 percent. See Gene Koretz, "Will the Boom Need Bucks?," *BusinessWeek,* 21 February 2000, 25. Now there are even CEO temp agencies. The dramatic rise in the use of temps will accelerate throughout the next decade. According to estimates by economists at the Bureau of Labor Statistics, the temporary help industry is expected to increase by more than 40 percent to 4.6 million workers. See Gene, Koretz, "America's Jobs Are Changing," *BusinessWeek,* 24 January 2000, 32.

9. Following his coauthorship of the blockbuster *In Search of Excellence* (with Tom Peters), Bob Waterman wrote a sleeper that was way ahead of its time. See Robert H. Waterman Jr., *Adhocracy* (W. W. Norton & Co., 1993). In this book, Waterman argues that due to the accelerating pace of change, organizations must be able to adjust and adapt quickly. He offers a wonderful set of guidelines that are still applicable for circumventing bureaucracy and creating ad hoc teams—that is, task forces and independent business units that come together quickly for the sole purpose of solving an acute problem or seizing an acute opportunity. *Adhocracy* is a gem.

10. For an overview of Professor Leavitt's work, see http://gobi.stanford.edu/facultybios/bio.asp?ID=188. For supporting research conducted by Professor Leavitt's colleagues at Stanford, see Margaret Neale, Gregory B. Northcraft, and Karen A. Jehn, "Exploring Pandora's Box: The Impact of Diversity and Conflict on Work Group Performance," *Performance Improvement Quarterly* 12, no. 1 (1999); Katherine Williams, Deborah H. Gruenfeld, Elizabeth A. Mannix, and Margaret A. Neale, "When Social and Knowledge Ties Are Incongruent: Effects on Group Information Sharing," Stanford GSB Research Paper no. 1514, August 1998; and Jeffrey Pfeffer, Robert B. Cialdini, Benjamin Hanna, and Kathleen Knopoff, "Faith in Supervision and the Self-Enhancement Bias: Two Psychological Reasons Why Managers Don't Empower Workers," Stanford GSB Research Paper no. 1432, April 1997.

11. See "Dawn of the E-Lance Company," *Harvard Business Review,* September/October 1998, 145. Also see http://mitsloan.mit.edu/research/centers.html for an overview of Malone's research.

Chapter 4: Pay for Performance, and Nothing Else

1. See "Commitment without Loyalty," *Harvard Business Review,* January/February 2000.

2. One 1999 study by Federal Reserve Board economists argues that there is "a fundamental shift" by employers toward flexible compensation, including production bonuses and other forms of variable pay. Close to 90 percent of companies surveyed by the Fed now offer some form of variable pay to nonexecutive employees. This study is reported in the 13 December 1999 issue of *BusinessWeek.*

3. Alfie Kohn's *Punished by Rewards: The Trouble with Gold Stars, Incentive Plans, A's, Praise, and Other Bribes* (Houghton Mifflin Co., 1999 [current edition]) argues against behavior-based reward systems on the basis of humanistic psychology. He offers instead the proposition that collaboration

(teamwork), content (meaningfulness), and choice (autonomy) are more effective human motivational factors.

4. Abraham Maslow (1908–1970) was an American psychologist and behavioral scientist who has been called the father of humanist psychology. He coined the term *hierarchy of needs* to account for the roots of human motivation. See his book *Motivation and Personality* (Harper & Row, reprint, 1970). Douglas McGregor (1906–1964) was an American social psychologist who specialized in human behavior within organizations. He is famous for his formulation of Theory X and Theory Y. See his books *The Human Side of Enterprise* (McGraw-Hill, reprint, 1960), *Leadership and Motivation* (MIT Press, reprint, 1966), and *The Professional Manager* (McGraw-Hill, reprint, 1967). Frederick Hertzberg is an American clinical psychologist whose work on human motivation separates the elements of a job into those serving animal or economic means ("hygiene" or "maintenance" factors) and those meeting deeper aspirations ("motivation" factors). See his books *The Motivation of Work* (John Wiley & Sons, Inc., reprint, 1959), *Work and the Nature of Man* (World Publishing, reprint, 1966), and *Managerial Choice: To Be Efficient and to Be Human* (Dow Jones-Irwin, reprint, 1976). Victor Vroom is an American psychologist whose work on the psychological analysis of behavior in organizations examines occupational choice, work satisfaction and behavior, and the role of motivation in work performance. He proposed that people asked three questions to motivate themselves: (1) Can I do what I am being asked to do? (2) Would I be rewarded for doing it? (3) Do I want the reward offered? See his books *Work and Motivation* (Jossey-Bass, 1994—originally published in 1964 by John Wiley & Sons, Inc.) and *Manage People, Not Personnel: Motivation and Performance Appraisal* (McGraw-Hill, 1990). For additional thinkers who take a humanistic approach to management, all well-worth reading, see the works of Elton W. Mayo, Chris Argyris, and Rosabeth Moss Kanter.

5. I believe he was referring here to Maslow, as well as Erik Erikson (1902–1994), the German-born American psychoanalyst whose work on social psychology and individual identity is related to behaviorism. Erikson's eight stages of psychosocial development describe the physical, emotional, and psychological stages of development and relate specific issues, or developmental work or tasks, to each stage. A person who is thwarted in mastering a task may go on to the next stage but carries with him the remnants of the unfinished task. An excellent overview of his work can be found in *The Erik Erikson Reader,* Robert Coles, ed. (W.W. Norton & Co., 2000).

6. From Stuart Crainer, *A Freethinkers's A-Z of the New World of Business* (Capstone, 2000), 23.

7. Patrick Mirza, "Continental's CEO Shares Secrets of Success," *HR News,* November 1999, 5.

8. See Jim Harris and Joan Brannick, *Finding and Keeping Great Employees* (AMACOM, 1999).

9. From Louisa Wah, "Pay Design Influences Company Performance," *Management Review,* March 2000, 8. From my ongoing discussions with compensation experts at the leading human resources consulting firms, including the Hay Group, Hewitt Associates, and William M. Mercer, among many others, I can tell you that this finding is regularly confirmed by their extensive field experience.

10. I have to explain why, while stock options are all the rage, I don't emphasize them more as a form of compensation. Real equity can be a very important form of performance-based compensation when the market value of services (skill, time, energy, goals, deadlines) is hard to determine or even speculate, or when the contracting employer has limited present resources but substantial future potential and the talent is willing to trade risk for increased upside return. What it really comes down to is that one way to give people real performance-based compensation is simply to give them a "piece of the action" in some way or another. The problem with long-term equity stakes is that usually the ultimate value of the reward will not be directly related to the individual's actual contribution. Sometimes the stock plummets, as we've seen in the first half of 2000, and then the risk side of the deal becomes more evident to everybody involved. Still, equity stakes (real risk for real return) is what some people want. If that's what the employer–employee negotiation yields, so be it. An alternative is simulated equity, a piece of the action that tracks equity stakes.

11. See "Keep It Simple, Keep It Cheap," *Forbes,* 19 June 1997.

12. Edward Lazear "Performance Pay and Productivity" (Hoover Institution and Stanford Graduate School of Business, December 1995). See also Edward Lazear, *Personnel Economics* (MIT Press, 1995) and *Personnel Economics for Managers* (John Wiley & Sons, Inc., 1997).

13. "Performance Management: Performance Pay—An Evolving System at Spectrum Center" (from *Performance Management* magazine), at http://members.xoom.com/PMhome/artjan1.htm.

14. Some of the preceding examples come from Bob Nelson, *1001 Ways to Reward Employees* (Workman Publishing, 1994).

15. Stanford professor Edward Lazear, cited earlier, makes one of the strongest

arguments I have seen that performance-based pay should be based on absolute performance (compared to a clear goal), rather than relative performance (compared to others).

16. Allow me to recommend the best sources I know on performance-based compensation: The Institute of Management and Administration (IOMA) publishes a broad range of information products for business professionals, including over forty-eight different newsletters, a list of which can be found online at IOMA's Web site: www.ioma.com/products/newsletters.shtml. IOMA's monthly "Pay for Performance Report" is an excellent general resource that provides information on how to improve productivity through the use of variable pay-and-bonus programs. Two other good sources of information are my clients the American Compensation Association and the Canadian Compensation Association. There are also many fine books on the subject. Among them, I would especially recommend Tom Wilson's book *Innovative Reward Systems for the Changing Workplace* (McGraw-Hill, 1995). Also, on nonfinancial rewards, see Bob Nelson, *1001 Ways to Reward Employees* (Workman Publishing, 1994) and Rosalind Jeffries, *101 Recognition Secrets* (Performance Enhancement Group Publishing, 1996).

Chapter 5: Turn Managers into Coaches

1. Tony Robbins has authored and coauthored numerous books, including the best-selling *Awaken the Giant Within: How to Take Immediate Control of Your Mental, Emotional, Physical & Financial Destiny!* (Fireside, 1993).

2. From Michael Jordan, *I Can't Accept Not Trying* (Harper San Francisco, 1996).

3. From *Executive Excellence,* November 1999, 17.

4. There is a short answer to the question, How many individuals can one person manage? Experts disagree, because different people can handle different numbers of direct reports. Typically, more than six is pushing it.

5. In a study of more than one hundred thousand employees in twelve different industries, the Gallup Organization, based in Princeton, New Jersey, identified factors with a "consistent, reliable relationship" to corporate productivity, profitability, and employee retention. Six of the twelve factors they identified link directly to the coaching competency of managers:
    —goals are made clear;
    —supervisors encourage the development of individual employees;
    —performance is recognized at least every seven days;
    —each individual's overall performance is evaluated regularly;
    —employees feel their supervisors care about them as people;
    —individuals feel they are learning and growing in their work.

Source: "Twelve Attitudes—Not Incentive Pay Programs—That Lead to a More 'Profitable, Productive' Workplace," Pay for Performance Report (IOMA), December 1998. See also Marcus Buckingham and Curt Coffman, *First, Break All the Rules* (Simon & Schuster, 1999). In a study by the Minneapolis consulting firm Personnel Decisions International it was found that "96 percent of employees say they'd be more likely to stay with their current employer if the company worked to provide better management." Source: "How to Use Pay to Compete During Full Employment," Pay for Performance Report (IOMA), March 1999, www.ioma.com/nls/archives.shtml?pfp_03_99. See also *What's New in Benefits & Compensation,* 13 January 2000.

Chapter 6: Train for the Mission, Not the Long Haul

1. This composite is based on our in-depth interviews with Enterprise trainees.

2. See the work of Wharton School of Business professor Peter Capelli as well as that of MIT professor Thomas Malone (both cited earlier in the book). See also "Commitment without Loyalty," *Harvard Business Review,* January/February 2000.

3. The leading thinker on continuous learning and the role of the organization is Peter Senge, author of *The Fifth Discipline: The Art and Practice of the Learning Organization* (Doubleday, 1994). See also Peter M. Senge, et al., eds., *The Fifth Discipline Fieldbook: Strategies and Tools for Building a Learning Organization* (Currency Doubleday, 1994). While Senge set the mainstream snowball in motion on the matter, the debate has evolved. See, for example, Bob Guns and Kristin Anandsen, *The Faster Learning Organization: Gain and Sustain the Competitive Edge* (Jossey-Bass, 1998). See also Bernard Saunders and Peter Kline, *Ten Steps to a Learning Organization* (Great Ocean Publishers, 1998), and Robert Louis Flood, *Rethinking the Fifth Discipline: Learning within the Unknowable* (Routledge, 1999).

4. As quoted in *USA Today,* 23 May 2000, p. B1.

5. Stuart Crainer, *A Freethinkers's A-Z of the New World of Business* (Capstone, 2000), 63, 77, 200. See the Corporate University Collaborative's *Corporate University Review,* which is a bimonthly "best practices" newsletter for corporate university and training professionals that details actions, strategies, and opportunities for corporate universities—it is available at www.traininguniversity.com/benefits.html. Also see *USA Today,* 23 May 2000, p. B2.

6. *Management Review,* January 2000, 7.

7. *USA Today,* 23 May 2000, p. B2.

8. For an overview of Professor Hansen's work see www.people.hbs.edu/mhansen.

9. From *Training & Development,* May 2000.

10. Terri Griffith, John E. Sawyer, and Margaret A. Neale, "Information Technology as a Jealous Mistress: Competition for Knowledge Between Individuals and Organizations," Stanford GSB Research Paper no. 1611, December 1999.

11. One interesting example of instant mentoring can be found in a Microsoft pilot study with their Microsoft Certified Solution Providers (see Chapter 3), which showed that along with self-paced computer-based training, online mentors were a valuable complement. Scholars.com (a Microsoft Certified Technical Education Center) is the first online learning company to offer twenty-four-hour mentoring; it features daily e-mailing, online chatting, discussion groups, help-desk scenarios, and online lab exercises.

Chapter 7: Create as Many Career Paths as You Have People

1. Elizabeth Perle McKenna, *When Work Doesn't Work Anymore: Women, Work, and Identity* (Delacorte Press, 1997).

2. For a copy of the study, go to www.radcliffe.edu/news/pr/000503ppc_harris.html. See also Mary Beth Grover, "Daddy Stress," *Forbes,* 6 September 1999; "Work and Family," *Business Week,* 15 September 1997; and Suzanne Braun Levine, *Father Courage: What Happens When Men Put Family First* (Harcourt Brace, 2000).

3. From Lawrence Ragan Communications, Inc., "Flexible Scheduling Increases Employee's Attendance—and Productivity," *Employee Recruitment & Retention* (www.ragan.com/pdf.ERR.pdf), adapted from articles in *Leading Companies Magazine.*

4. See http://knowledge.wharton.upenn.edu/articles.cfm?catid=2&articleid=45 for an overview of Professor Friedman's work in this area.

5. See Christopher P. Winner, "Commuting to War," *USA Today,* 12 May 1999, p. 1A.

6. See Karen Morrell and Michael Simonetto, "Managing Retention at Deloitte Consulting," *Journal of Management Consulting* 10, no. 3 (May 1999): 55.

7. Rhonda Fleming, an assistant director in the Center for People Process Innovation at CGEYC, provided much of these details about CGEYC's role-based system and other career alternatives.

8. See Jennifer Reingold with Diane Brady, "Brain Drain," *BusinessWeek*, 20 September 1999.

9. According to a 1999 survey by Scudder Kemper Investments, one-third of adults sixty-six and older are in the workforce. More than half of adults age fifty-three to sixty-five are also planning on continuing employment into their golden years. Almost three out of four baby boomers also plan to work after retirement. Regardless of whether these (future) retirees are motivated by financial concerns or anticipated boredom, the trend towards postretirement employment seems to be growing with each generation. Source: "Aging Work Ethic," *American Demographics*, November 1999, 23. Wells Fargo and Company has been busing Sun City retirees to their operations center in Tempe, Arizona, to help process monthly statements on an as-needed basis. Companies like McDonald's Corporation gear their recruiting campaigns to senior workers. John Challenger of the outplacement firm Challenger, Gray and Christmas, even foresees wired oldsters telecommuting to work from senior centers. Source: "Will Retirement Centers Turn into Hiring Halls?," *Wall Street Journal*, 29 February 2000, p. A1.

10. As companies become more sophisticated about work–life policies, they continue to gain bottom-line benefits. The comprehensive resource and referral program at Prudential saved the company $7 million in reduced absenteeism and turnover. Another insurance giant, CIGNA, confirmed that its lactation program reduced new moms' absences by 27 percent. Benjamin Group's on-site child care and twenty-four-week maternity leave, combined with a company culture that values women's contributions (after all, the company's founder and CEO, Sheri Benjamin, is female), keep turnover very low. Each time Benjamin fills a job at her seventy-two-person company without using a headhunter—which is 98 percent of the time—she saves $20,000. See "100 Best Companies for Working Mothers," *Working Mother*, 9 September 1999.

11. See "100 Best Companies for Working Mothers," *Working Mother*, 9 September 1999.

Appendix 1: "Employer of Choice" Life Resources

1. Hewitt Associates, a management-consulting firm in Illinois, reports that the benefits most commonly offered as of 1998 were:
   Flexible scheduling arrangements—73 percent offer flex-time
   Child care assistance—up to 85 percent
   Elder care programs—33 percent
   Family and medical leave—20 percent exceed federal mandated minimums
   Adoption benefits—26 percent
   Employee assistance programs (EAPs)—85 percent
   Source: F. John Reh, "Employee Benefits as a Management Tool," www.about.com, 1 October 1998.

2. Joe Heim, "They Do Your Chores," *Seattle Times,* www.time-unlimited.com/seattletimes.html, 2 November 1998.

3. See Joy Loverde, *Complete Eldercare Planner: Where to Start, Which Questions to Ask, and How to Find Help* (Times Books, 2000).

Appendix 2: What about Unions?

1. See Joann Muller, "The Auto Talks: Who Really Won," *BusinessWeek,* 25 October 1999, 98.

ACKNOWLEDGMENTS

As always, I must thank first and foremost the thousands and thousands of incredible people who have shared with me and my company over the years the lessons of their own experiences in the workplace. Every single interview has been a profound learning experience, and I want to thank every single person who has taken the time to talk about your work. Without your insights, there would be no RainmakerThinking.

Special thanks to the dozens of people who consented to interviews specifically for this book.

I also want to thank all of the business leaders and managers who have expressed so much confidence in my work and given me the opportunity to learn from the real management challenges they deal with and opportunities they seize on a daily basis. Thank you for all that you have taught me and for the opportunity to work with such fine people. I am honored by your faith and thrilled to be included in your efforts to make your organizations even better than they are.

And to the tens of thousands who have attended my seminars, as I have said before: Thanks for listening, for laughing, for sharing the wisdom of your experience, for pushing me with the really tough questions, for all of your kindness, and for teaching me.

To my colleagues at RainmakerThinking—especially Cynthia Conrad, Jeff Coombs, Mark Kurber, Carolyn Martin, and Heather Neely—thank you for your hard work and commitment and your valuable contributions to this enterprise every single day. Jeff Coombs is referred to at some length in Chapter 2 as my metaphor for the most valuable talent you can possibly imagine, so I'm not sure what else to say except this: I am ever grateful, my friend. Cynthia Conrad also deserves special thanks because she has been my reliable, insightful, diligent, and patient research assistant for the book. Without her efforts, the book would not be as strong.

The book is much stronger because of several other individuals. I want to thank Nikki Sabin and Carol Franco for their great advice and support while my project was still at Harvard. But the most important editorial input came from Drake McFeely and Sarah Stewart at W. W. Norton, my publisher. Sarah dazzled me with her very good and very fast work on the manuscript, recommending rewrites, inserts, chapter reorganizations, and more. Wow. Thank you. To Drake McFeely, who is the president at W. W. Norton and my current hero: I don't know what I would have done without your leap of faith in this book. Your advice on the manuscript has been dead-on and I've tried to follow it to the letter.

And then there is Susan Rabiner, my agent (and my wife's agent too). Susan has changed my life (and Debby's). When I first met Susan Rabiner, she said, "I'll represent you, but only if you want to write a really important book." That's when I knew she was perfect. Susan helped me translate all that I have been learning in the last seven years into the ideas and the basic structure for this book. Susan: There are simply not enough words to thank you for what you have done and all that you are. I am so deeply indebted to you, it's a little bit scary. Maybe someday I can repay you in a way that comes close to what you deserve.

To my family and friends, I owe my deepest thanks for being you and for allowing me to be who I am. Thanks to my parents, Henry and Norma Tulgan; my other parents (in-law), Julie and Paul Applegate; my nieces, Elisa, Erin, Frances, and Perry; my nephew, Joey; my sisters, Ronna and Tanya; and my brothers, Jim and Shan and Tom.

Finally, I reserve my most special thanks always for my wife, Debby Applegate—to whom this book is dedicated. Debby is my intellectual partner in every way, and it is hard to separate my own thoughts, and thus my work, from her because I never think or say or write or do anything without running it by her. Debby is my best friend, my smartest friend, my most loving friend, my toughest friend, my partner in all things, half of my soul, owner of my heart, and the person without whom I would be lost indeed. Thank you, my love.

INDEX

accountability, 111, 121, 123
accuracy, of feedback, 124,
    126–27
Adhocracy (Waterman), 200
advertising industry:
    coaching in, 109–10
    conformity to schedules in,
        158–61
    outsourcing in, 60
Aetna Insurance Company, 173
aging of population, 170–71
ambidextrous organizations, 66
Applegate, Paul, 82–83, 103
architecture, team-based bonuses
        in, 99–100
Argyris, Chris, 201
Army, U.S., 72–74
art:
    coaching as, 121
    everything in life as, 121
    work as, 121, 124, 160
Arthur Andersen, 153–55
Asea Brown Boveri (ABB), 100–101
athletic facilities, corporate, 184
Austria Mikro Systeme Internation-
        al AG, 98–99
authority vs. power, 21

Baptist Healthcare System, 73
Barea, Al, 73
Barnes & Noble, 60

Bartolone, Mark, 99–100
Benjamin Group, 206
best-practice migration, 70
best-teams approach, 64–67
Bethune, Gordon, 100
bidding wars, 16–18, 56, 84
Blanton, Don, 151
boot camp approach to training,
        129–30, 139–43, 179
Bridges, William, 22, 191
"buddy" training approach, 142–43

Capelli, Peter, 25–26
Cap Gemini Ernst & Young Con-
        sulting (CGEYC), 157,
        167–68
capitalism, 24, 26–27; *see also* free
        markets
"career downshifting," 166–67
career paths, 153–74
    alternatives to, 70, 166–68
    customization of, 66–67, 68–70,
        155–57, 160–61, 168–71
    dream jobs and, 153–57, 160–61,
        169
    nontraditional, 68–70, 167–68,
        169
    power over, 13, 162, 169
    responsibility for one's own,
        19–20, 23, 25, 92
    social comparisons in, 41

traditional, 16–18, 19, 28, 56,
    67–68, 136, 154, 155,
    169–70
cartels vs. labor unions, 189
Carter, Deborah, 50–52
case-study method, 141
Castle Harlan, 170
casual dress, 9–11
celebrity, and free agency, 40–41
Central Intelligence Agency (CIA),
    132
Chambers, John, 61
change leaders:
    career paths and, 174
    as coaches, 128
    in compensation system, 108
    in effective utilization of talent,
        52–53
    in management roles, 29–30
    in staffing, 81
    in talent acquisition, 52–53
    in training programs, 152
child-care programs, 185
CIGNA, 206
Cisco Systems, 61, 101, 163
climb-the-ladder model, see old-
        fashioned employment
        model
coaching, 109–28
    accountability and, 111, 121, 123
    art of, 121
    best practices of, 124–28
    customization of, 127
    downside of, 117
    effectiveness of, 115, 128
    executive, 114–18
    feedback in, 123–28
    first efforts in, 126–28
    functions of, 121, 122
    as leadership style, 121–22
    management by fear vs., 27
    methodology of, 121–22
    motivation via, 110, 117
    mutual, 47
    for ongoing improvement, 123,
        179
    performance, 83, 107–8, 110–11,
        112

personal, 114–18
    personal therapy vs., 117–18
    professional skills and, 119–21
    for self-help, 116–17
    for short-term goals, 118–19, 124
    teaching skills of, 113–14
    by trial and error, 127–28
collective bargaining, 186–89
Comcast Cable Communications,
    109–10
compensation systems:
    base pay in, 107
    behavior following rewards in,
        85, 102
    bonuses in, 97–101, 104, 107, 179
    changes needed in, 28
    commission-based, 102–3
    employee control of, 106, 107
    flexible, 198
    in free markets, 85–93, 96, 101
    management of, 96–100, 105,
        106–8
    milestones for, 83
    motivation and, 86–87, 89–93
    nonfinancial rewards in, 104–6,
        156–57, 162, 163–64, 181
    opportunity cost and, 94–96
    pay-for-performance, 85, 88, 89,
        93, 97–108, 112
    philosophical bases for, 88–90
    for piecework, 102
    profit sharing, 100
    seniority-based, 86–88
    stock options in, 101
    team-based, 99–101
    wage negotiation, 24
concierge services, 182–83
conformity, 158–61
consulting business:
    as career option, 19–20
    career paths in, 153–55, 168–70
    compensation systems in, 101
    conformity to schedules in,
        158–61
    k-nets in, 148–49
    personal coaches from, 114–18
    relief from schedule in, 161–64
    role-based reconfiguration of

consulting business (*continued*)
organization structure in,
167
sharing knowledge in, 170–71
training in, 141–42
"up or out" mentality in, 162, 169
in utilities, 82–83
work-life balance in, 157–58,
161–63
Continental Airlines, 100
Coombs, Jeff, 32
core competencies, 59
core group:
filling positions in, 78–79
fluidity and, 78–80
strengthening of, 178
use of term, 77
corporate culture:
casual dress in, 9–11
changes needed in, 28
constant learning in, 150
of dot coms, 10, 157
free agency in, 11–12
knowledge sharing in, 151
life resources in, 181–85
mission and, 176
power in, 13
transformation of, 114
corporate meetings, as special
events, 62–63
corporate universities, 138–39, 204
corporate wellness programs,
183–84
Countrywide Home Loans, Inc.,
31–32
customer service, rewards for, 101

day-care programs, 183
Dayton Hudson Corporation, 67
Dell, Michael, 45–46, 52
Dell Computer Corporation,
45–46
Deloitte Consulting:
career customization in, 168–70
training in, 141–42
work-life balance in, 161–63
Delphi Saginaw Steering Systems,
35–36

Dow Chemical Company, 144
downsizing:
accelerated pace of, 23
effects of, 18, 25, 125–26, 190–91
labor unions and, 189
and technological advances, 33,
37–39
dream jobs, 153–57, 160–61, 169–70
employee commitment and, 156,
171
employee expectations and,
153–55, 160
negotiation of, 155–57, 160, 168,
169, 170, 172
scheduling flexibility in, 163–64,
170
dress codes, 9–11

Ecolab, Inc., 42–46
e-commerce, in new economy, 46, 84
e-lance, coining of term, 77
e-mail, mentoring via, 147–48
employees:
careers of, *see* career paths
coaching for retention of, 128
compensation of, *see* compensation systems
cross-training of, 71, 139
downsizing of, *see* downsizing
entrepreneurship of, 61, 78, 130
hiring of, *see* hiring process
job security of, 14, 22–23, 24, 25,
113, 188–89
as knowledge workers, 134–36
labor unions and, 186–89
lifelong learning of, 138, 150
low-skill, fewer opportunities
for, 33
loyalty of, 131, 180
meaningful work for, 133–34
mobility of, 14–15, 18–20, 24–25,
44–45, 66–67, 79
motivation of, 86–87, 89–93
new stresses on, 14
part-timers becoming full-
timers, 48, 80
and proprietary information, 132
public, 184

quit rate of, 192
relocation of, 164–66
reserve army of, 178
retired, knowledge shared by,
    170–71
sole, 62–63
speed and accuracy required of,
    33, 36
talented and powerful, see talent
training of, see training
tuning in to frequency of, 124
turnover rates of, 18–20, 67, 104
value added by, 21–22, 24, 32–33,
    39–41, 70, 141
employer-employee relationships:
    development of, 48–49, 64
    exclusive, 55
    fluid and flexible, 49–52, 78, 161
    fundamental basis of, 89
    golden handcuffs in, 16, 56
    hiring process and, 15–17
    labor unions and, 186–89
    long-term, 16–18, 22, 32, 46, 52,
        55, 80, 175–77
    market forces and, 18, 26, 27
    mutual trust in, 80
    negotiation in, 11, 20, 176–77
    paradigm shift in, 10, 25–27
    power in, 20–22
    short-term, results-based, 85,
        111, 169, 177
    talent-network/best-teams
        approach in, 66–67
    test-drives in, 80
    transactional nature of, 83–84, 112
    turnover and, 18–20
employment, see employer-employ-
    ee relationships; work
energy flow, basic law of, 28–29
engineering, compensation systems
    in, 100–101
Enterprise Rent-A-Car, 129–30, 134
entrepreneurship:
    of all employees, 78, 130
    in hiring process, 41–46, 55
    start-ups by former employees,
        61

in technical jobs, 55
Erikson, Erik, 199
Ernst & Young, 157, 167–68
exclusive employment, use of term,
    55
executive coaches, 114–18

family, time for, 158
family support programs, 184–85
Fannie Mae, 75
FAST feedback, 124–27
fear:
    as basic obstacle, 29, 175, 177
    management by, 13, 27, 110, 112
feedback:
    accuracy of, 124, 126–27
    in coaching, 123–28
    for corrective action, 123–24, 127
    customization of, 124, 127
    FAST, 124–27
    frequency, 124, 127
    goal-setting in, 124–25
    specific, 125, 126–27
    styles of, 127
    timely, 125, 126
    trial and error in giving, 127
Fernandez, Roberto, 33
finance industry:
    coaching in, 112–14
    fluid staffing in, 46–47, 75
    job customization, 173
    outsourcing in, 61–62
    retirees as temps in, 170–71
    work environment in, 10–11
flexibility, organizational, 11, 46,
    113, 161
flexible scheduling, 162–63, 184–85
focus:
    feedback and, 123, 127
    learning how to, 124
    on today, 118–19, 124
free agency:
    and career paths, 13, 154–55
    celebrity and, 40–41
    as e-lancers, 77
    flexible management and, 27, 66,
        160–61

free agency (*continued*)
fluidity and, 48–52, 64, 66–67, 78
in free market, 10, 11–12, 24–26, 50, 154, 160
job security vs., 14, 25
motivation and, 92–93
role of manager tied to, 30
self-selection of, 77–78
transparent value in, 40–41
free markets:
capitalism and, 24, 26–27
chaos in, 22
compensation in, 85–93, 96, 101
efficiencies of, 26, 84–85
fluidity of, 18, 27, 46–52, 56, 66, 134
free agency in, 10, 11–12, 24–26, 50, 154, 160
labor unions and, 188–89
negotiation in, 50, 83–84, 155–56
online, 84
results rewarded in, 96–100
risks and costs in, 26
success defined by, 24
talent in, *see* talent
Freiman, Terri, 48–49
Friedman, Stewart, 163

Gallup Organization, 127–28
GE Capital, 61–62
gender bias, 158
General Electric Company:
corporate university of, 138
employee relocation in, 164
retirees as temps in, 170
wage negotiation in, 24
General Motors, 35, 187
Generation X, 11
Gerry (health-care executive), 89–92
Gislason, Walt, 175–76
golden handcuffs, 16–18, 56
Gorman, Frank, 118–19, 121

Hamada, Robert, 138
Hamel, Gary, 12, 198
HammerStrength, 97–98
Hansen, Morten, 139, 203

Hartford Insurance Company, 112–14
Harvard Business School, 77, 138
Hayat-Dawoodi, Kambiz, 98–99
health and wellness, 183–84
health-care industry:
compensation in, 89–92
conformity to schedules in, 160
staffing in, 73
Hertzberg, Frederick, 90, 201
Higgins, Monica C., 41
hiring process, 15–18, 54–81
ad hoc, 22, 58–59, 69, 70, 76
alternatives to, 15, 47, 64, 66–67, 70
bidding wars in, 16, 17–18, 56, 84
of core group, 77, 78–79, 178
employee poaching, 21, 70
entrepreneurship in, 41–46, 55
flexibility in, 27, 28, 39, 45–52, 56, 78, 79, 161
negotiation in, 42, 158–61
outsourcing vs., 59–62, 177
recruitment and, 74, 79, 84, 178
selection in, 43, 58, 77–78, 79, 158–61, 178
traditional, 55, 57
wage process in, 26
Home Depot, 71
horizontal integration, 60
human resources:
compensation and, *see* compensation systems
critical nature of, 121
just-in-time acquisition of, 22, 58–59, 69, 70, 71, 75–76
maximizing of, 66
opportunity cost in, 94–96
outsourcing of, 74, 177
proprietary talent database of, 75
staffing and, *see* hiring process; staffing
vs. technology, 151

Iams, pet food, 92
IBM, outsourcing by, 61

information, proprietary, 132
information overload, 136
information sources, 40–41, 84
insight vs. knowledge, 12
Institute of Management and
    Administration (IOMA),
    201
Intel Corporation, 144
Internet:
    B2B applications, 196
    information from, 41
    recruitment via, 74, 84

J.C. Penney:
    nonfinancial rewards in, 104–5
    relocation in, 165
    training program of, 149–51
job descriptions, 22
job placement, labor unions and, 188
jobs:
    control over one's schedule in,
        68, 105
    dream, 153–57, 160–61, 163–64,
        169, 170, 171, 172
    joint ventures in, 51, 55
    matching people to, 74–75
    seasonal, 56
    squeezing people to fit, 45
    streamlined, 56
    unbundling tasks in, 45–46,
        133–34, 172
    see also career paths; work
job security:
    expectation of, 113
    free agency vs., 14, 25
    labor unions and, 188–89
    in old-fashioned employment
        model, 22–23, 113
    options and, 24
    responsibility for one's own, 14
Johnson & Johnson, 9–10, 163
joint ventures, 51, 55
Jones, Gary, 97–98
Jordan, Michael, 118
J.P. Morgan, 10–11
judgment:
    as basic requirement, 33, 38–39

as "killer app," 35–37, 40
    in performance evaluation, 104
Kanter, Rosabeth Moss, 201
Ketchum, Inc., 64–67
k-nets, 148–49
knowledge:
    company-specific, 21–22
    deep learning of, 137–38, 139
    from experience over time, 133
    gaps in, 137
    insight vs., 12
    resource library of, 144
    searchable repository of, 149
    sharing of, 70, 146–49, 151,
        170–71
    transferability of, 22, 151
knowledge workers, all employees
    as, 134–36
Kohn, Alfie, 89–90
Kotcher, Ray, 64–66, 75

labor unions, 186–89
Larsen, Ralph, 9–10, 11
Lazear, Edward, 102
LesConcierges, 182
life resources, 181–85
    concierge services, 182–83
    family support programs, 184–85
    labor unions and, 188
    wellness services, 183–84
lifetime employment, 175–77
Lipton, Thomas J., Company, 105
location of work, 164–66
Lopez, Filemon, 109–10, 123–24,
    125

McGregor, Douglas, 90, 91
McKenna, Elizabeth Perle, *see*
    Perle, Elizabeth
Madigan, John, 112–14
Malone, Thomas, 76–77
management:
    authority vs. power of, 21
    benevolent, 112
    change leaders in, *see* change
        leaders
    coaching by, *see* coaching

management (*continued*)
of compensation systems, 96–100, 105, 106–8
constraints on, 28
de facto, 126
deputizing others in, 126
of discretionary resources, 21, 28, 113
eliminating levels of, 126
by fear, 13, 27, 110, 112
flexibility of, 27–28, 66, 160–61
by good example, 112
high-maintenance, 111
intense personal engagement in, 127
labor unions and, 186–89
of market value, 39
of numbers of people, 125–26, 201
organization chart and, 20–22, 84, 111, 125–26
performance driven by, 121
power lost and recovered by, 20–21, 27–29
professional skills leading to, 119–21
roles of, 20–22, 30
strategies and best practices for, 178–80
traditional, 111–14
transformation of, 114
of vendor performance, 103–4
manager shopping, 71
Managing Generation X (Tulgan), 11
manufacturing:
changing nature of, 36
compensation systems in, 97–98
just-in-time, 35–37
quality in, 36–37
robots in, 35
training in, 135–36
work assessment in, 171–72
Marine Corps, U.S., 121–22, 139–41
market differentiation, excellence and, 59
market forces, *see* free markets
Maslow, Abraham, 90, 201
Masten, Deborah, 149, 150

Mayo, Elton W., 201
men, new parenting standards for, 158
mentors, one-minute, 146–48
Mervyn's, 67–70, 71
Metamor Technologies, 101
Microsoft:
flexible schedules in, 163
resource library in, 144
Microsoft Certified Solution Providers (MCSPs), 54–55
Microsoft Certified Systems Engineers (MCSEs), 54–55
Minnesota Technologies, 160–61
money, interchangeability of, 156
Monsanto, 170
morale:
coaching and, 128
flexible scheduling and, 163
life resources for, 181–85
most-frequently-asked-questions approach to training, 145–46
motivation:
coaching for, 110, 117
and compensation, 86–87, 89–93
free agency and, 92–93
intrinsic, 90–93
in tangible rewards, *see* compensation systems
Motorola, Inc., 105, 196
mutual coaching, 47

National Guard, U.S., 72
negotiation:
constraints on, 28
day-to-day, 112
of dream jobs, 155–57, 160, 168, 169, 170, 172
in free markets, 50, 83–84, 155–56
in hiring process, 42, 158–61
labor unions and, 186–89
life resources for, 181–85
in lifetime employment, 176–77
nonnegotiable elements and, 171–73

power in, 11, 20, 39, 79, 84, 169, 170
wage, 24
and work assessment, 82–83
new economy, 13–30
access to talent in, 32–33, 64–67, 84
e-commerce in, 46, 84
employee mobility in, 14–15, 18–20, 24–25, 44–45, 66–67, 79
employee stress in, 14
entrepreneurship in, 41–46, 61, 78, 130
executive power in, 20–22, 27–29
free agency in, see free agency
high-maintenance management in, 111
hiring process in, 15–17, 54–81
labor unions in, 186–89
macroswings in, 26–27
old work models ineffective in, 22–24
organization structure in, 76–80
organizing principles for, 12
performance in, 112
prosperity and, 23
results needed in, 39–41, 96–100
speed as important in, 96, 98–99
staffing challenges in, see staffing
transition to, 11–12, 25–27, 177
work-life balance in, 157–58, 163

obsolescence, 21, 134, 136
Ogilvy & Mather, 60
old-fashioned employment model, 10, 21–24
career paths in, 16–18, 19, 28, 56, 67–68, 136, 154, 155, 169–70
company-specific knowledge in, 21–22
conformity in, 158–61
constraints of, 21–22
experience gained over time in, 133
hiring process in, 55, 57

job descriptions in, 22
job security in, 22–23, 113
knowledge acquisition in, 133
labor unions and, 188
leaders identified in, 79
long-term career planning in, 16–18, 136, 139
management in, 111–14
organizational flexibility vs., 11, 46, 113, 161
power in, 21, 121
relocation in, 164–66
rewards for time in, 93–96
schedule pressures in, 162
seniority system in, 86–88
social/cultural norms in support of, 22
stability in, 21–22, 113
success in, 21, 22
wage pressure in, 26
work-life balance and, 158, 163
see also organization chart
Omnicom Group, 158–60
one-minute mentors, 146–48
online learning, 143–44
online talent auction sites, 84
opportunity cost, 94–96
O'Reilly, Charles, 66
organization chart:
adjusting to fit available talent, 45–46
career paths and, 166–68
chain of command in, 28, 111, 126
of downsized organizations, 126
letting go of, 46
power and, 20–22, 84, 88, 112
reporting relationships on, 126
role-based reconfiguration of, 167–68
squeezing people to fit, 44
success and, 24
organization structure, new, 76–80
orientation, as boot camp, 179
outsourcing, 59–62, 177
to former employees, 60–61, 67, 78, 178
as horizontal integration, 60

outsourcing (*continued*)
  of human resource work, 74–75
  of lease financing, 61–62
  market differentiation and, 59
  to outside vendors, 59–60
  to professional service firms, 63,
    65–66, 74
  of sales, 45
  in strategic alliances, 60
  in talent-network/best-team
    approach, 66–67
  as test-drive relationships, 80

parenting, 158, 172, 184–85
pay-for-performance systems,
    82–83, 85, 88, 89, 93,
    97–108, 112
pay-your-dues model, *see* old-fash-
    ioned employment model
"peer mentor" training, 142–43
Peoplesoft, 37–39
performance, 82–108
  benchmarks of, 107
  coaching for, 83, 107–8, 110–11,
    112
  and customized jobs, 173
  expectations of, 107
  extraordinary, as goal, 140
  feedback for, 123–28, 179–80
  incentives for, 101, 104–6,
    156–57, 181
  management-driven, 121
  measurement of, 41, 83, 93,
    103–4, 107
  in new economy, 112
  pay for, 82–83, 85, 88, 89, 93,
    97–108, 112, 179–80
  standards for, 104, 107, 179–80
  team-based bonuses for,
    99–101
perks, 181–85
Perle, Elizabeth, 157
Persian Gulf War, 72
personal coaches, 114–18
personnel economics, 102
Peters, Tom, 190
piecework, compensation for, 102
population, aging of, 171

Portland General Electric Company
    (PGE), 82–83
production company model, 63
productivity:
  coaching for, 128
  flexible work schedules and,
    162–64
  increases in, 23, 190
  job customization and, 173
  reward-driven, 97–99, 101, 102,
    104
  technology and, 23
professional services firms:
  alternative career paths in,
    166–68
  client needs as first priority in,
    65
  partnership structures of, 166–67
profit sharing, 100
proprietary information, 132
prosperity, and new economy, 23
Prudential Insurance Co., 170, 206
psychology, self-esteem movement
    in, 114
public employees, 184
public relations industry, 64–67
Publix Super Markets, 47–48
Punished by Rewards (Kohn), 89–90
purchasing contracts, elements of,
    107–8

quality:
  commitment to, 134
  judgment and, 36–37
quit rate, 190

Radcliffe Public Policy Center, 158
recruitment:
  fluidity and, 79
  via Internet, 74, 84
  see also hiring process
reengineering:
  effects of, 18, 23, 25, 39, 125–26
  via technology, 37–39, 56
relocation, 164–66
repayment contracts, 131–32
resources:
  critical, 121

human, *see* employees; human resources; talent
    just-in-time acquisition of, 22, 35–36
responsibility:
    immediate, 134
    need for, 33
    new, 68
    for one's own career path, 20, 23, 25, 92
    unbundling for available talent, 45–46, 133–34, 172
    and value added, 39–40
restructuring:
    and changing work, 111
    effects of, 18, 23, 25, 38–39, 125–26
    role-based, 167
results:
    delivery of, 82, 83, 156
    focus on, 118–19, 169
    management for time vs., 93–96
    market value of, 39–41
    milestones and, 83
    reputation tied to, 134
    rewards and, 85, 88, 96–100
    skill or knowledge gaps as obstacles to, 137, 148
    tangible, 24, 134
retail sector:
    compensation systems in, 104–5
    fluidity in, 47–49, 71
    relationship development in, 48–49
    SWAT teams in, 67–70
    training in, 131–32
    turnover in, 47
retirement, flexible work programs in, 169–71
Rick (technical sales), 42–46
Robbins, Tony, 114
role models, 112

sales force:
    coaching of, 109–110, 123–24
    compensation of, 94–95
    retraining of, 37–38

Samantha (new employee), 129–30, 134
Sandia National Laboratory:
    energy flow and, 28–29
    knowledge transfer in, 151
    SWAT team of, 70–71
schedule:
    conformity to, 158–61
    flexibility in, 162–64, 170, 184–85
    relief from, 161–64
    self-management of, 68, 105
    work-life balance in, 157–58, 161–63
Schultz, Howard, 125
self-actualization, 90–92
self-esteem movement, 114
self-help, 116–17, 184
Senge, Peter, 134–35
seniority-based compensation, 86–88
Senior Leaders Program, 169–70
Six Sigma, 36, 196
Smith, John F., 35
social/cultural norms, 21–22, 157–58
Sofco, Inc., 44–46
Spectrum Center, 104
staffing:
    flexible, 45–52, 76–80, 132, 161, 177
    gaps in levels of, 57–59, 69–70, 79
    HR department and, 74–76
    just-in-time, 22, 58–59, 69, 71, 75–76
    networks for, 64–67
    organization structure and, 76–80
    outsourcing in, 59–62, 177
    production company model of, 63
    reserves, 70, 72–74
    SWAT teams and, 67–71
    technology and, 54–55, 57–59, 73, 77
    by temporary agencies, 74–75
    training investment paradox and, 130–32

staffing (*continued*)
    work-focused vs. job-focused,
      54–81
    see also hiring process
staffing crisis:
    free agency and, 12
    reengineering and, 56
    training time and, 133
Stanford Business School, 46
Starbucks, 60, 125
stock options, 101
strategic alliances, 60
success:
    access to talent and, 32–33, 47
    in free markets, 24
    leading to success, 118–19
    leanness and, 77
    new definitions of, 162
    in traditional work model, 21, 22
Sun Microsystems Finance (SMF),
    61–62
SWAT teams, 67–71

talent, 31–53
    access to, 32–33, 47, 55, 64–67, 84
    best-teams approach with, 66–67
    bidding wars for, 16, 17–18, 56,
      84
    careers of, *see* career paths
    commitment of, 156
    communicating with, 63, 75, 180
    compensation of, *see* compensa-
      tion systems
    core group of, 77, 179
    as critical resource, 121
    data pool for, 63, 178
    entrepreneurship of, 41–46
    expectations of, 153–55, 160, 162,
      165
    fluid staffing of, 45–52, 76–80,
      132, 161, 177
    and free agency, 10, 11–12,
      24–26, 50, 154, 160
    judgment and, 33, 35–37, 38–39,
      40
    leveraging of, 52
    life resources for, 181–85

    mobility of, 14–15, 18–20, 24,
      44–45, 66–67, 79
    and negotiation power, 11, 20,
      39, 79, 84, 169, 170
    nonfinancial rewards for, 104–6,
      156–57, 162, 163–64, 181
    online auction sites for, 84
    outsourcing, 45, 59–62, 177, 178
    power over careers of, 13, 39–40,
      162
    proprietary database of, 63, 75,
      178
    at remote locations, 31–32, 163,
      165–66, 172
    self-selection of, 77–78
    SWAT teams of, 67–71
    test-driving of, 80
    training of, *see* training
    transparent value of, 40–41
    tricks of, 160
    unbundling tasks for utilization
      of, 45–46, 133–34, 172
    upping the ante for, 37–39
    as worth the hassle, 161
    see also employees
Target Corporation, 67–70, 71
team-based compensation, 98–101
technology:
    added, and downsizing, 33, 37,
      39
    human factor vs., 151
    nontechnical skills added to,
      33–34, 36–37
    obsolescence and, 136
    organizational change and, 23,
      134
    productivity and, 23
    reengineering via, 37–39, 56
    robots and, 35
    skill levels and, 33, 40
    speed to market of, 98–99
    staffing and, 54–55, 57–59, 73, 77
    training and, 38
    visualization, 144
telecommunications industry, com-
    pensation systems in,
    85–86

telecommuting, 31–32, 163, 165–66, 172, 173
temporary agencies, 74–75
Texas Instruments, 141
Thelian, Lorraine, 65–67
Theory X and Theory Y, 90–92
Theraldson Enterprises, 102
Thomas J. Lipton Company, 105
time:
  conformity to schedules and, 158–61
  control over one's schedule, 68, 105
  as equalizer, 93
  for feedback, 125, 126
  flexible schedules and, 162–64, 184–85
  management for results vs., 93–96
  and opportunity cost, 94–96
  and speed to market, 98–99
time logs, 116
Time Unlimited, 182–83
today, focus on, 118–19, 124
Towers Perrin, 101
trade unions, 188
tradition, see old-fashioned employment model
training, 129–52
  allocation of resources in, 135–36
  boot camp approach to, 139–43, 179
  "buddy" or "peer mentor" approach to, 142–43
  case-study method of, 141
  changes needed in, 28
  coaching skills, 113–14
  in corporate universities vs. graduate business programs, 138
  cross-training, 71, 139
  deep learning and, 137–38, 139
  desktop access to, 144, 150–51
  diversity of exposure in, 139
  of everybody, 136, 179
  of executives only, 135–36
  human factor in, 151
  for immediate meaningful roles, 133–34
  information infrastructure for, 143–44
  investment paradox of, 130–32
  J.C. Penney's system of, 149–51
  just-in-time, 137, 139, 143–44, 150
  knowledge-sharing networks for, 148–49, 151
  of knowledge workers, 134–36
  leadership, 122
  and learning curve, 132
  for lifelong learning, 138, 150
  lost investment in, 45, 79, 130–32
  and loyalty, 131
  most-frequently-asked-questions approach to, 145–46
  new opportunities for, 68
  one-minute mentor approach to, 146–48
  for one mission at a time, 136–39
  online, 143–44
  philosophy of, 140, 142
  professional businesses for, 138–39
  realignment with flexible work, 139
  repayment contracts for, 131–32
  retraining, 37–38
  self-directed, 129–30, 144
  for short term vs. long haul, 129, 133, 139
  for specific tasks and responsibilities, 139, 142, 143–44
  value of investment in, 72–74
  in vocational schools, 196–97
turnover, employee, 18–20, 67, 104
turnover-reduction programs, focus of, 16
Tushman, Michael, 66

uncertainty, becoming accustomed to, 23
unemployment, downsizing and, 23
uninterrupted employment, use of term, 55

unions, 186–89
United Auto Workers, 187
University of Phoenix, 138–39
utilities, pay for performance in,
  82–83

Van Dusseldorp, Monique, 51
Van Dusseldorp & Partners, 51–52
vocational schools, 196–97
Vroom, Victor, 90, 201

Walker Digital, 61
Warner, Douglas "Sandy," 11
Waterman, Robert H. Jr., 200
Weiser, Katie, 142
Welch, Jack, 24, 164
Welcome, Chris, 31–32
wellness services, 183–84
West Point Market, 48–49
Whaley, Sgt. Maj. William, 122,
  127, 140
Wharton School of Business,
  25–26, 85, 163
*When Work Doesn't Work Any-
  more* (Perle), 157
will, force of, 119
women, and work-life balance,
  157–58
work:
  as art, 121, 124, 160
  assessment of, 64, 78–79, 82–83,
    171–72
  balance of lifestyle and, 157–58,
    161–63

customizing, 156–57, 160–61,
    171, 172
  de-facto managers of, 126
  flexible scheduling of, 163–64,
    170, 184–85
  greatness connected with, 123,
    124
  information-related, 165–66
  location of, 164–66
  management's understanding of,
    120
  meaningful, 133–34
  as moving target, 76, 111
  nature of, 89, 160
  negotiated arrangements of,
    155–57, 160, 168, 169, 170,
    172
  nonfinancial compensation for,
    104–6, 156–57, 162, 163–64,
    181
  nonnegotiable elements of,
    171–73
  outsourcing of, 45, 59–62, 66, 74,
    78, 80, 177, 178
  ownership of, 134
  specific jobs in, *see* jobs
  SWAT teams and, 68–70
  training realigned to match,
    139
  see also career paths
work environment, *see* corporate
  culture

Xerox Corporation, 163